APPLIED ORGANIZATIONAL BEHAVIOR AND LEADERSHIP DEVELOPMENT

AN IDENTITY APPROACH

GRETCHEN VOGELGESANG LESTER
PAUL B. LESTER

Cover image © Shutterstock, Inc.

Kendall Hunt
publishing company

www.kendallhunt.com
Send all inquiries to:
4050 Westmark Drive
Dubuque, IA 52004-1840

Copyright © 2023 by Kendall Hunt Publishing Company

Print ISBN 978-1-7924-9445-1
eBook ISBN 979-8-7657-5695-9

All rights reserved. No part of this publication may be reproduced, stored in a retrieval system, or transmitted, in any form or by any means, electronic, mechanical, photocopying, recording, or otherwise, without the prior written permission of the copyright owner.

Published in the United States of America

Table of Contents

Preface... xiii

Part One: Meaning of Identity

Chapter 1   Identity in Leadership and Organizational Behavior.................................1

Chapter 2   Attribution Theories in Leadership and Organizational Behavior 17

Chapter 3   Your Working Self-Concept...37

Part Two: Level of Identity

Chapter 4   Individual-Level Identity: Character, Traits, and Motivation 55

Chapter 5   Relational-Level Characteristics and Influence Processes 81

Chapter 6   Collective-Level Leadership and Teams..99

Part Three: Strength of Identity

Chapter 7   Behavioral Theories..119

Chapter 8   Competency and Skills-Based Theories 135

Part Four: Integration of Identity

Chapter 9   Integration of Leadership Identity 159

Chapter 10 Authenticity and Ethicality in identity..179

Chapter 11 Launching Your Identity Development..201

Contents

Preface xiii

Part One: Meaning of Identity

Chapter 1   Identity in Leadership and Organizational Behavior 1
    Chapter Outcomes 1
    Purpose of this Chapter 1
    What is Identity? 2
        Activity 1: Sub-identities (I see myself as Statements) 2
    Identity Construction 3
        Activity 2: Possible Self Inventory 4
        Activity 3: Sub-Identity and Possible Self Motives 4
    Identities in Multiple Domains 6
    Leader Identity 7
    Leader and Manager Identity—Born or Made? 7
    Leader Identity—Meaning, Level, Strength, Integration 9
    Sensemaking and Sensebreaking 9
    Organizational Behavior and Leadership 10
    Evidence-Based Approach 10
    Scientific Method 10
    Outcomes of Identity Work 11
    Implicit Leader/Organization Theories 12
    In Review 13
    Learning Objectives 14
    Key Terms 15
    Critical Thinking Questions 15
    Chapter Summary 15
    References 15

Chapter 2   Attribution Theories in Leadership and Organizational Behavior 17
- Chapter Outcomes 17
- Purpose of this Chapter..17
- What are attributions?..17
  - Activity 1: Self-Serving Bias 18
- Implicit Leadership Theories..20
  - Activity 2: Leader Identity Meaning 20
- Prototypes..20
  - Activity 3: Leader Prototype/Antitype Rating Activity 21
- Attribution Theories of Leadership 23
  - Activity 4: Do You Romanticize Leaders? 24
- Self-Fulfilling Prophecies 25
- Theory X and Theory Y 26
- Pygmalion Effects 27
- Galatea Effects 27
  - Activity 5: Pygmalion/Galatea...28
- Avoiding Attributional Errors 29
- Using Attributions to Your Advantage 30
- In Review 30
- Learning Objectives..32
- Key Terms 33
- Critical Thinking Questions 33
- References 33

Chapter 3   Your Working Self-Concept 37
- Chapter Outcomes 37
- Purpose of this Chapter..37
- What is the "Self"? 37
  - Activity 1: Life Roles and Schemas..38
- What Is the Working Self-Concept? 39
- Self-Views..41
- Possible Selves...41
- Current Goals...42
- Motivations 43
  - Activity 2: Motivation to Lead 43
- The Working Self-Concept and Identity Development 44
  - Activity 3: Describing your Working Self-Concept 45
- Complexity and Identity..46
- Efficacy and the Working Self-Concept...47

	In Review	48
	Learning Objectives	49
	Key Terms	50
	Critical Thinking Questions	51
	References	51

Part Two: Levels of Identity

Chapter 4 Individual-Level Identity: Character, Traits, and Motivation 55
- Chapter Outcomes 55
- Purpose of this Chapter 55
- What Is the Individual-Level of Identity? 55
- Traits and Trait Theories 56
- Physical Characteristics 58
- Intelligence 58
- Education 60
- Wisdom and Judgment 61
    - Activity 1: After Action Review 62
- What Is Personality? 64
- Core Self-Evaluations 64
- The Big Five 65
    - Activity 2: Assessing your Big Five Personality Traits 67
- HEXACO 67
- The Dark Triad 68
- Summary of Leader Traits 70
- Individual-Level Motivation 71
    - Activity 3: The Motivation Process 71
- Summary of Individual-Level Motivations 73
- In Review 73
- Learning Objectives 74
- Key Terms 75
- Critical Thinking Questions 76
- References 76

Chapter 5 Relational-Level Characteristics and Influence Processes 81
- Chapter Outcomes 81
- Purpose of this Chapter 81
- What is the Relational-Level of Identity? 82
- Consideration and Initiating Structure—The Ohio State Studies 82
    - Activity 1: Complete the LBDQ 83

Situational Leadership Theory 84
    Activity 2: Situational Leadership Activity 85
Path-Goal Theory 87
    Activity 3: Path-Goal Reflection 88
Vertical Dyad-Linkage 89
Leader-Member Exchange 90
Followership Theories 91
    Activity 4: Complete the Followership Questionnaire 92
    Activity 5: Tango: The Dance of the Leader and the Follower 94
In Review 94
Learning Objectives 96
Key Terms 97
Critical Thinking Questions 97
Conclusion 97
References 97

Chapter 6   Collective-Level Identity: Leadership and Teams 99
Chapter Outcomes 99
Purpose of this Chapter 99
What Is Collective-Level Identity? 100
    Activity 1: Collective Identity Inventory 101
Social Identity Theory 102
Group Prototypes 103
    Activity 2: Creating a Team Charter 104
Team Mental Models 105
    Activity 3: Team Mental Models 106
Social Identity Theory of Leadership 107
Charismatic Leadership 107
    Activity 4: Charismatic Leadership Scale 108
Personalized Charismatic Leadership 110
Socialized Charismatic Leadership 110
Servant Leadership 110
    Activity 5: Servant Leadership Scale 112
Levels of Leader Identity 112
In Review 113
Learning Objectives 114
Key Terms 115
Critical Thinking Questions 115
References 116

Part Three: Strength of Identity

Chapter 7 Behavioral Theories 119
    Chapter Outcomes 119
    Purpose of this Chapter 119
        Activity 1: Leader Meter 119
    What Is Leader Identity Strength? 120
    Claiming and Granting 122
        Activity 2: Claiming and Granting Activity 123
    Classic Leadership Behavioral Studies 123
    Lewin, Lippitt, & White (1939) Studies 124
    Ohio State and Michigan Studies 124
    Blake and Mouton's Managerial Grid™ 126
        Activity 3: Managerial Grid Examples 127
    Leading Change Behaviors 127
        Activity 4: Complete the Self-Survey 128
    In Review 129
    Learning Objectives 130
    Key Terms 131
    Critical Thinking Questions 131
    References 131

Chapter 8 Competency and Skills-Based Theories 135
    Chapter Outcomes 135
    Purpose of this Chapter 135
    What Are Competencies? 135
    Management Systems Theory 136
    Skills-Based Model of Leader Performance 138
        Activity 1: Leadership Identity Strength—Identity Circles 139
    Social Intelligence 140
    Emotional Intelligence 140
    Skill Development 142
    Decision-Making 143
    Influence Tactics and Power 144
    Political Skill 146
        Activity 2: Political Skill Inventory 146
    Negotiation and Conflict Management Skills 148
        Activity 3: Lunar Survival 150
        Activity 4: Leader Identity Strength—Identity Circles 152
    In Review 153

Learning Objectives 154
Key Terms 155
Critical Thinking Questions 156
References 156

Part Four: Integration of Identity

Chapter 9 Integration of Leadership Identity 159
Chapter Outcomes 159
Purpose of this Chapter 159
What is Leader Identity Integration? 159
    Activity 1: Domain Circles 160
Introduction 161
The Full-Range Leadership Model 162
Transformational Leadership 165
The Case *against* the Full-Range Leadership Model 168
The Case *for* the Full-Range Leadership Model 170
    Activity 2: Assessing Transformational and Transactional Readership 171
In Review 173
Learning Objectives 174
Key Terms 175
Critical Thinking Questions 175
References 176

Chapter 10 Authenticity and Ethicality in Identity 179
Chapter Outcomes 179
Purpose of this Chapter 179
Introduction 179
Impression Management 180
Dramaturgical Approach 181
Ethical Leadership 183
    Activity 1: The Ethical Leadership Scale 187
Authentic Leadership 188
    Activity 2: Carlos the Inspired Case Study 190
In Review 194
Learning Objectives 196
Key Terms 197
Critical Thinking Questions 197
References 198

Chapter 11 Launching Your Identity Development 201
    Chapter Outcomes 201
    Purpose of this Chapter 201
    What are Bandura's Social Learning and Social Cognitive Theories 201
    Mentoring—A Specific Learning Opportunity 204
    Transformative Learning 205
        Activity 1: ILT Frame of Reference 205
    Positive Organizational Outcomes 206
        Activity 2: Organizational Citizenship Scale 208
    Goal setting as Identity Development 209
        Activity 3: Action Planning 211
    Your Personal Leader Identity Timeline 212
        Activity 4: Culmination of Leader Identity in Your Development Timeline 213
    In Review 214
    Learning Objectives 215
    Key Terms 216
    Critical Thinking Questions 216
    References 217

Preface

We are leadership and organizational scholars and educators, so we've dedicated much of our professional lives to researching, teaching, and practicing those topics. Yet, for the better part of two decades, we have witnessed a paradox in our own classrooms as well as the classrooms of many of our peers. Engaging students in animated discussions about leadership and human behavior at work is the easy part. Regardless of demographic or experience, people get excited and want to talk about leadership and organizations; the good, the bad, and the ugly—it doesn't matter, everyone seems to have a story they want to tell.

Yet, when we turned towards what is "under the hood" within leadership and organizational behavior—the theory, foundational concepts, and history—student enthusiasm rapidly waned. By its nature, theory is an abstraction, and teaching abstractions in an engaging way to a room full of emerging leaders is a tall order. After all, upper-level undergraduates or MBA students probably are not taking an applied organizational behavior or leadership course to learn about theory, but rather they are there to gain practical knowledge. We needed to offer them something useful and personal, something that would generate excitement for these theories that help explain behavior in organizations. When we talked with our peers teaching at other universities, their experience was largely the same. Most told us that, like us, they did the best they could to balance passion with rigor; first by attracting students' interest and then using momentum to get them through the dry stuff (the theory). Many candidly admitted that they often traded rigor for engagement because engagement led to happier students

Over time and after many long walks around our neighborhood during the COVID pandemic, we began to realize that we did not need to accept this tradeoff. Rather, we needed a different approach to framing rigorous theory in a way that people would *want* to learn about it. *How do we do that?* We make it about them.

When working with colleagues on a leader identity project that would go on to win a Best Paper Award at Journal of Management Education, Gretchen organized organizational behavior and leadership theories to map onto the four dimensions of leader identity. As we revised syllabi and re-oriented the material to coincide with leader identity meaning, strength, levels, and integration, the student response was overwhelmingly positive. We could see the students start to relate to the theories in a personal, developable way. After customizing textbooks, collecting articles for readers, and designing our courses to meet the needs of our students, we realized a need for a textbook the students could use in their active learning to help further apply these concepts.

This text is written with the goal of helping students personalize their learning and connecting deeply to the material given their personal experiences. In each part of the text, we relate the theories to how an individual could incorporate the ideas as part of their identity construction and development. The end goal is a student who understands there are many paths to effectiveness in organizational behavior and leadership, and they should adopt the theories that resonate with them as they launch or continue their careers. In addition, we highlight the cross-domain nature of these concepts, so we encourage students to think more broadly about leadership and organizational behaviors—finding ways to practice with their friends and family and in their communities. This book is the result of many years researching and evaluating identity within an organizational behavior and leadership framework.

The identity-based framework of the text: meaning, strength, level, and integration across domains, is an engaging way to examine organizational behavior and leadership development. Each section includes theories that relate to each of those dimensions. To our knowledge, this is a new approach that seeks to integrate OB and leadership theories as a robust field instead of disparate theories that compete to explain human behavior.

This textbook is targeted for upper-division undergraduate or early graduate courses on applied organizational behavior (a step beyond "Introduction to Organizational Behavior" or "Principles of Management") or leadership courses. Many Business, Public Policy, Project Management, Nursing, International Business, Psychology, Hospitality, and other programs include such applied OB and leadership development courses. This text is specifically aimed for instructors interested in adopting an approach focused on students' organizational behavior skills and leader identities in multiple domains (work, family, community), and how they can hone their current competencies to be successful in their chosen fields.

The class size may range from 10 students for a graduate-level course to over 50 for larger undergraduate courses. Since the course is focused on individual identity OB skills and leadership development, the instructor should be prepared to give personalized feedback on the reflection materials.

It is recommended but not required that students have some knowledge of human behavior through a prerequisite introductory psychology, organizational behavior, or principles of management course or through their own personal experience leading and managing people.

Approach

The key focus of the text is helping the student generate awareness and develop their leader identity to effectively motivate human behavior. Students are challenged in this course to conduct thorough self-reflection and generate self-awareness about their specific OB and leadership skill set. Initially, some students may be skeptical of this approach, but the exercises included in the text are designed to break down this skepticism and create respect for the individual nature of OB and leadership development. The text is grounded in leader identity literature and highlights multiple pathways for development that are not always available in the workplace. A challenge for instructors is balancing the need for personalized feedback with the time commitment necessary to get to know each student well enough to provide guidance.

The material here is the basis for a redesigned a course for upper-division undergraduates, informed by expertise in coaching MBA students and working professionals, and employed in corporate consulting projects—all focused on the identity-based approach to OB and leadership development across domains. This approach immediately personalizes leadership theory and development for each individual by exploring their individual meaning of leadership, their leader identity strength, their level of leader identity, and their integration of leader identity with their other identities. Through several experiential exercises, I have seen individuals flourish in their approach to and utilization of their OB and leadership skills. At the completion of the course, coaching, or training session, each individual continues a personalized path towards OB and leader development that is based in leadership theory but is applied to their personal leadership challenges—whether in the workplace, a family setting, or within a community. The deep reflection and self-awareness that accompany this method offer outcomes not available when teaching these topics in a traditional approach.

Guiding principles

There are many individuals who may not have access to development opportunities within their workplace but may not realize they have options for leadership development *outside* their workplace. The exercises and cases are readily accessible for any individual seeking to learn more about their leader identity.

Features

This textbook includes embedded activities throughout each chapter. Students can complete the activities on their own, or the instructor can guide them through the activities in class, where they can reflect and discuss their results with their classmates. Some activities are repeated throughout the chapters, asking the students to revisit their earlier work and reflect upon changes they may see as they gain more knowledge regarding leader identity.

Learning objectives

Each chapter begins with 4-5 learning objectives, written at the higher levels of Bloom's taxonomy. As this book is geared towards upper division and Master's-level classes, the focus is on analyzing, evaluating, and creating connections between the concepts.

Exercises

The exercises can be reflective in nature, may involve drawing or articulating a vision, include many self-assessments, and offer opportunities for teamwork throughout the course. Sometimes, the students will work in teams and then evaluate and give feedback regarding their peers' behaviors.

Critical thinking questions

Each chapter ends with critical thinking questions to help the students apply the knowledge to scenarios they may encounter after they complete their schooling.

Key terms

Key terms for each chapter are provided in line with the text to help students quickly review and understand these terms as they read through the content.

End materials

Chapter reviews reiterate the learning objectives and reinforce the main content from each chapter.

Online resources

- **Test banks** built using Bloom's Taxonomy that cover the textbook content in detail. There are both multiple choice and essay questions an instructor may choose for assurance of learning, a key component of AASCB accreditation.
- **MS PowerPoint slide presentations** available for each chapter. They include content and activities from the chapters but are customizable for you to add or take away content. Each deck covers about three hours' worth of content. The slides also include visually appealing graphics.
- **Teaching notes** provide ideas for how the instructor can cover the material, structured to cover three hours of content. Some activities can be completed in a shorter time frame; others can take more time depending on how in-depth the requirement is.

Acknowledgements

We would like to express our sincere gratitude to our research partners, colleagues, and our family, whose expertise, dedication, and unwavering support have made this textbook possible.

The contributions of countless researchers, scholars, educators, and practitioners have advanced the fields of organizational behavior and leadership, and their work has been instrumental in shaping the content and approach of this book. Their passion, dedication, and tireless efforts have helped elevate our understanding of how people approach their work and shape their leadership identities and have opened new avenues for exploration.

From Gretchen: I would like to extend my thanks to my very close colleagues, Dr. Michelle Hammond, Dr. Rachel Clapp-Smith, and Dr. Michael Palanski. Our collaborations generated the ideas behind the organization for this book, and your Academy of Management Research paper provided the structure and lens through which I approach leader identity. I have learned so much through working with you all and continue to think of you as my brain trust.

This book is the fruition of too many pomodoro writing sessions to count, all with the support of the Women of Organizational Behavior (WOB) group. I do not have the words to describe how much I have enjoyed getting to know all these amazing women, sharing my challenges and frustrations, and giving updates on the book's progress. They are a cheering section with whom any scholar would be thrilled having in their corner.

I also want to thank my colleagues at San Jose State University for supporting me throughout this endeavor. Finally, I want to thank my family—my parents, Reed, and Riley—for your understanding throughout this book writing process. Paul, this has been an amazing experience and you have carried a heavy load in our personal life to help us manage the work and bring this project into reality.

From Paul: I thank my family—Mom, Reed, and Riley—for your patience and support. Additionally, I thank the faculty and military students at the Naval Postgraduate School: You have been a great source of inspiration throughout this process. Finally, I thank my wife, Gretchen, for surfacing this idea and offering to bring me on as her co-author. This book is hers through-and-through, she deserves the credit.

This textbook has been a passion project, and we are so thankful to have collaborated as a wife-husband team. Teaming with your spouse to write a textbook alongside having two young children and independent careers is not for the faint of heart.

We also would like to thank the following reviewers for their thoughts on early chapters of the manuscript:

Dr. Angelo Brown
Kennesaw State University

Dr. Sheng Wang
UNLV

Dr. Alice Camuti
Tennessee Tech University

Ms. Lara Hobson
Western Michigan University

The remarkable visuals were generated by the creative team at Kendall-Hunt. Our editorial team, including the wonderful Brenda Rowles and Paul Carty at Kendall-Hunt, managed to keep this project running smoothly. The layout and organization of the online resources, particularly the slides, were perfected by Dr. Peter Hammond. Teaching assistants, David Poirier and Alexander Colmenaro, provided support to allow us to address editorial comments while maintaining our teaching load and commitment to students. Three cohorts of undergraduate and graduate students at San Jose State University provided feedback and constructive criticism on the content and the teaching approach; their assessment has been critical in adapting the content to suit different learning styles. Pam Wells has been an enthusiastic early adopter of this approach, and we cannot thank her enough for her attention to detail and thoughtful questions regarding the pedagogy. Evan M. line edited this book, and we thank him for his meticulous review of the text.

Finally, we would like to thank the readers of this book for their enthusiasm and participation in interacting with the content. It is our hope that this work will serve as a valuable resource for students, educators, and professionals alike, and that it will inspire a deeper appreciation for the subject matter. Sometimes it is possible to feel like leadership is for other individuals who have different opportunities; the goal of this book is to make knowledge accessible to a wider audience and provide everyone with a starting place given their own self-identity. It is our hope that this work will help to disseminate knowledge and promote knowledge equality, enabling more people to benefit from the insights and practices of leader identity development.

Thank you all for your support and encouragement.
Sincerely,
Gretchen Vogelgesang Lester, Ph.D.
Paul B. Lester, Ph.D., PMP

CHAPTER 1

Identity in Leadership and Organizational Behavior

CHAPTER OUTCOMES

1. Identify and define identity
2. Analyze your leader identity
3. Examine a multi-domain approach to identity
4. Apply personal identity to organizational behavior outcomes

Purpose of this Chapter

In this chapter, we begin where we hope you ultimately end: Incorporating *leader* as part of your identity. In and out of the classroom, we are often asked if being a leader is a combination of behaviors, a role someone performs, or if it is simply being who you are. The answer is that leading incorporates all three—it is a process, a performed role, and a property or part of someone's identity. **Leadership** is "the exertion of social influence between and among multiple loci of leadership (leader, follower, leader-follower dyad, collective, and context) working toward a common goal, via the leadership mechanisms of traits, behaviors, affect, and cognition, through a series of event cycles that may or may not include the same mechanisms and/or loci." Leadership is constructed both inside and outside of the workplace, and it impacts everyone's organizational behavior (i.e., how an individual interacts with people in a working environment). The best organizations offer opportunities to lead at all levels of their organizations, even for those serving in follower roles. While we will periodically touch on the process of leadership, this book mainly focuses on what it means to be a leader or follower, what it takes for each of us to incorporate being a leader or follower into our identity, and how we enact behaviors to impact those around us. Thus, the purpose of this introductory chapter is to dive into the topic of **identity**— what it is, how it is formed, and how it changes over time. We also embed this identity work in the broader field of **organizational behavior** and the research evidence that gives insight into predicting, analyzing, and making sense of how individuals come together to accomplish goals and tasks.

LEADER:
A person who has commanding authority or influence. (Merriam Webster)

LEADERSHIP:
The exertion of social influence between and among multiple loci of leadership (leader, follower, leader—follower dyad, collective, and context) working toward a common goal, via the leadership mechanisms of traits, behaviors, affect, and cognition, through a series of event cycles that may or may not include the same mechanisms and/or loci. (Eberly, Johndon, Hernandez, & Avolio, 2013)

Chapter 1: Identity in Leadership and Organizational Behavior

IDENTITY:
The sum total of one's values, experiences, and self-perceptions. (Vogelgesang Lester, Palanski, Hammond, Clapp-Smith, 2017)

ORGANIZATIONAL BEHAVIOR:
The field directly concerned with the understanding, prediction, and control of human behavior in organizations. (Fred Luthans, 2002)

What is Identity?

Identity is foundational to who we are as individuals. It is shaped in various ways, including the roles we take on in life—student, spouse or partner, sibling, parent, professional, and so on. We often take an individual approach to each of these roles, but generally, they have agreed-upon meanings. For example, most people would agree that a student is someone who is at least mildly interested in a particular topic and therefore dedicates time and effort toward learning. The process of *how* we go about being a student varies from person to person, but the core meaning is generally accepted. Thus, identity is comprised of "meanings that individuals attach to themselves" (Gecas, 1982; Dutton, Roberts, & Bednar, 2010).

These meanings are the tools we use to explain ourselves to others, the attributes we use to define ourselves, and the descriptions through which we experience our lives. Our work identities are the meanings we attach to our job-related activities and can relate to the overall organization, our job duties, or our careers. People can adopt multiple identities, known as sub-identities—some are specific to a particular role or domain, others can exist across multiple roles. Identities can be adopted or discarded as our experiences and contexts change. Some identities can even linger after we no longer actively access them (Wittman, 2019).

Activity 1: Sub-identities (I see myself as Statements)

In this activity, use each line to highlight a different sub-identity, or aspect of your self, that you adopt across the domains in which you live, work, and relax. This exercise is based upon the Twenty Statements Test, originally created by Kuhn & McPartland (1954) to catalog the breadth of one's self-concept.

In the spaces below, finish the beginning of each "I see myself as" statement with a different sub-identity or role you enact. You can include aspects of your current self, along with dormant sub-identities.

I see myself as _____
I see myself as _____
I see myself as _____
I see myself as _____
I see myself as _____
I see myself as _____
I see myself as _____
I see myself as _____
I see myself as _____
I see myself as _____
I see myself as _____
I see myself as _____
I see myself as _____
I see myself as _____
I see myself as _____

I see myself as _____
I see myself as _____
I see myself as _____
I see myself as _____
I see myself as _____

Activity 1: Learning Outcomes

If you are a full-time student, you may have identified with your university or your chosen major ("I see myself as… [insert your mascot here]" or "I see myself as… a management major"). You might shed your student identity after graduation, but your university may encourage the construction of an alumni identity.

If you are currently working, you might have included statements describing your position at work (I see myself as… a team lead) or a particular skill set you use in your working life (I see myself as… a problem-solver). Completing this exercise will enhance your self-awareness of your own personal sub-identities.

Please be sure to save your responses to this activity for future activities, particularly in Chapters 4-7.

Identity Construction

Identity construction is the "process through which actors come to define who they are" (Ashforth & Schinoff, 2016). Throughout our lives we adopt **possible selves**. Some last only for a short period, while others are adopted as part of our core identity. Young adults continually try out possible selves as they prepare to move on from their traditional family roles. Possible selves create motivation and action towards specific goals and life experiences, which reinforces self-perceptions, values, and beliefs. Some identities may be chosen consciously (e.g., choosing to learn a musical instrument or trying out for a sports team), while others may be chosen for us due to circumstances beyond our control (e.g., adopting a caretaking role for an ailing relative). Some may derive identities through membership in groups, job titles, exposure to sports or media figures, or personal relationships. These possible selves are specific and are narrowly connected to an individual's desired future—one which can be visualized as a state to achieve or avoid. As the possible selves become integrated into the current self, they motivate future performance and fulfill progress towards specific aspirations. A workplace identity creates a framework through which we adapt and redirect our self-meaning as we pursue occupational fulfillment. How we choose to integrate these identities governs our actions in different domains. Thus, the possible selves serve to interpret events as they occur, either strengthening or weakening the self-concept. We will discuss this in greater depth in Chapter 4.

IDENTITY CONSTRUCTION: People being engaged in forming, repairing, maintaining, strengthening or revising their identities. (Sveningsson & Alvesson, 2003, p.1165)

POSSIBLE SELVES: Derive from representations of the self in the past and they include representations of the self in the future. They are different and separable from the current or now selves, yet are intimately connected to them. (Markus and Nurius, 1986)

© Unitone Vector/Shutterstock.com

Activity 2: Possible Self Inventory

Envision your possible future selves. First, use some descriptors to detail what you see for your self in each area. Then, write down your achievement and avoidance intentions in each area.

Area	Examples	Achievement Intentions	Avoidance Intentions
General Life Descriptors	*Happy, Innovative, Stable*		
Physical Descriptors	*Athletic, Strong*		
Life-Style	*Social, Adventurous*		
General Abilities	*Dual-Language, Artsy*		
Occupational Options	*Entrepreneur, Corporate Position, Non-Profit*		
Other-Focused Opinions	*Followed, Appreciated*		

Activity 2: Learning Outcomes

The Possible Self Inventory helps you visualize how you want your life to look, how you envision yourself, your abilities, occupations, and perceptions of you by the community. Clarifying these aspects may help you identity the possible selves you are most interested in fostering and give direction and motivation towards specific goals. This activity is a first step towards more intensive action planning for your leadership development discussed in Chapter 11.

Activity 3: Sub-Identity and Possible Self Motives

In the following activity, please refer back to your "I see myself as…" statements from earlier in the chapter and to the intentions you just listed. Using the table below, choose the motives driving each identity. Once you have explored the central identity motivations behind your sub-identities and your possible selves, you can begin to prepare the necessary resources required to enact these sub-identities across domains.

Figure 1: Why and How Individuals are Motivated to Construct Their Identity

Central identity motives	Definition of motive
Belonging	A need to feel close to, connected to, and accepted by others
Belonging: personalized	A need to feel known or liked as an individual based on interpersonal attraction
Belonging: depersonalized	A need to feel known and liked as a member of a collective based on social attraction
Need for identification (see, also, self-construal)	A need to define oneself in terms of a given target (i.e., another individual, role-relationship, collective)
Self-enhancement (see, also, self-expansion, self-improvement)	A need to hold valued identities and a desire to grow toward a positive conception of oneself
Self-knowledge (see, also, self-assessment)	A need to accurately understand more about oneself, particularly in the context in which the identity is enacted and salient to others
Self-expression (see, also, authenticity)	A need to display one's sense of self and to enact identities that are valued
Self-coherence	A need for an integrated sense of self
Self-continuity	A need for a consistent sense of self over time
Optimal distinctiveness	A need to strike a balance between seeing oneself as similar to and different from others
Reduction of subjective uncertainty	A need to resolve, manage, or avoid a perceived lack of clarity
Self-verification	A need to be seen by others as one sees oneself
Self-presentation	A need to externally project a socially desirable self to influence others' perceptions
Identity-relevant but more peripheral motives	
Meaningfulness	A need to find significance or purpose
Self-efficacy	A need for a sense of capability and competence
Control	A need to influence domains perceived as important

Used with permission of Annual Reviews, Inc., from Annual Review of Organizational Psychology and Organizational Behavior, B.E. Ashforth, B.S. Schinoff, vol. 3, © 2013; permission conveyed through Copyright Clearance Center, Inc.

Activity 3: Learning Outcomes

The central and peripheral identity motives listed in Activity 3 can help you recognize what motivates you towards identity construction. Once you identity the drivers of motivational effort, you can use those motives to help direct attention and resources towards specific goal attainment. For example, if you acknowledge that you have a need for belonging, you may recognize that you enact behaviors within your roles that emphasize a group's social identity. Alternatively, if you find that you have a need for self-continuity, you may recognize behaviors that connect your past actions to your future actions and avoid behaviors that take you in a different direction.

Identities in Multiple Domains

Humans often organize identities by situations, or domains—the areas in which our daily behaviors are enacted. As we reach adulthood, complete full-time education, and launch working careers, these domains typically fall into three categories: work, family/friends, and community. In organizational behavior, researchers explore work-related identities enacted mainly in the work domain. Data presented in the book *Happiness at Work* (Pryce-Jones, 2010) estimates that the average American spends over 90,000 hours of their life at work. Research suggests that adopting positive work identities can increase self-esteem and help one identify as part of a social group (Dutton et al., 2010). Furthermore, constructing these identities based on one's ideals and standards can enhance the meaningfulness one finds in their work (May, Gilson, & Harter, 2004).

© ESB Basic/Shutterstock.com

Organizational behavior research often treats these work identities as a persona left at one's place of business and explores work outcomes such as job satisfaction and performance. However, the shifting nature of work, technology, and our approach to life in the twenty-first century is expanding those boundaries. Some professional identities have always spilled over from the work domain—think of a doctor or nurse who jumps into action at the scene of an accident, or a writer who consistently scans the environment for stories or characters. However, more workers than ever are being asked to enact their identities outside of a typical workday—perhaps because they have clients in other time zones, they work with a team that needs answers after hours, or they are able to work remotely on occasion. Scheduling demands for adults or working parents, organizing community activities, and collaborating with friends' groups are further examples that can impose upon traditional work hours—especially when decisions are time sensitive. In addition, the increasing use of technology before, during, and after working hours activates multiple sub-identities, which may create challenges in the work-family interface. As people elect to continue to adapt to telework opportunities, the

© fizkes/Shutterstock.com

barriers between domains become less clear, meaning additional self-awareness and cognitive agility to negotiate cross-domain interruptions are required. This text focuses on these cross-domain interactions, allowing for the theoretical and empirical findings from leadership and management sciences to be applied to real-world challenges and situations.

Leader Identity

While identity seeks to answer the question "Who am I?", the idea of **leader identity** poses "Who am I as a leader?" (Clapp-Smith, Hammond, Vogelgesang Lester, & Palanski, 2018). As noted above, some identities cross domains. A leader identity is one such identity, as it can straddle multiple domains like work-to-community or friends/family-to-work (DeRue, Ashford, & Cotton, 2009; Hammond, Clapp-Smith, & Palanski, 2018; Vogelgesang Lester, Palanski, Hammond, & Clapp-Smith, 2017). A leader identity is activated in multiple domains by situations that require an individual to make decisions or support others in the decisions they make. Thinking about leadership from an identity standpoint can help novice leaders in the work domain build upon their prior skills and abilities from other domains. In this approach, the leadership skills encountered as a member of a sports team, drama club, gaming group, or any community-based organization can make up one's leader identity. Those skills can then be applied to the family domain, the work domain, or the community domain, where they are reinforced and will then spur further development. Too often, we treat leadership in the work domain as a skill that can only be acquired after a manager bestows potential on an individual and puts them on the "leadership track". But this approach may end up ignoring the leadership skills already in existence within the organization, and it can be demotivating for the individuals who are not singled out for development.

> **LEADER IDENTITY:** The self-perception one has of themselves as a leader. (Derue, Ashford, & Cotton, 2009)

Leader and Manager Identity—Born or Made?

Successful leaders evoke powerful emotions, and history tends to place leaders on a pedestal to be admired and emulated. In most societies leaders are seen as infallible, heroic change agents who make the world a better place. In other societies—like Australia—such individuals are singled out for scrutiny and viewed from the outset as untrustworthy (Peeters, 2004). Some leaders are objective change agents. But via the explosion of social and other media modalities, we as individuals reinforce the mythology of leadership (e.g., we "follow" other people on social media, which implies that those we are following are leaders operating under the *nom de guerre* of "influencer"). Leadership is seductive—many inherently want to trust leaders, and over time an emotional attachment grows, which is why we react so negatively when we learn just how human these leaders really are. After all, one of the earliest conceptualizations of leadership was called "The Great Man Theory," which mythologized leaders and held that some people are simply born to be great leaders.

This view is as pervasive as it is wrong. Throughout our teaching undergraduate and graduate leadership courses, coupled with our own experiences working in corporate and government contexts, we continue to find that the "made or born?" question is alive and well. This debate rages among practitioners despite convincing scientific evidence, which answered the question years ago. Subsequent research continues to add weight to what we know about the made-or-born

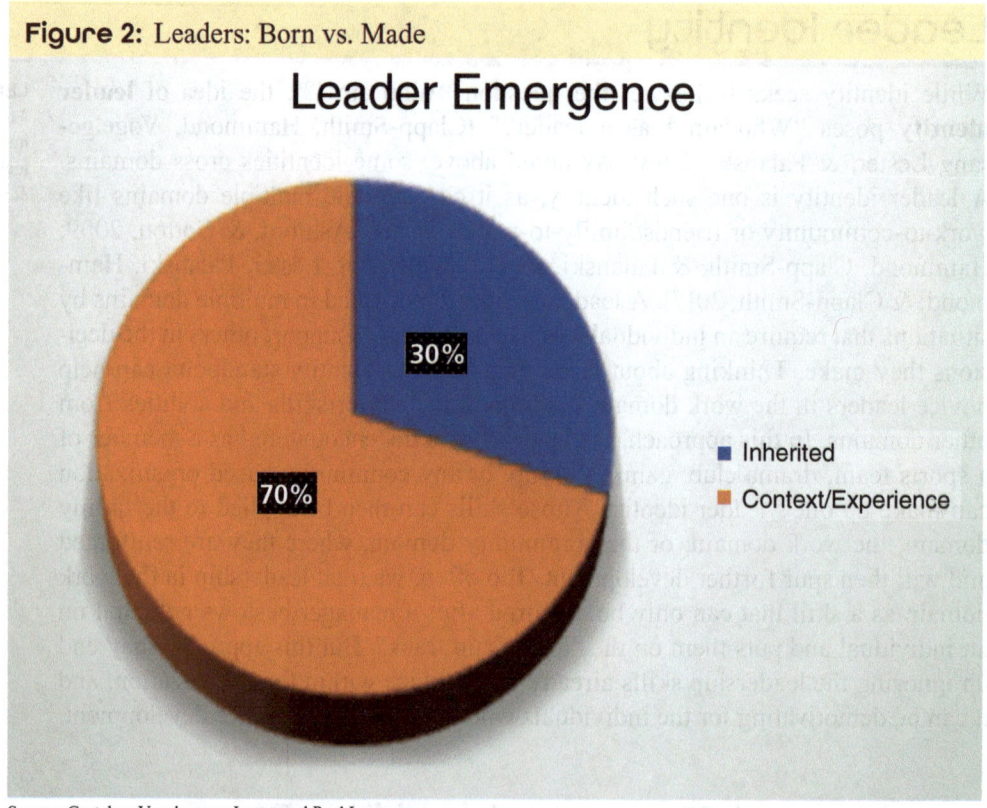

Figure 2: Leaders: Born vs. Made

Source: Gretchen Vogelgesang Lester and Paul Lester

question. In short, yes, some people are born with certain qualities that help them emerge and perform as leaders. Yet, the environment—what we learn, how we are raised, our level of education, the opportunities presented to us—plays a much larger role than genetic gifts.

Just how much bigger? Leadership researchers have studied identical and fraternal twins in several studies. This is important because identical twins share nearly identical genetic material, while fraternal twins share approximately half of their genetic material. So, if leaders really are "born" and we hold all other factors constant, identical twins *should* emerge in tandem as leaders. On the other hand, different trajectories of leader emergence *should* manifest within fraternal twins (i.e., within fraternal twin pairs, one sibling might become a leader while the other does not). However, the research does not support this notion. Instead, it offers much more nuance. If we think of leadership as a pie, with the two ingredients being heritability (what we're born with) and context (environmental factors that shape us), about 30% of leader emergence can be attributed to heritability, while 70% can be linked to the environment (for a review of several studies, see Avolio & Hannah, 2020).

This is especially important when you consider that while we cannot readily change what we are born with, we can absolutely shape our environment. However, both are important to leader development. While we can learn new skills, receive training as leaders, and strive for an outstanding education about leadership, we can also leverage the heritable strengths that we have (such as certain aspects of our personality) provided we are sufficiently aware of them and understand how to properly use them to influence others. We will dive deeper into these areas in Chapter 4.

Leader Identity—Meaning, Level, Strength, Integration

A leader identity is made up of four components: meaning, level, strength, and integration (Hammond et al., 2018). The **meaning** of leadership stems from personalized beliefs about leadership, and what we expect and demand from leaders. Our **level** of leadership identity encompasses the types of leadership behaviors we enact, either through personal characteristics, interpersonal influence, or membership in a group. Our **strength** of leadership identity determines the extent to which we define ourselves as leaders. Finally, our **integration** of leader identity refers to how easily we adapt our leader skills across different domains—or if we choose instead to splinter our identity across domains. While we will thoroughly investigate each of these components throughout the text, for now, take a moment to analyze your leader identity based on these facets. How do you illustrate leadership with your actions? How do you prefer to lead—with innate skills, by working with another person, a small team, or as part of a collective? How strongly do you identify as a leader? Finally, do you act as a leader across domains or partition leader behaviors based on domain-specific roles? Answering these questions will give you a baseline analysis of your leader identity.

Sensemaking and Sensebreaking

We often see the greatest development of leader identity when experiencing new situations. We may have to adopt different identities until we have made sense of our new environment. Sometimes, we have to break down our belief systems in a sensebreaking process to create new meanings (Pratt, 2000). For example, if your meaning of leadership includes a directive leader barking orders at a willing group of employees, but you realize you feel more comfortable and effective leading with interpersonal influence for the good of the team and organization, you must break your initial meaning to construct a new one. Doing so will increase your strength of leader identity. This breaking down of meaning requires the individual to question their initial understanding of leadership and to pursue trying on new and different possible leader selves (Pratt, 2000). And this process serves as a catalyst for a new identity construction phase towards leading with influence instead of coercive power.

Alternatively, one can embrace a sensemaking process to foster a leader identity. Sensemaking includes noticing, interpreting, authoring, and enacting behaviors. Instead of breaking down and rebuilding one's initial understanding of leadership, they might instead practice observing successful leaders, **noticing**, for example, that inspirational appeals as an influence tactic are more effective in fostering commitment than pressure tactics. They then **interpret** an additional meaning of leadership (leaders can be directive *and* lead with influence), perhaps adding detail to their initial understanding. They can then seek to include leading with influence by **authoring** their own personal leader identity, which may then bring forth the **enactment** of such behaviors. As their leader identity continues to develop, new behaviors can be adapted and eventually enacted.

In this text, we embrace the idea that humans are always adapting and thus, learning new knowledge, skills, and abilities needed to move through life. Leader identity provides the opportunity to use life lessons and experiences within our careers to achieve success.

Organizational Behavior and Leadership

Organizational behavior is the study of humans at work. It encompasses research from psychology, sociology, political science, anthropology, and several other fields to help us predict and explain why humans enact the behaviors they enact in the work environment. But given that the work environment is changing and the boundaries between domains are becoming less distinct, this book focuses on all domains of life to provide even greater insight into how we can harness all facets of development and enable workers to find meaningful work. The study of organizational behavior can include cases, experiments, observations, and qualitative research to inform processes and policy for the working environment. Throughout the text, we will include research findings from all of these areas to explain the content.

Evidence-Based Approach

EVIDENCE-BASED MANAGEMENT: Setting aside the accepted conventions and hierarchy of opinion, and instead, using critical thinking and the best available evidence to make decisions. (Pfeffer & Sutton, 2006)

This text adopts an evidence-based approach to organizational behavior. Thousands of researchers across the globe conduct research into human behavior and organizations. This text seeks to include activities, theories, examples, and applications that provide evidence of efficacy (in essence, the things that actually work). While there are many "gurus" who purport methods that work, the reality is that many thought leaders in business have not run scientific studies of their approaches. What worked in their personal experience may not apply to the broader business of management. Therefore, we include the most cohesive evidence from the latest research to present theories that govern behavior in as many situations as possible. As Pfeffer and Sutton note, "Managers can practice their craft more effectively if they are routinely guided by the best logic and evidence" (2006, p. 2). Knowing where to look for evidence-based management as you begin your working career will set you apart from the millions of managers and leaders who do not have formal management education. The first step to understanding the evidence is to acknowledge the importance of the scientific method in organizational behavior and leadership research.

Scientific Method

Organizational behavior and leadership are social sciences. Due to the complexity of human beings, these sciences are not as concrete or predictable as disciplines like biology and chemistry. Still, researchers use data-driven approaches to find evidence that either supports or disproves hypotheses. The scientific method guides organizational behavior and leadership research.

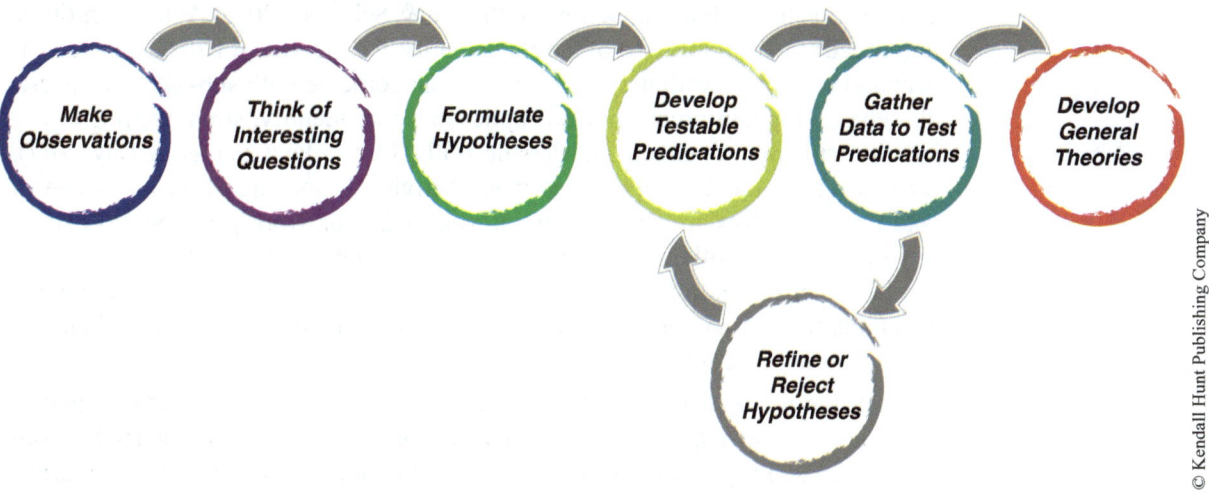

Figure 3: The Scientific Method

Like any scientific experiment, one first **makes observations** about a particular phenomenon, then **devises questions** to help focus the attention on the driving force behind the phenomenon. From those questions, one **formulates hypotheses** that are **testable**. Researchers **gather data** through surveys, observations, experiments, case studies, interviews, or other data-collection methods. The data determine if the hypotheses are supported or contradicted, which then leads to refinement and additional data gathering. Amassing data allows for **generalizing the theories** to the larger population... until **new observations** occur. As noted above, the content included in this textbook includes general theories observed over decades of organizational behavior and leadership research. While these theories are particularly interested in work-focused outcomes like performance and job satisfaction, the identity approach includes outcomes that not only affect the whole person, (e.g., stress, engagement, self-confidence) but also the domains in which they operate (team performance, community engagement, cross-domain learning, and performance). The more identity work we undertake, the more we can understand the broader repercussions both inside and outside the work domain.

Outcomes of Identity Work

Research into identity work strongly supports taking this approach regarding organizational behavior and leadership. Not only can your work shape your identity, but your identity can also shape and change your work. A study of medical residents found that those who saw themselves as primary caregivers enriched their original work identity to include not just the treatment of maladies, but also an emotional connection with their patients. The demands of the work required a shift in identity—they changed the way they conducted their work by taking a more caring approach with patients (Pratt, Rockmann, & Kaufmann, 2006). Identity construction can help move individuals towards a promising future by serving as a motivational tool for goal-setting (Ashforth & Schinoff, 2016). When identity is reinforced as a desirable part of the core identity, the individual will be more confident and seek out additional opportunities that coincide with sub-identities/possible selves. This reinforcement also applies to leader identity: strengthening leader identity will enhance enacted leadership skills (Miscenko, Guenter, & Day, 2017). As you reflect upon your motives from Activity 3, you may find that some of your possible selves are already guiding your behavior, from your course of study to your choice of college to your selected career field. Envision how powerful it can be to engage individuals in the identity construction process from the earliest points in their careers, thus setting the conditions for positive individual and organizational outcomes.

From the management perspective, understanding how individuals construct identities can also help explain performance. For example, females tend to be more complex in identity formation and construct fluid identities that span boundaries, while males tend to create separated, bounded selves (Jordan, 1997). Organizations and leaders who understand the different processes of identity construction for their workers can better motivate and foster desired identities.

Implicit Leader/Organization Theories

IMPLICIT LEADERSHIP THEORIES: Assumptions, beliefs, and expectations regarding the causes, nature, and consequences of leadership. (Lord & Emrich, 2001)

We mentioned earlier that people tend to either set leaders upon pedestals or increase their scrutiny. These ideas communicate an outsized influence on the leader role. Such expectations are called **Implicit Leadership Theories (ILTs)**, "assumptions, beliefs, and expectations regarding the causes, nature, and consequences of leadership" (Lord & Emrich, 2001). Each individual carries their own unique implicit leadership theories—basically, their picture of what a leader is supposed to do or how a leader is supposed to act. These ILTs are formed through experiences, behavioral models, cultural understandings, representations of leaders in the media, fiction and nonfiction content, and role models. Our ILTs change through exposure to different managers and leaders, but often we seek to match leaders to the prototypes we already envision. When pattern matching, we may overlook negative attributes and forgive poor performance or unsuccessful decision-making because our ILTs override our lived experience. It is important to understand, then, what our ILTs look like—this will be the focus of Chapter 2.

IMPLICIT ORGANIZATIONAL THEORIES: Expectations regarding models or organizations imprinted into the firm. (Eden & Leviatan, 2005)

We also have **Implicit Organization Theories (IOTs)**: our expectations for how organizations should be structured. We often attribute more power to leaders in organizations because of our IOTs. We hold an idea that the person in charge should wield significant power. This idea manifests as the Romance of Leadership, where individuals tend to over-attribute responsibility to leaders instead of the market, the government, or human capital within the organization. Becoming aware of our implicit theories is the first step in claiming a leader identity and preparing for leadership emergence. Noticing how humans overestimate and over-attribute responsibility in some cases, and underestimate in others, is an important part of the sensemaking process regarding applied organizational behavior.

In Review

The opening chapter creates a foundation for using your identity in leadership and organizational behavior. As we note in the first paragraph "leadership is the exertion of social influence…working toward a common goal". Your identity, made up of your values and experiences is what allows you to exert leadership or followership both in and outside of organizations. Throughout the book, we will explore your identity as a leader and as a person, noting the meanings you attach to it, the strength of it, and how you integrate your identity across domains. We will also conduct many self-report assessments to help you increase your self-awareness and your self-reflection abilities. The more you can understand your identity as it is and what you hope to become, the more aware you are of the environment surrounding you and the opportunities that may present themselves. Seeing the connections between the ways people behavior in different types of organizations will help you apply leadership knowledge, skills, and abilities, regardless of your actual position.

The statistic regarding whether leaders are made (about 70%) or born (30%) underscores our approach. Leaders are constantly honing their skills, accepting new challenges, including serving in follower roles when required. The interplay between leaders and followers in organizations is a key driver of performance outcomes and personal satisfaction. The evidence shows that anyone can emerge as a leader if they have a developmental mindset and seek out opportunities to hone their leadership abilities.

Understanding how you see yourself and the roles you take on, how you relate to others, and how you see your future possibilities is a key driver of identity development. The activities in this chapter capture your current state, your desired future states, and the motivations attached to your identities. Approaching your possible selves with a sensemaking and sensebreaking mindset will help you notice opportunities, interpret self- and other reactions, author your own narrative, and enact behaviors that move you closer to your desired state. We ground all of this in the scientific method because organizational behavior and leadership are social sciences with decades of evidence supporting the relationship between variables and the outcomes generating performance and satisfaction. We encourage all those who are in a leadership or followership relationship to use the scientific method to observe what and how things work, the influence processes amongst organizational members, and the potential actions to take based upon the challenges that arise.

If you are motivated to lead and seek to understand organizational behavior, the first step is awareness regarding your own identity. This is your opportunity to author your own development journey; this is not the time to act out a role someone else has created for you. You don't need to wait for a supervisor to bestow you with a promotion or nominate you for a leadership development program, you can do this yourself. The environment around you—your community, your classes and classmates, your friends and family—they all present leadership opportunities. The challenge is noticing those opportunities, acting, and then communicating the skills you have developed to those instrumental to your success.

The next chapter explores how we attribute success and failure to individuals in organizations. Learning about these attributions and your own cognitive shortcuts will provide insight into how you can use these predictable actions to your benefit.

Learning Objectives

Identify and define identity

Identity is the sum total of one's values, experiences, and self-perceptions. We explain ourselves to others by describing our identities and sub-identities, which can exist across multiple roles and multiple domains. Activity 1 asked you to complete the question stem "I see myself as…" to help you identify your identities.

Analyze your leader identity

A leader identity is the self-perception you have regarding your self as a leader. You may have included aspects of a leader identity in your possible self-inventory, noting central identity motives related to a leader identity, such as belongingness, identification, or self-enhancement. Understanding the motives behind constructing a leader identity can help you determine the outcomes you expect to achieve.

Examine a multi-domain approach to identity

A multi-domain approach to identity describes the meaning, level, strength, and integration of an identity. The meaning is based upon our personalized beliefs about leadership and expectations we hold. The level of identity varies based upon personal skills, interpersonal influence, and group membership or social identity. The strength of identity indicates how much we define ourselves as leaders and may be derived from the skills, abilities, and competencies we develop through different experiences. The integration of identity illustrates how intertwined or splintered our identity is across domains; how easily we may enact behaviors in multiple domains.

Apply personal identity to organizational behavior outcomes

Identity work explores how both dispositional and situational factors combine to construct your identity. This means incorporating your traits, emotions, and abilities alongside the requirements placed upon you by the organizations with which you associate. Your work, community, family, or your friendships can shape your identity but also can be *shaped by* your identity. Your possible selves can motivate certain actions towards desirable outcomes. The extent to which you understand your identities, sub-identities, and possible selves will lend you confidence, encourage emergent leader behaviors, and enhance your skill sets.

Key Terms

Leader (Pg. 1)

Leadership (Pg. 1)

Identity (Pg. 2)

Organizational Behavior (Pg. 2)

Identity Construction (Pg. 3)

Possible Selves (Pg. 3)

Leader Identity (Pg. 6)

Evidence-Based Management (Pg. 10)

Implicit Leadership Theories (Pg. 12)

Implicit Organizational Theories (Pg. 12)

Critical Thinking Questions

1. As a manager, how can you help your employees construct their identities and sub-identities? Describe the ways in which you could use different central identity motives to incentivize certain behaviors.

2. In your own words, describe the steps of the sensemaking process. Give an example of a time you have used this process in your own development.

3. Why do you think we employ evidence-based management approaches and include a scientific method section in this text? Why is this approach important to leadership and organizational behavior?

4. What are the outcomes of identity work for organizations? As a manager, why should you be concerned about the relationships between different variables and these outcomes?

Chapter Summary

In this chapter, we have introduced the concept of identity in relation to leadership and organizational behavior. Identities are constructed from possible selves and are informed by experiences and challenges throughout our lives. Most identities are role-based in that they are enacted only in a particular domain. A leader identity is a unique identity that informs actions in multiple domains. Leader identity is derived from our meaning, level, strength, and integration of leader behaviors across domains. As we seek to understand how to enact the leader identity both in and outside of work, we can use our knowledge of organizational behavior to determine which behaviors are appropriate for specific situations.

References

Ashforth, B. E., & Schinoff, B. S. (2016). Identity under construction: How individuals come to define themselves in organizations. *Annual Review of Organizational Psychology and Organizational Behavior, 3*(1), 111–137.

Avolio, B. J., & Hannah, S. T. (2020). An enduring leadership myth: Born a leader or made a leader?. *Organizational Dynamics, 49*(4), 100730.

Clapp-Smith, R., Hammond, M. M., Lester, G. V., & Palanski, M. (2019). Promoting identity development in leadership education: A multidomain approach to developing the whole leader. *Journal of Management Education, 43*(1), 10–34.

DeRue, D. S., Ashford, S. J., & Cotton, N. C. (2009). Assuming the mantle: Unpacking the process by which individuals internalize a leader identity. *Exploring positive identities and organizations: Building a theoretical and research foundation, 213–232.*

Dutton, J. E., Roberts, L. M., & Bednar, J. (2010). Pathways for positive identity construction at work: Four types of positive identity and the building of social resources. *Academy of Management Review, 35*(2), 265–293.

Eden, D., & Leviatan, U. (2005). From implicit personality theory to implicit leadership theory: A side-trip on the way to implicit organization theory. In B. Schyns, & J. R. Meindl (Eds.), *The Leadership Horizon Series: Implicit Leadership Theories—Essays and Explorations.* IAP: Greenwich, CT.

Gecas, V. (1982). The self-concept. *Annual Review of Sociology*, 1–33.

Hammond, M., Clapp-Smith, R., & Palanski, M. (2017). Beyond (just) the workplace: A theory of leader development across multiple domains. *Academy of Management Review, 42*(3), 481–498.

Jordan, J. V. (1997). A relational perspective for understanding women's development. *Women's growth in diversity: More writings from the Stone Center*, 9–24.

Kuhn, M. H., & McPartland, T. S. (1954). Twenty Statements Test. *American Sociological Review*.

Markus, H., & Nurius, P. (1986). Possible selves. *American Psychologist, 41*(9), 954.

May, D. R., Gilson, R. L., & Harter, L. M. (2004). The psychological conditions of meaningfulness, safety and availability and the engagement of the human spirit at work. *Journal of Occupational and Organizational Psychology, 77*(1), 11–37.

Miscenko, D., Guenter, H., & Day, D. V. (2017). Am I a leader? Examining leader identity development over time. *The Leadership Quarterly, 28*(5), 605–620.

Peeters, B. (2004). Thou shalt not be a tall poppy: Describing an Australian communicative (and behavioral) norm. *Intercultural Pragmatics*, 1, 71–92.

Pfeffer, J., & Sutton, R. I. (2006). Evidence-based management. *Harvard Business Review, 84*(1), 62.

Pratt, M. G. (2000). The good, the bad, and the ambivalent: Managing identification among Amway distributors. *Administrative Science Quarterly, 45*(3), 456–493.

Pratt, M. G., Rockmann, K. W., & Kaufmann, J. B. (2006). Constructing professional identity: The role of work and identity learning cycles in the customization of identity among medical residents. *Academy of Management Journal, 49*(2), 235–262.

Pryce-Jones, J. (2011). *Happiness at work: Maximizing your psychological capital for success*. John Wiley & Sons.

Vogelgesang Lester, G., Palanski, M., Hammond, M., & Clapp-Smith, R. (2017). Multi-domain leadership: A whole person approach to leading in the workplace... and beyond. *Organizational Dynamics, 46*(3), 133–139.

Wittman, S. (2019). Lingering identities. *Academy of Management Review, 44*(4), 724–745.

CHAPTER 2
Attribution Theories in Leadership and Organizational Behavior

CHAPTER OUTCOMES

1. Define and explain attributions
2. Differentiate between attribution errors and self-serving biases
3. Explore your personal implicit leadership theories
4. Describe attribution theories of leadership
5. Examine Self-Fulfilling Prophecies

Purpose of this Chapter

In this chapter, we explore how **attributions** shape our understanding of behavior in organizations and in our everyday lives. We define attributions, explore how our brains use attributions to explain experiences and events, and then detail leadership theories that are rooted in attribution theory. We highlight the common attribution biases that are often self-serving and illustrate methods by which we can question our attributions. Finally, we will discuss how individuals can navigate the tendency for humans to use attributions.

ATTRIBUTIONS: The interpretive process by which people make judgments about the causes of their own behavior and the behavior of others. (Merriam Webster)

What are attributions?

Attributions are how we make sense of the world around us. They help us interpret the behaviors we witness and guide how we judge our own behaviors in response. Attributions are a cognitive shortcut, meant to limit the amount of effort required to take in new information (Wiener, 1985). Our attributions are affected by many different factors, including temperament, personality traits, moods, emotions, experiences, and knowledge. Attributions are a filter through which we see the world, sometimes distorting actual events. While attributions can be helpful in speeding up our decision-making processes, they can also be harmful by increasing our potential to make judgement errors. Let's observe a common example as a demonstration.

Activity 1: Self-Serving Bias

First, think of a time you arrived early or exactly on time to an event. Did you attribute your expected arrival to your own personal effort and planning (e.g., leaving on time, accounting for public transportation schedules, previewing the parking situation, etc.)? If so, enter your explanation in the "Internal" column below. Or did you feel that you were lucky or only arrived on time because you had the resources available (e.g., personal car, public transportation worked, a parking spot magically appeared, etc.)? If so, enter your explanation in the "External" column below.

Now, think about a time you were late for class or a meeting. Why were you late? Was it due to some external factor outside of your control (e.g., traffic, parking, a friend stopped you along the way, another class that ran late, etc.)? Or did you think it was your fault (e.g., improper planning, lack of interest)? Again, enter your explanation into the "Internal" or "External" column.

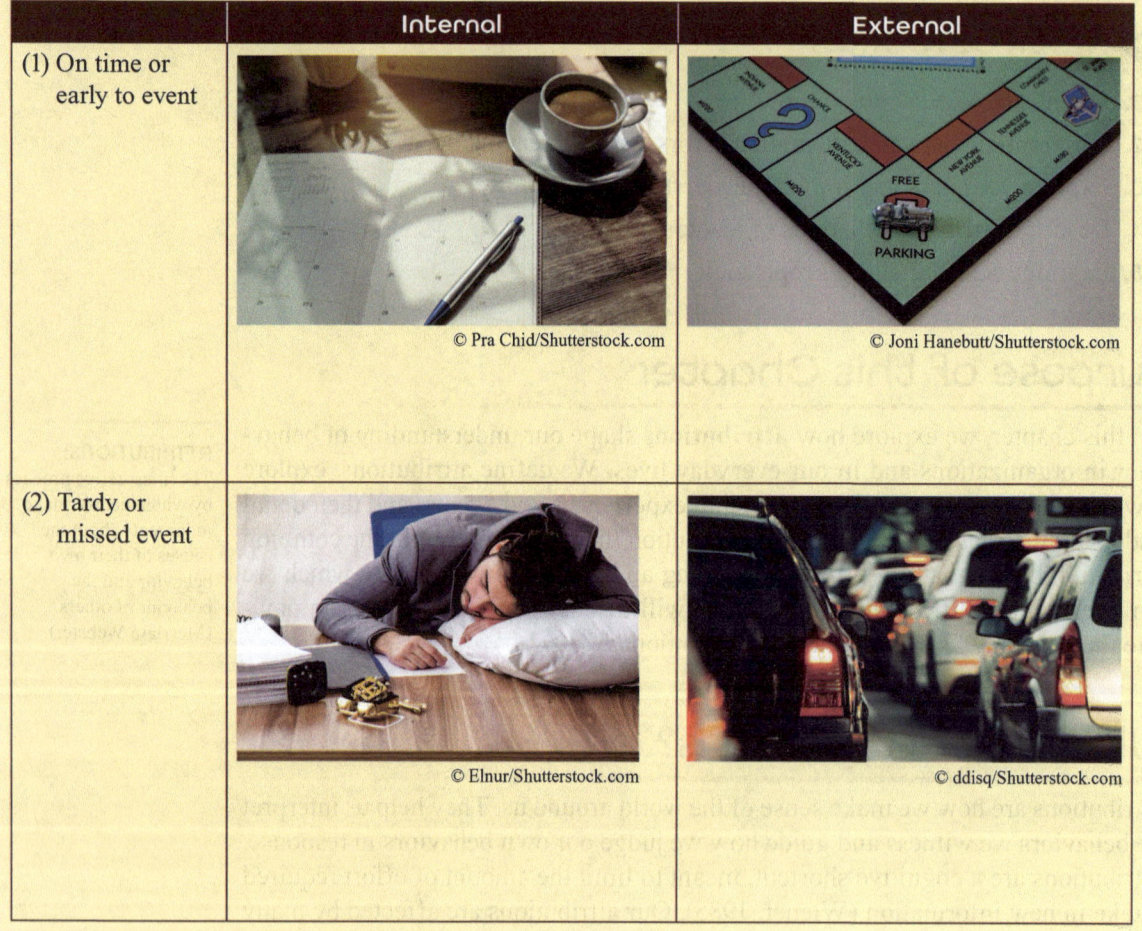

Activity 1: Learning Outcomes

Now, compare your results to your classmates, peers, or family members. In general, are explanations in (1) mostly internal or external? How about those in (2)?

If you are like most individuals, you congratulated yourself on proper planning in section (1) but, used external or situational excuses for (2).

We often use internal explanations for something that goes well, and external explanations to justify a failing—this is called a **self-serving bias** (Miller & Ross, 1975). This tendency varies due to personality characteristics and core-self evaluations such as self-esteem and locus of control, all of which is covered in Chapter 4. For example, those with high levels of self-confidence are more likely to use a self-serving bias (Silver, Mitchell, & Gist, 1995), while individuals with low self-esteem or who hold a negative self-view are less likely to be self-serving (Mezulis, Abramson, Hyde, & Hankin, 2004). As a manager or leader, you must recognize not only your own tendencies to employ a self-serving bias, but also to observe how your followers incorporate such explanations. Incorporating a simple activity like the one above can provide insight into how an individual takes credit or assigns blame for expected versus unexpected outcomes.

SELF-SERVING BIAS: People view their positive outcomes as primarily internally caused, yet view their negative outcomes as primarily externally caused. (Shepperd, Malone, & Sweeny, 2008)

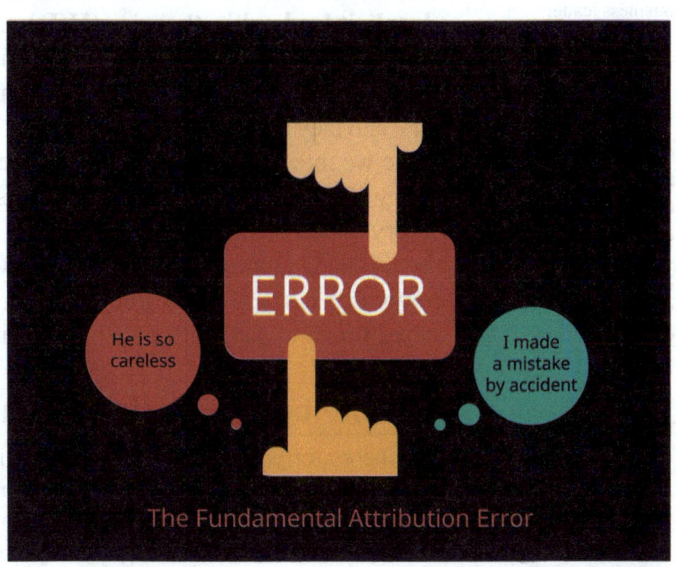
© Piscine26/Shutterstock.com

The self-serving bias is activated while interpreting our own behavior, but we often employ different attributions when evaluating the behavior of others. To illustrate, take the same example as above, but instead of observing yourself in the situation, think about a time a teammate was late. While you were sitting there wondering where your teammate was, did you think they were lazy or didn't care about attendance? Did you think they would rely on you to get them the work from the day? Or did you blame illness, family issues, or another external factor on their behalf? If you immediately thought it was a disposition or personality characteristic (lazy, uncaring, inconsiderate), you have made the **Fundamental Attribution Error**, meaning you attributed the cause of an action to the person rather than the situation. **Disposition** generally refers to how an individual acts or thinks. The Fundamental Attribution Error is the inverse of self-serving bias—when no potential explanation is offered, we tend to attribute others' achievements to a situation or external factors (such as luck) and their failings to personal traits or abilities. Again, it is important to question the attributions we make regarding our own and others' behaviors and performance. Doing so ensures we make the effort to properly review incidents from multiple perspectives.

FUNDAMENTAL ATTRIBUTION ERROR: The tendency for attributors to underestimate the impact of situational factors and to overestimate the role of dispositional factors in controlling behavior. (Ross, 1977, p. 183)

DISPOSITION: A person's inherent qualities of mind and character. (Oxford Languages)

Our attributions take on additional importance in an organizational context. Actors in organizations can either be helped by self-serving biases or derailed by misplaced fundamental attribution errors. The expectations created for those in decision-making roles (i.e., leaders and managers) can create structural issues for our organizations. Uncovering individuals' different meanings of leader identity will clarify expectations and set the conditions for enhanced decision-making processes to help avoid these potential errors.

We will now explore the meaning of leader identity, where one's expectations mold a particular type of leader (Implicit Theories). We will also examine the circumstances around an organization's attributed success or failure (Romance of Leadership). Throughout this process, we must be aware of how our attributions shape an individual's ability to progress as a leader (Self-Fulfilling Prophecies). Finally, we will explore how leaders can attribute certain behaviors to followers (Theory X/Theory Y).

Implicit Leadership Theories

IMPLICIT LEADERSHIP THEORIES: Personal assumptions about the traits and abilities that characterize an ideal business leader. (Epitropaki & Martin, 2004)

MEANING OF LEADER IDENTITY: the characteristics and knowledge, skills, and abilities one includes as part of their understanding of effective leadership.

Implicit leadership theories (ILTs) are "personal assumptions about the traits and abilities that characterize an ideal business leader" (Epitropaki & Martin, 2004, p. 293). They are expectations that determine how we view current and potential leaders, and they are shaped by experiences and stimuli throughout our development. Any time we interact with an individual we perceive as a leader, our ILTs are activated. They shape our behavior and reactions to the events occurring around us. Leaders everywhere—teachers, scout leaders, parents, community members, siblings, the heroes and heroines in pop culture movies, the protagonists in books—serve as prototypes that shape ILTs throughout our lives. Each successive leader behavior is filtered through these patterns, thus shaping our perceptions of their effectiveness.

Activity 2: Leader Identity Meaning

Your implicit leadership theory, or your **meaning** of leadership is personal. It is the same for your implicit management theory. These meanings inform how you see yourself and others as leaders and managers. This exercise should help you uncover your meaning of leadership and management and highlight variability across domains (e.g., in your view, does a leader or manager act differently at work than they should when working with volunteers in the community?).

Step 1: Draw what effective leadership looks like in different domains (work, community, school, friends/family, etc. Draw what management looks like.
Step 2: Describe what is occurring in your pictures. Explore visuals, sounds, tones of voice, etc.
Step 3: Write down your personal meaning of leadership based upon the images portrayed across domains.
Step 4: Compare drawings with your classmates, peers, or family members. Review similarities and differences.

Source: Gretchen Vogelgesang Lester and Paul Lester

Activity 2: Learning Outcomes

Your illustration represents your current understanding and meaning of leader identity. It may include prototypical behaviors, but also may include unique qualities that you believe are important for effective leadership.

Prototypes

PROTOTYPE: An abstract conception of the most representative member or most widely shared features of a given cognitive category. (Phillips, 1984, p. 126)

ILTs are **prototypes**. A prototype is an "abstract conception of the most representative member or most widely shared features of a given cognitive category" (Phillips, 1984, p. 126). When we find that a person's demeanor, physical attributes, or behavior match our ILT, we are more likely to conflate our expectations with effectiveness. When you picture a super hero, a specific image likely comes to mind. Take a moment to draw that image in the picture frame provided.

Chapter 2: Attribution Theories in Leadership and Organizational Behavior

Humans are more likely to view someone as an effective leader when there is a pattern match between that person and one's ILT. This can create issues when someone who does not fit our "leader mold" moves into a leadership position, as we are less likely to view that person as effective (Schyns, 2006). From an evolutionary standpoint, pattern matching allows for quick judgements that can be helpful when under stress. In current society, we must take the time and effort to ensure that our pattern-matching tendencies don't ignore potential leaders or innovators just because they do not fit generalized expectations. There are financial consequences as well—entrepreneurs who do not fit the "pattern" of upstart innovators (e.g., women or people of color) are less likely to receive funding. Even when they do, it is for smaller amounts (Hebert, 2019). Thus, it is imperative we continue to seek out diverse representations of leaders in many different segments of society and at multiple levels in organizations to maximize opportunities for success.

© NoraVector/Shutterstock.com

Research on ILTs established four universal prototypes and two anti-types. Those prototypes and anti-types may vary by individual and by organization, but it is still helpful to know how your co-workers or peers feel about certain leader prototypes so you can evaluate whether your ILTs match. If you work in an environment where one prototype is commonly held but you do not hold that same prototype, you may find it difficult to progress your career (Schyns, 2006).

Activity 3: Leader Prototype/Antitype Rating Activity
(Epitropaki & Martin, 2004)

Step 1: Please rate the extent (from **not at all** to **extremely**) to which you find that each descriptor is a characteristic of a business leader.

	Not at all			Somewhat			Extremely
1. Understanding							
2. Helpful							
3. Sincere							
4. Intelligent							
5. Knowledgeable							
6. Clever							
7. Educated							
8. Dedicated							
9. Motivated							

10. Hard-working									
11. Energetic									
12. Strong									
13. Dynamic									
14. Domineering									
15. Pushy									
16. Manipulative									
17. Loud									
18. Selfish									
19. Conceited									
20. Masculine									
21. Male									

Source: Adapted from Epitropaki & Martin, 2004.

Activity 3: Learning Outcomes

Scoring:

Prototypes: Items 1-3 are Sensitivity; 4-8 are Intelligence; 8-10 are Dedication; 11-13 are Dynamism.

Anti-types: 14-19 are Tyranny; 20-21 are Masculinity.

Higher scores indicate the importance of the characteristic to your ILT.

Step 2: Compare your pattern to your leader identity drawing from Activity 2. Does your illustration integrate the prototypical behaviors that you scored the highest? If not, there may be a mismatch between your espoused meaning of leadership and your enacted meaning of leadership.

Source: Adapted from Epitropaki & Martin, 2004.

Implicit theories can be helpful for us. They lead to efficiencies in evaluating leader behaviors. However, they can cause us to miss out on potential leaders who do not fit our expectations. Consequently, we should routinely examine the prototypical behaviors that are rewarded to ensure they match the espoused goals of the organization. For example, if an organization highlights its participative nature towards decision-making but selects domineering individuals for management positions, there is a disconnect. However, if that same organization selects sincere and dynamic individuals for management positions, the culture will be reinforced.

Aligning perceived leader attributions with follower ILTs positively corresponds with the quality of leader-follower relationships. (Epitropaki & Martin, 2005). Thus, the more your leader matches your ILT, the likelier you are to develop a strong relationship with that leader. The greater the difference between the leader and your ILT, the weaker your relationship will be. Whether this difference can be overcome or not depends on your intrinsic motivation. Basically, the more you work toward overcoming the perceptual differences between your ILT and your leader, the less that difference will matter. From the leader's perspective, it is necessary to uncover followers' ILTs in order to understand and fulfill their expectations. From an organizational perspective, it is important to provide diverse representation of leaders. Doing so will create the motivation to overcome any ILT mismatches to ensure objective performance evaluations.

Attribution Theories of Leadership

Given our nature to use prototypes, we sometimes allow our expectations for leaders to override objective criteria regarding performance. This is another way in which attributions impact our decision-making. The **romance of leadership** theory describes how individuals over-attribute responsibility to leaders for organizational performance (Meindl, 1990). It is both an implicit organizational theory (organizations succeed or fail due to its leaders) and an implicit leadership theory (the leader generates organizational performance). Romance of leadership is a cognitive shortcut to explain organizational performance. It glosses over complexities of the industry, the global economic environment, workers' performance, etc. As with all attributions and attribution errors, it is much more efficient to reward or blame the leader than it is to stop and think through all the other factors. Think of how many times the coach of your favorite sports team is either rewarded handsomely with a new contract for a string of wins or fired immediately for a string of losses. Often, those decisions do not account for the following factors: investments franchise owners may or may not have made in the team; advances in technique the players may or may not be able to apply; decisions on salary negotiations or player trades; governing body rules that assist or disadvantage certain teams; or even something as simple as the weather. Fair or not, the coach is the one who symbolizes the effectiveness of the team.

When individuals romanticize leadership, their instinct is often to default to the prototype of a male leader. For example, a recent research study included an unnamed leader. In tweets that respondents were asked to write, if they included a gender, they gendered the leader as male. Interestingly, masculinity presents (as seen in the ILT activity above) as a leader anti-type—while masculine behaviors such as competitiveness and assertiveness do predict leader emergence, those behaviors are often at odds with leader effectiveness. And in times of crisis, individuals often prefer female leaders (Haslam et al., 2011). However, while female leaders are preferred in these precarious positions, they often end up taking the blame for poor performance, even if the failure preceded their organizational tenure. This phenomenon is known as the "**Glass Cliff**." Here, women tend to find their leadership positions associated with risk and potential failure. Further research supports a pattern where women are elevated to leadership positions after a company has encountered poor performance, but then the woman's leadership becomes an explanation for the poor performance (Ryan & Haslam, 2007). Romance of leadership—over-attribution to a leader's influence—can lead to the celebration or sacrifice of a leader, irrespective of his or her actual abilities and responsibility for the success or failure of the firm.

ROMANCE OF LEADERSHIP:
An over-attribution to leaders for responsibility over organizational performance. (Meindl, 1990)

GLASS CLIFF:
Women's positions of leadership are associated with greater risk of failure. (Ryan & Haslam, 2007)

Some individuals tend to romanticize leaders more than others. Research findings suggest that less experienced workers are more likely to romanticize leadership (Bligh & Schyns, 2007). In addition, self-efficacy, conscientiousness, self-esteem, and extraversion are among the characteristics that may increase the likelihood of romance of leadership.

Activity 4: Do You Romanticize Leaders?

Please read the following statements and, using the following scale, indicate how much you agree with them: strongly disagree = 0, disagree = 1, slightly disagree = 2, neither agree or disagree = 3, slightly agree = 4, agree = 5, strongly agree = 6

1	When it comes right down to it, the quality of leadership is the single most important influence on the functioning of an organization.
2	Anybody who occupies the top-level leadership positions in an organization has the power to make or break the organization.
3	The great amount of time and energy devoted to choosing a leader is justified because of the important influence that person is likely to have.
4	Sooner or later, bad leadership at the top will show up in decreased organizational performance.
5	High- versus low-quality leadership has a bigger impact on a firm than a favorable versus unfavorable business environment.
6	It is impossible for an organization to do well unless it has high-quality leadership at the top.
7	A company is only as good or as bad as its leaders.
8	With a truly excellent leader, there is almost nothing that an organization can't accomplish.
9	Even in a bad economy, a good leader can prevent a company from doing poorly.
10	Top-level leaders make life-and-death decisions about their organizations.
11	It's probably a good idea to find something out about the quality of top-level leaders before investing in a firm.
12	When a company is doing poorly, the first place one should look to is its leaders.
13	The process by which leaders are selected is extremely important.
14	When the top leaders are good, the organization does well; when the top leaders are bad, the organization does poorly.
15	There's nothing as critical to the "bottom-line" performance of a company as the quality of its top-level leaders.
16	Leadership qualities are among the most highly prized personal traits I can think of.
17	No expense should be spared when searching for and selecting a leader.

*From a scoring perspective, 0-35 is in the low range, 36-70 is moderate, and 71-101 is in the high range. If you scored in the high range, you may tend to over-attribute responsibility to leaders.

Birgit Schyns, James R. Meindl, Marcel A. Croon, *Leadership*, vol. 3, issue 1, pp. 29-46, copyright © 2007 by SAGE Publications. Reprinted by Permission of SAGE Publications.

Activity 4: Learning Outcomes

Increasing self-awareness of a tendency to romanticize leadership attribution is crucial for reducing over-attribution. (The same is true for any form of self-assessment.)

While romance of leadership explains behaviors with attributions to the leader or the situation; the next section details self-fulfilling prophecies, which can drive certain behavioral outcomes.

Self-Fulfilling Prophecies

Self-fulfilling prophecies are processes "through which the expectation that an event will occur increases its likelihood of occurrence" (Eden, 1992). Now, imagine you are a manager at a retail store. You know your regional manager is planning on reviewing your store's performance, and you make it known to your employees that in advance of the regional manager's visit, they should focus on ensuring a clean aesthetic in the store and on delivering excellent customer service. The following day or week, the regional manager comes to the store and notices an uptick in sales and more satisfied customers. Is the performance due to the management skills of the store manager, the visit from the regional manager, or the overall skill level of the employees? Perhaps it was the focus on the basics (a clean store and improved customer service) that allowed for the enhanced performance. Perhaps the expectation of the regional manager's visit increased the chances of enhanced performance.

A similar effect became apparent even from the earliest management research—studies from the well-known Hawthorne experiments. Initially, the researchers were interested in learning which level of illumination in the workplace led to the best performance. Researchers were very interested in the scientific approach to management, where every variable could be controlled to optimize output. Instead, they found no variation in performance related to the amount of light—but did find that the attention from both management and the researchers had a positive effect on output. The "Hawthorne Effect," as it is now known, is typically used to explain any unexpected outcome where the presence or attention of a researcher/outside influence can impact the outcome. This increase in output or productivity may raise the expectations of the population under study, making them then perform in accordance with those expectations (Roethlisburger & Dickson, 1939; Wickstrom & Bendix, 2000). A similar effect occurred in early leadership studies where teachers' enhanced expectations of students' performance subsequently raised performance (Rosenthal & Jacobson, 1968). Whether through increased attention to employees or an increase in expectations, self-fulfilling prophecies and the Hawthorne Effect help explain the impact that outside influences can have on performance. We will now discuss a few common self-fulfilling prophecies that occur in organizations: Theory X/Y, the Pygmalion effect, and the Galatea effect. Each of these theories follow the same pattern as illustrated in Figure 1. Supervisor beliefs regarding follower abilities and skills lead to supervisory support behaviors and resource allocation. The support and resources coupled with supervisor beliefs generate performance achievements and also impact follower beliefs, self-confidence, and expectations. The effort put forth by followers also impacts performance, which affirms supervisor beliefs.

> **SELF-FULFILLING PROPHECIES:** Expectations of another person or entity eventually result[ing] in the other person or entity acting in ways that confirm the expectations. (Encyclopedia Britannica)

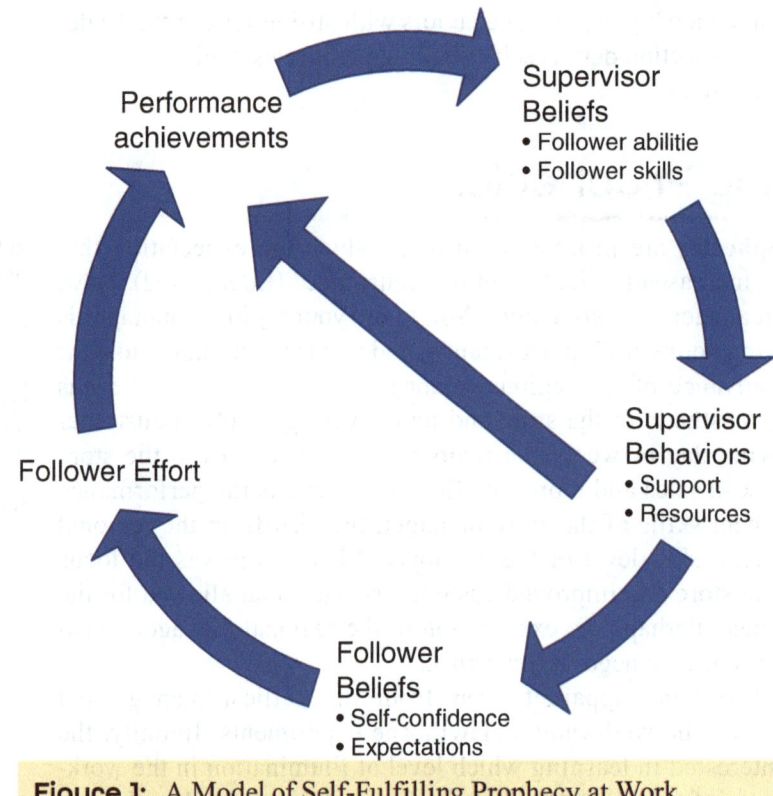

Figure 1: A Model of Self-Fulfilling Prophecy at Work

Theory X and Theory Y

Theory X

In Theory X and Theory Y, McGregor (1960) theorized that assumptions about followers drive different types of manager expectations. So, a manager who believes that followers are lazy and untrustworthy would enact hands-on management behaviors, which leads to achievements obtained through intimidation and potentially lowered goals.

On the other hand, if a manager believes that followers can complete their work autonomously and that they have the skills necessary to deliver a sufficient product, then they would enact empowering behaviors and create pathways for followers to exceed their performance goals.

Consider how you think about "followers." Many students already have experience in organizations, whether they were through full- or part-time work, educational structures, sports teams, or community groups. Now, reflect upon how you view the people who work around you and with you in those organizations. Do you think of those individuals as trustworthy and worthy of investment? Do they have ideas you could put into practice? Or do they need to be watched closely because they are untrustworthy and need constant supervision to achieve their tasks?

Chapter 2: Attribution Theories in Leadership and Organizational Behavior

The way you think about and act towards other individuals, particularly followers, can impact individual, team, and organizational performance. If you believe others are untrustworthy and you create structures that reinforce that untrustworthiness, then they may be inclined to act untrustworthy as a self-fulfilling prophecy. On the other hand, if you treat people as responsible and you challenge them to contribute their knowledge, skills, and abilities, they may work harder to deliver on those expectations, perhaps even overachieving. We will discuss these approaches to motivation in Chapter 5.

Theory Y

Pygmalion Effects

The **Pygmalion Effect** occurs when leaders' expectations of followers are raised, which in turn improves the leadership they exhibit and incentivizes stronger performance (Eden, 1992). It is so named because of the Greek myth of Pygmalion, a king and sculptor who fell in love with a statue he carved out of ivory (Ovid, 43 B.C., 17 A.D., 18 A.D.). The statue came to life after the goddess Aphrodite granted his wish for a living likeness of his ivory statue. Pygmalion's expectations created the transformation of his statue into a real woman, just as a leader's expectations can create transformation in followers. Hence, the Pygmalion effect. This self-fulfilling prophecy is a powerful example of one of the most consistent methods of leadership development (Eden, 1992). Many different organizations—for-profit companies, defense forces, caregivers like nurses and doctors—use the Pygmalion effect in their training. In essence, raising your expectations of your followers is a small intervention that can lead to excellent outcomes.

PYGMALION EFFECT: Raising manager expectations improves leadership, which in turn promotes subordinate performance. (Eden, 1990)

As illustrated in Figure 2, our beliefs influence our actions, which impact the beliefs and actions of others. In other words, if a leader has high expectations of their team, that leader can enact more motivating actions towards that team, and the team will absorb the knowledge the leader conveys, and then seek to fulfill the leader's expectations.

Figure 2: The Self-Fulfilling Prophecy Process

Galatea Effects

Further research explored whether it is always necessary for the leader's beliefs to start the cycle. Evidence from this research supports the idea that directly raising followers' expectations of their own performance is also quite effective.

GALATEA EFFECT: Directly inducing subordinates to expect more of themselves [to enhance] performance. (Eden, 1992).

GOLEM EFFECT: Any negative Pygmalion Effect, when expectations function as self-fulfilling prophecies having negative consequences. Oxford Reference

This was dubbed the **Galatea Effect** (although Ovid did not name the statue in the original Pygmalion myth, over the years, she became known as "Galatea") (Reinhold, 1971). The Galatea effect refers to the ability of the follower to draw on their own beliefs and abilities to achieve high performance. The positive outcomes from incorporating the Galatea effect can depend on many personality and state-like factors such as self-esteem, self-confidence, and emotional stability.

While it sounds like self-fulfilling prophecies have no negative effects, it is important to note that leaders' expectations can also be negative (much like Theory X, which we discussed above). This is known as the **Golem Effect**, which can be debilitating to performance (Golem in Hebrew implies one is stupid). If in your leadership role you raise expectations for some of your followers, you should be careful not to lower expectations for the rest.

Activity 5: Pygmalion/Galatea

Think about a situation when you achieved more than you initially thought—perhaps it was strong performance in a sports event, a time you overcame stage fright to perform in front of an audience, or maybe when you received a higher grade than you thought you could earn on an assignment. Think about the expectations your team leader, drama coach, or teacher placed on you beforehand. Did they encourage or motivate you? How? Or did they perhaps underestimate you, leading you to respond with persistence?

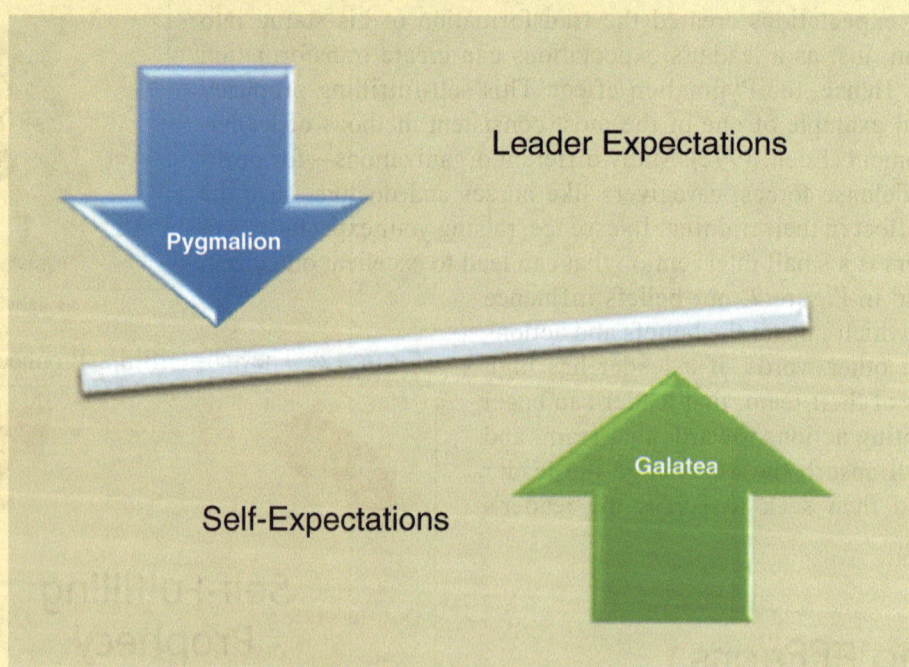

Source: Gretchen Vogelgesang Lester and Paul Lester

Now, think of a time you under performed. Did your coach, teacher, or team leader place any negative expectations on you? Did you feel any negative self-doubt creep in? What did you do after the poor performance to counter that effect?

Activity 5: Learning Outcomes

Recognizing the impact that our own and others' beliefs can have on performance can help you adopt these positive self-fulfilling prophecies into your leadership skill set. It should also help you become more aware of how negative expectations can limit performance.

Pygmalion, Galatea, and Golem raise or lower performance not only in knowledge-based work environments, but also of tasks that require manual labor and physical fitness. Thus, the power of expectations can enhance or inhibit even more objective measures such as strength or endurance. The research into such self-fulfilling prophecies presents evidence that the positive and negative effects are generalizable to many populations and cultures. Many of these outcomes are rooted in self-efficacy, which is a belief in the self's capability to achieve goals. Self-efficacy will be discussed in much detail in Chapter 3.

The Pygmalion, Galatea, and Golem effects show how our attributions can alter our expectations. While Pygmalion and Galatea can have extremely positive outcomes on follower performance, we must remember that our expectations are motivating the higher performance and that while some followers benefit, others may be left out. Those who experience lowered expectations—the Golem effect—may not be able to overcome those negative beliefs.

Avoiding Attributional Errors

Attributions are common in the workplace, and errors or inattentiveness due to these judgements can range from minimal to not impactful to causing significant harm. Making a fundamental attribution error could lead to additional training costs, disciplinary steps, or employee separation even though the actual error could be due to the workplace environment and not the employee. Self-serving biases could blind a leader to their own shortcomings and inhibit process improvements. Romance of leadership allows individuals to enshrine or scapegoat a leader or leadership group—*without* examining the structural issues that may lead to either excellent or poor performance. As seen repeatedly with sports teams, firing the coach does not often fix the problem, especially if the underlying issues are due to resource constraints or time/financial investments. Finally, the Golem effect can be debilitating to those who only see reduced expectations in relation to those of peers who enjoy the Pygmalion or Galatea effect.

Therefore, the question remains—how do individuals slow down and prevent these shortcuts from disadvantaging organizational actors? The first step is to encourage a clear view of the self-concept. As we discussed in Chapter 1, identity is key to developing better knowledge, skills, and abilities. The act of understanding attributional errors draws attention to these processes, which in turn can slow them down. One method to help you evaluate the problem from multiple perspectives is to take the opportunity *in the moment* to question whether the explanation is dispositional or situational. Then evaluate who benefits from that explanation. Creating awareness around the impact that expectations can have on others' actions can help make the activity of goal-setting more intentional.

Seeking feedback from others can also help you avoid attributional errors. Humans tend to seek out agreement, so it is important to solicit feedback from multiple parties that do not feel pressure to conform. The manifestation of feedback in electrical systems is often an unpleasant sound or unexpected spark, something that immediately draws attention until you fix the problem (imagine a sound engineer setting up a microphone and amplifier). In human actions and communication, we often do not complete the final stage of feedback (i.e., ensuring the system is set up correctly and running smoothly). We may transmit the feedback signal without waiting to ensure that the signal is received correctly or interpreting the signal that is sent back to us. To avoid attributional errors, one must ask for and incorporate the feedback they receive from others.

Using Attributions to Your Advantage

Understanding the tendency humans have to make attributional errors can provide an individual with insight into organizational behavior. If one understands that explanations for others' failures are often attributed to the person's disposition, it is important to speak up and describe the situation. Further, if one can employ the self-serving bias to maintain self-esteem, then use this attribution as an advantage. Romance of leadership offers an opportunity to take outsized responsibility for success—but be wary of the equally strong tendency to scapegoat a leader for poor performance. In fact, romance of leadership can also backfire, particularly if you are tasked to fix a problem. Even if you fix it, that problem may become attached to you.

Inviting an employee into a leadership position is a perfect opportunity to create or reinforce an implicit leadership theory in the population. Seek out and publicize diverse representation. Doing so will broaden the patterns and prototypes people carry. Allow organizational members to observe different leaders, leadership styles, and responses to both success and failure across time and across various projects.

Finally, employ the positive self-fulfilling prophecies liberally. Allow your manager to believe that their followers have the required knowledge, skills, and abilities. Take it one step further—allow those followers themselves to believe that their efforts will lead to success. Espouse a Theory Y mindset for the organization to avoid Theory X or the Golem effect.

In Review

This chapter describes attributions, a fundamental process by which individual create judgements and generate expectations regarding their own and others' behaviors. As we note in the first paragraph, "attributions are how we make sense of the world around us". Your attributions drive your interpretations and responses to the behaviors you observe and enact. Part of your leader identity includes the meaning you attach to leadership and followership behaviors in different domains. The activities and self-report assessments in this chapter are provided to help you increase your self-awareness of your own attributional processes and biases, your meaning of leadership, your tendency to over- or under-attribute behaviors to individuals, and to introduce additional interpretation into your experiences. The more you can understand your attributional processes as they exist and what they may become, the clearer you can be in introducing additional explanations and interpretations to broaden your perspective. Seeing these connections between the ways people attribute behavior in different types of organizations will help you apply your knowledge, skills, and abilities as you navigate your career and life paths.

The first activity highlighted the differences between self-serving bias and the fundamental attribution error. We tend to give ourselves a pass and blame the situation when we make an error or fail to follow through, but we give ourselves extra credit when something positive occurs. Conversely, we blame others when they make errors, but give the situation credit when they make positive strides. This tendency can have an impact in organizations, so we must be sure to use multiple interpretations of an event before we assign blame that may derail someone's progress in an organization or attribute additional credit where it may not be warranted.

We also should recognize our implicit leadership theories (ILTs), the assumptions we have regarding the traits and abilities that characterize an ideal leader. First, we should recognize that each individual manifests unique ILTs based on their experiences, role models and cultural stimuli. Activity 2 is designed to elicit your own, unique ILT. When comparing to classmates, you may find a variety of behaviors and actions portrayed in the leadership drawings. You may also find some prototypes, or abstract conceptions of leaders, that are widely shared across your classmates. You should be aware of the tendency to "pattern-match", the process of seeking out leaders who portray the behaviors illustrated in your ILT. While pattern matching can create strong ties between leaders and followers, it can also ignore leaders or followers who have unique skills sets that are uncommon or untested but may allow for disruptive approaches that can lead to positive outcomes. Activity 3 is provided to help you compare your ratings on the most common leader prototypes and antitypes to others to see how well your expectations match up with the overall group ratings.

The next sections detail theories driven by attributions. Romance of leadership (RoL) is the tendency to over-attribute leader responsibility, even when the leaders may not have as much control as perceived. We use RoL to explain organizational performance and may allocate rewards or punishments based off this cognitive shortcut. Some individuals are naturally predisposed to over-attribute responsibility to leaders, Activity 4 allows you to rate yourself on this predisposition. While RoL is a retroactive way to explain performance, self-fulfilling prophesies can assist in producing future behavior. Supervisor or self-beliefs motivate the allocation of support and resources that can provoke effort towards performance goals. If those beliefs are positive (Theory Y, Pygmalion, Galatea), then the aid and encouragement from the organizational leadership should evoke positive outcomes. If those beliefs are negative (Theory X, Golem), then the lack of belief will lead to reduced effort and poorer outcomes.

Understanding how attributions work and how the beliefs systems of yourself and others can impact your own knowledge, skills, and abilities are key drivers of how you can navigate multiple domains. Learning and understanding how you and those around you make sense of actions will allow you to use these forces to your benefit. If you are motivated to lead and seek to understand organizational behavior, the recognition of attributions is a positive step towards your own leadership skill development. The challenge is slowing down the automatic cognitive processes that drive these behaviors and creating self-awareness regarding your own approach to interpreting actions and events.

The next chapter explores your working self-concept. Learning about your self and your working self-concept will provide insight your motivations, your approach to self-development, how you organize your thoughts and memories, and how you can align your current and possible goals.

Learning Objectives

Define and explain attributions

Attributions are judgements people make about the causes of their own and others' behaviors. The attribution process is an automatic cognitive process that speeds up how we perceive and interpret information. While attributions are efficient, we sometimes make mistakes. Activity 1 asked you to think through your own attributions regarding common events as related to your own versus others' behaviors.

Differentiate between attribution errors and self-serving biases

As highlighted in Activity 1, self-serving biases blame the situation for negative events, and give credit to the person for positive events. The fundamental attribution error is the inverse, where you place the blame on another individual for a negative event and use the situation to explain their positive outcomes. Self-serving biases are often amplified by high self-confidence and negated by low self-esteem or negative self-views. These errors can be avoided by inviting multiple perspectives in an event where an attribution may be made, slowing down the cognitive processes in an effortful and methodical manner.

Explore your personal implicit leadership theories

The drawing you created as part of Activity 2 represents your implicit leadership theory (ILT) or your meaning of leader identity. Each individual will generate a unique ILT, although it may include prototypical behaviors that are similar across individuals, groups, and cultures. ILTs are our personal assumptions regarding effective leadership traits and abilities.

Describe attribution theories of leadership

Individuals can over-attribute responsibility and organizational performance to leaders in a phenomenon called romance of leadership. By romanticizing the leader's influence, individuals ignore the complexity that drives organizational performance. Another example of how we attribute responsibility to leaders includes the glass cliff phenomenon, where women and people of color often are looked to as potential leaders only when the risk of failure is already high, but then eventually become responsible for the potential failure. Activity 4 highlights the predispositions individuals might have in over-attributing responsibility to leaders.

Examine self-fulfilling prophecies

Self-fulfilling prophecies exist when expectations regarding an event will increase the chance that it will occur. The self-fulfilling prophecies covered in this chapter include the positive outcomes associated with Theory Y, the Pygmalion effect, and the Galatea effect. The supervisor or self-held high expectations have a strong relationship with positive performance. Theory X and the Golem effect describe the negative effect low expectations can have on organizational outcomes.

Key Terms

Attributions (Pg. 17)

Self-Serving Bias (Pg. 19)

Fundamental Attribution Error (Pg. 19)

Disposition (Pg. 19)

Implicit Leadership Theories (Pg. 20)

Meaning Of Identity (Pg. 20)

Prototypes (Pg. 20)

Romance Of Leadership (Pg. 23)

Glass Cliff (Pg. 23)

Self-Fulfilling Prophecies (Pg. 25)

Pygmalion Effect (Pg. 27)

Galatea Effect (Pg. 27)

Golem Effect (Pg. 28)

Critical Thinking Questions

1. In your own words, describe the attribution processes. Give an example of a time you have used the self-serving bias or fundamental attribution error.
2. As a manager, how can you help your employees discover their implicit leadership theories? How can you compare prototypes within your organization?
3. Why do you think individuals romanticize leadership? Why is this important to recognize? Can leaders use romance of leadership in a positive manner?
4. What are the potential outcomes of self-fulfilling prophecies for organizations? As a manager, why should you be concerned about the positive or negative outcomes associated with these processes?

References

Bligh, M. C., & Schyns, B. (2007). Leading question: The romance lives on: contemporary issues surrounding the romance of leadership. *Leadership, 3*(3), 343–360.

Clapp-Smith, R., Hammond, M. M., Lester, G. V., & Palanski, M. (2019). Promoting identity development in leadership education: A multidomain approach to developing the whole leader. *Journal of Management Education, 43*(1), 10–34.

Eden, D. (1990). *Pygmalion in management: Productivity as a self-fulfilling prophecy.* Lexington Books/DC Heath and Com.

Eden, D. (1992). Leadership and expectations: Pygmalion effects and other self-fulfilling prophecies in organizations. *The Leadership Quarterly*, *3*(4), 271–305.

Epitropaki, O., & Martin, R. (2004). Implicit leadership theories in applied settings: Factor structure, generalizability, and stability over time. *Journal of Applied Psychology*, *89*(2), 293.

Epitropaki, O., & Martin, R. (2005). From ideal to real: A longitudinal study of the role of implicit leadership theories on leader-member exchanges and employee outcomes. *Journal of Applied Psychology*, *90*(4), 659.

Ryan, M. K., Haslam, S. A., Hersby, M. D., & Bongiorno, R. (2011). Think crisis–think female: The glass cliff and contextual variation in the think manager–think male stereotype. *Journal of Applied Psychology, 96*(3), 470.

Hebert, C. (March 20, 2020). Gender Stereotypes and Entrepreneur Financing. 10th Miami Behavioral Finance Conference, Available at SSRN: https://ssrn.com/abstract=3318245 or http://dx.doi.org/10.2139/ssrn.3318245.

McGregor, D. (1960). Theory X and theory Y. *Organization Theory*, *358*(374), 5.

Meindl, J. R. (1990) 'On Leadership: An Alternative to the Conventional Wisdom', in B. M. Staw & L. L. Cummings (eds) *Research in Organizational Behavior*, pp. 159–203. Greenwich, CT: JAI Press.

Mezulis, A. H., Abramson, L. Y., Hyde, J. S., & Hankin, B. L. (2004). Is there a universal positivity bias in attributions? A meta-analytic review of individual, developmental, and cultural differences in the self-serving attributional bias. *Psychological Bulletin*, *130*(5), 711.

Miller, D. T., & Ross, M. (1975). Self-serving biases in the attribution of causality: Fact or fiction? *Psychological Bulletin*, *82*(2), 213.

Ovid, 43 B. C.-17 A. D. or 18 A. D. (2004). *Ovid Metamorphoses* (R. J. Tarrant, Ed.). Oxford University Press.

Phillips, J. S. (1984). The accuracy of leadership ratings: A cognitive categorization perspective. *Organizational Behavior and Human Performance*, *33*(1), 125–138.

Reinhold, M. (1971). The Naming of Pygmalion's Animated Statue. *The Classical Journal*, *66*(4), 316-319.

Roethlisberger, F. J. (1939). and WJ Dickson. *Management and the Worker*.

Rosenthal, R., & Jacobson, L. (1968). Pygmalion in the classroom. *The Urban Review*, *3*(1), 16–20.

Ross, L. (1977). The intuitive psychologist and his shortcomings: Distortions in the attribution process. *Advances in Experimental Social Psychology* (Vol. 10, pp. 173–220). Academic Press.

Ryan, M. K., & Haslam, S. A. (2007). The glass cliff: Exploring the dynamics surrounding women's appointment to precarious leadership positions. *Academy of Management Review*, 32, 549–572.

Schyns, B. (2006). Are group consensus in leader-member exchange (LMX) and shared work values related to organizational outcomes? *Small Group Research*, *37*(1), 20–35.

Schyns, B., Meindl, J. R., & Croon, M. a. (2007). The romance of leadership scale: Cross-cultural testing and refinement. *Leadership*, 3, 29–46.

Shepperd, J., Malone, W., & Sweeny, K. (2008). Exploring causes of the self-serving bias. *Social and Personality Psychology Compass*, *2*(2), 895–908.

Silver, W. S., Mitchell, T. R., & Gist, M. E. (1995). Responses to successful and unsuccessful performance: The moderating effect of self-efficacy on the relationship between performance and attributions. *Organizational Behavior and Human Decision Processes*, *62*(3), 286–299.

Weiner, B. (1985). "Spontaneous" causal thinking. *Psychological Bulletin*, *97*(1), 74.

Wickström, G., & Bendix, T. (2000). The" Hawthorne effect"—what did the original Hawthorne studies actually show?. *Scandinavian Journal of Work, Environment & Health*, 363–367.

Wilson, J., North, M., Morris, D., & McClellan, R. (2020). Rethinking implicit leadership theories: Tomorrow's leaders are collective, generative, and adaptive. *Journal of Leadership Studies*, *14*(3), 24–32.

CHAPTER 3
Your Working Self-Concept

CHAPTER OUTCOMES

1. Define and explain the self and the working self-concept
2. Understand how to use the working self-concept to influence leader development
3. Describe how identity relates to leader complexity
4. Identify requirements for building leader efficacy

Purpose of this Chapter

In this chapter, we explore who you are. We define the self and the working self-concept (WSC) and explore how it influences our development, the goals we pursue, and how we approach influencing and developing others. We start this chapter by exploring concepts of the self. Next, we present an overview of WSC as it relates to identity. We then describe identity and leader complexity. The chapter closes with a deep dive into leader confidence—known as leader self-efficacy.

SELF:
A very broad and deep structure of knowledge that helps organize the memories and behavior about ourselves. (Kihlstrom & Klein, 1994)

What is the "Self"?

Let's step back and consider the term *self*. Many people initially struggle with conceptually describing the self. Doing so requires the individual to express an idea of who they are, or at least who they *think* they are, as it pertains to reality and existence. There are several ways to describe the self, and doing so often bends towards the metaphysical (i.e., abstractly describing the nature of existence and the concept of reality as it pertains to you)—but for our purposes, we functionally define the **self** *as a very broad and deep structure of knowledge that helps organize the memories and*

© pathdoc/Shutterstock.com

behavior about ourselves (Kihlstrom & Klein, 1994). There are certainly other ways to conceptualize the self, but we approach the term from a cognitive point of view for two reasons. First, we agree with Susan Fiske's famous quote that "Thinking is for doing" (1992, p. 877). Second, because thinking is indeed for doing, and because this textbook is focused on your identity development, then becoming who you want to be requires an understanding that how you think, what you think, and to what degree you actually think, in turn, drives your behavior.

Using this frame of the self, when a person says, "I see myself as ..." he or she is activating a list of knowledge categories known as **schemas** and **scripts** (Lord & Brown, 2004), where schemas represent lists of knowledge about the person (i.e., memories) and scripts represent patterns of action that fit a particular context (i.e., behaviors). In other words, schemas are what you know about yourself, and scripts shape what you do.

Both schemas and scripts play central roles in how we think about and express ourselves to others. But two types of schemas—known as peripheral and core schemas—are particularly noteworthy. While your peripheral schemas hold information that you might occasionally activate (e.g., serving as a volunteer twice a year at a non-profit), core schemas are activated habitually (e.g., manager at work, parent, spouse). Please complete Activity 1 to establish your core schemas and behavioral scripts.

SCHEMAS:
A cognitive structure in memory that holds descriptive information about a person or thing. (Lord & Brown, 2004)

SCRIPTS:
A cognitive structure in memory that holds descriptive information about a process, which can be accessed to assist with behavior. (Lord & Brown, 2004)

Activity 1: Life Roles and Schemas

Think of the core schemas or roles you play on a regular basis. Then think of the scripts or behaviors that accompany those roles. You can use the illustration provided to frame your thinking about your core schemas and scripts. You can also add peripheral schemas to your drawing as well. Once you complete your list, please discuss with a classmate.

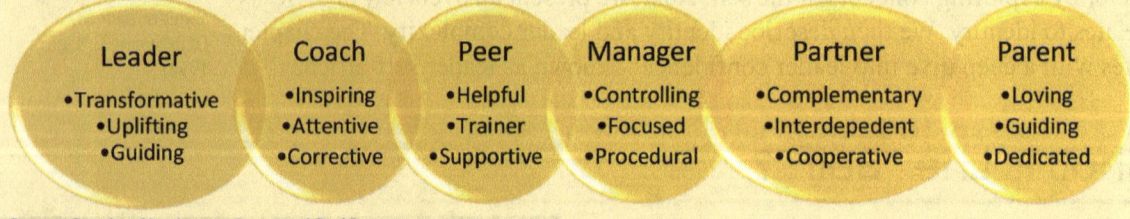

Leader
- Transformative
- Uplifting
- Guiding

Coach
- Inspiring
- Attentive
- Corrective

Peer
- Helpful
- Trainer
- Supportive

Manager
- Controlling
- Focused
- Procedural

Partner
- Complementary
- Interdepedent
- Cooperative

Parent
- Loving
- Guiding
- Dedicated

Source: Gretchen Vogelgesang Lester and Paul Lester

Activity 1: Learning Outcomes

This activity highlights the most salient schemas or roles that are present and perhaps also more peripheral schemas that become salient in certain circumstances. Identifying the behaviors that we enact alongside those roles can help us better predict how we will act in alignment with our roles.

Notes:

[1.] Adapted from Hannah, S. T., Woolfolk, R. L., & Lord, R. G. (2009). Leader self-structure: a framework for positive leadership. *Journal of Organizational Behavior: The International Journal of Industrial, Occupational and Organizational Psychology and Behavior, 30*(2), 269-290.

[2.] Words in the boxes represent schematic knowledge a person may hold about themselves as it pertains to specific roles they fill in their lives.

Knowledge categories about the self vary, and some are more important than others. As Hazel Markus and Elissa Wurf wrote, "[s]ome are positive, some negative; some refer to the individual's here-and-now experience, while others refer to past or future experiences. Moreover, some are representations of what the self actually is, while others are of what the self would like to be, could be, ought to be, or is afraid of being" (1987, p. 302). This last sentence is particularly important to leader development—our views of the self are not only about the facts we know and our memories of ourselves but also about our future orientation of the self or what we can see ourselves becoming. A review of your resume is likely a good illustration of your future orientation of the self. While every resume should apportion some space that describes what you have done in the past, the best resumes articulate a compelling vision of what you can do in the *future* for the organization that is considering hiring you. While you have not actually done the job yet, you envision yourself doing so and should use your resume to market yourself as such. Thus, a resume is a link between your past self to your possible selves.

© 145Patma/Shutterstock.com

The self is also malleable, meaning it can be deliberately or unintentionally shaped in a variety of ways (Markus & Kunda, 1986). For example, going to college is a deliberate, formative action that shapes one's views of the self via exposure to education, new social situations, and independence. The same can be said for volunteering for a company's leadership development and training program. On the other hand, being a child of divorce is without question an unintentional yet deeply formative experience that impacts the self—we know that children of divorce often face a variety of disadvantages they must overcome (Amato, 2001). These three examples are experiences that create indelible memories and which are easily and habitually recalled later. These memories represent the peaks and valleys of life, which in turn shape the self.

What Is the Working Self-Concept?

This malleability of the self leads us to the working **self-concept**, which is *the highly activated but contextually sensitive portion of the self that guides behavior and how we process information based on the context we are facing in the moment* (Lord et al., 1999; Lord & Brown, 2004). Two questions emerge from the WSC definition. First, what specifically becomes "highly activated" in our WSC? Returning to the previous material on the self, our WSC activates schemas (memories) and scripts (behavioral patterns), but keep in mind that our working memory can only hold a limited amount of information at any given time. Second, what exactly does "contextually sensitive" mean? Your WSC relies on salience (the relevant cues you identify from your environment) to activate useful schemas and scripts.

SELF-CONCEPT: The highly activated but contextually sensitive portion of the self that guides behavior and how we process information based on the context we are facing in the moment. (Lord et al., 1999; Lord & Brown, 2004)

Chapter 3: Your Working Self-Concept

Our working self-concept, be it in how we think about ourselves or what we tell others about ourselves, says a lot about who we currently are while also providing a preview of who we want to be in the future. Because humans fill so many roles in life, we are a lot of things. For example, since you are reading this textbook, you might be primed to say, "I'm a leader!" (Well ... we at least hope that's the case.) But if you were asked this question in a different context—say, at your child's school—you might start off by saying you are the parent of your child. Or maybe you'll mention if you have a co-parent and then discuss how well your child is doing in school before *finally* getting around to mentioning your professional affiliations if the conversation lasts long enough. However, in that same conversation, you would probably omit mentioning your occasional hobbies, or that in third grade you placed fourth in the local spelling bee, or that while in college you were once cited by the police for disturbing the peace. These snippets from your past may be part of your personal story, so why omit them? Aside from relevance and general contextual inappropriateness, these latter items are not part of your durable self-representation.

Turning towards our roles in organizations—our WSC may activate one set of schemas and scripts when we are providing developmental counseling to a follower but a *completely different* set of schemas and scripts when we are hosting a meeting to plan an upcoming training event. And the contents of those schemas and scripts may be shared across contexts but then significantly change as your role changes. For example, the language you used this morning to initiate structure at work might not be as effective when you transition later that day into your role as a parent and in knowing that you will activate a more appropriate set of schemas and scripts.

As described below and shown in Figure 1, there are three major components of the WSC: *self-views*, *possible selves*, and *current goals*. Additionally, there are three forms of motivation that shape how the WSC functions: *proximal motivation*, *distal motivation*, and *self-development motivation*. Each facet plays a role in your development as a leader, so let us discuss them one by one.

Figure 1: The Working Self-Concept (WSC)

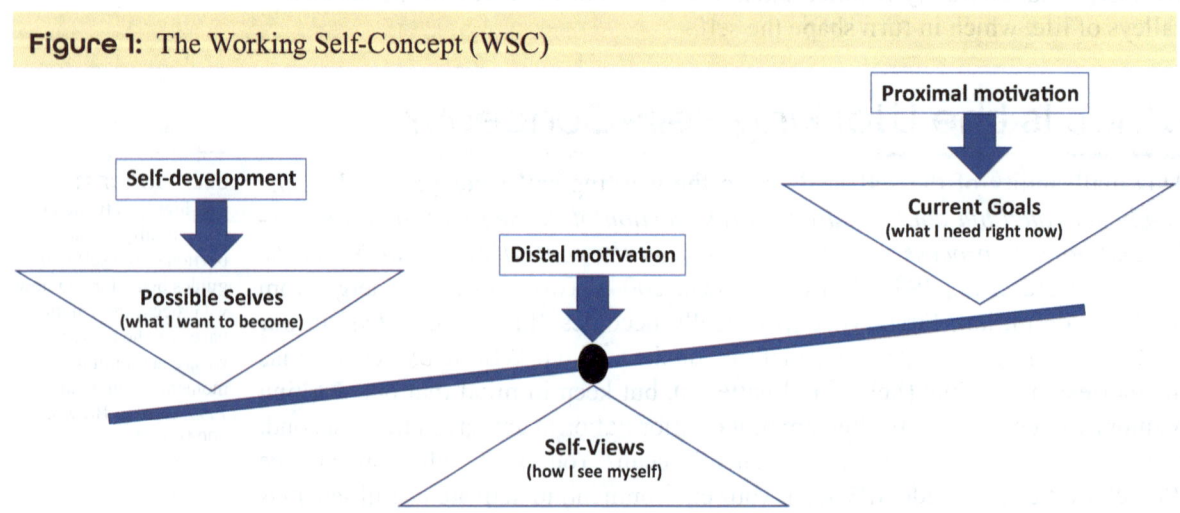

Source: Gretchen Vogelgesang Lester and Paul Lester.
Adapted from Lord, R. G., & Brown, D. J. (2004). *Leadership processes and follower self-identity*. Psychology Press.

Self-Views

Self-views are simply the way you see yourself within a particular context. While they tend to be positive, the degree of positivity will vary as the context changes (Lord & Brown, 2004). For example, maybe you're a highly intelligent person who excelled in high school—so much so that you received a scholarship to a great university. In this case, your self-view regarding your academic ability *before* you left for college was probably very positive. But then, like most college students, you quickly realized once you arrived that everyone around you was just as intelligent or perhaps even *more* intelligent, causing you to reassess your self-view as it pertains to academics. It is not as though you feel you are any less intelligent, but rather the context caused you to *re-anchor* your self-views within your new college reality. This is part of the identity construction process we discussed in Chapter 1.

Athletes go through a similar re-anchoring process as they move through increasingly higher levels of competition. A local standout might just be average at a state or national championship event. The same thought applies to leaders as they take on more responsibility across a career, with each new role representing a transition point where re-anchoring of self-views occurs. And recent research suggests this is especially true for individuals taking on a leadership role for the first time. Emerging leaders may initially experience short-term tensions and a drop in their self-esteem, but then over time, the new leadership experience can actually bolster their perceived well-being and self-esteem (Fletcher & French, 2021).

Possible Selves

We fill many roles in our current life. But there are many *other roles* we *could* fill if we were motivated to do so. Perhaps these roles are oriented towards a profession, such as an undergraduate biology student aspiring to go to medical school to become a doctor. Or the role could be oriented toward spiritual fulfillment, such as one day serving as a church deacon or working towards organizing support for a local homeless shelter. The linkage between conceptualizing what we could become and tapping into the motivation to work towards that is known as possible selves, which we discussed and defined in Chapter 1. Possible selves serve

© KieferPix/Shutterstock.com

a few purposes within the WSC—namely, to describe what you hope to one day become *and* what you fear becoming (Lord & Brown, 2004). This powerful tension between hopes and fears shapes goal creation and motivations (described in later passages) but remember that views of your possible selves direct in-the-moment behavior. For example, you have likely read many aspirational stories of leaders who "did it right" alongside the cautionary tales of leaders who abused their power, hurt others, and ultimately failed. In doing so, you learned about the characteristics and specific behaviors that made some leaders succeed while others failed. Recall from Chapter 2 that over time, these stories help us create our own implicit theories of what it means to be a prototypical successful or failed leader, which means you ascribe schemas and scripts to each. Throughout the typical workday, a leader's WSC activates both sets of schemas and scripts to direct how he or she should act to stay on the path toward becoming their possible self (the leader he or she wants to become) and simultaneously avoid derailing behaviors that might prevent reaching that goal.

Current Goals

Having a positive self-view and determining that a leader is one possible self then sets the conditions to form goals around doing just that: creating short- and long-term goals focused on developing and attaining an identity as a leader. In its simplest form, a goal is nothing more than an objective you are trying to reach. So, goals become standards you work towards meeting. This can mean obtaining an object, mastering a skill, or behaving a certain way in each context (Locke & Latham, 2006). Cognitively, though, goals serve a specific function within our WSC: They are highly contextualized schemas that shape how we think, the choices we make, and ultimately how we behave (Markus & Nurius, 1986). As depicted in Figure 1, there is a tension between current goals and self-views and a tension between current goals and possible selves. For developing leaders, the challenge is to harmonize these tensions. For example, an emerging leader must balance setting goals that enhance their self-views (i.e., leading in ways that result in short-term and admittedly selfish outcomes to enhance your standing within an organization) with goals that promote attaining a possible self (i.e., becoming the inspiring leader that others in the organization look up to).

Frankly, there may be times when tying current goals to either view of the self is warranted. Pursuing one form of goal does not necessarily mean that it comes at the significant expense of the other—rather, it means that at a particular moment in time, one form of goal is more important than the other and therefore has the greatest relevance within one's WSC. If you have ever worked on a sales team, you have likely had a boss who gave you a significant amount of autonomy and discretion to perform your work (provided you met your sales quotas). Here, your boss' goal is to lead in an empowering way, which is their way of working toward their idealized self of good leadership. However, if you were behind on your sales quota and the end of the business year was looming, your boss likely adopted a more directive style, which could feel like micromanagement. Here, the goal of making your sales figures was critical—doing so meant you both (you and your boss) kept your jobs, so the empowering management style was temporarily sacrificed to reap the necessary results.

Motivations

The above talking points (goals, examples of team leader) illustrate that while we may set developmental goals and swap the priority of attaining those goals based on what is important at any given time, the drive behind our decisions is rooted in our motivations (Day & Harrison, 2007). **Motivation** is the impetus that provides us with purpose and direction in what we do and pursue (APA, 2022). There are two distinct motivations at work within a leader's working self-concept, both of which are delineated by their time horizons. As shown in Figure 1, *proximal motivations* are those that drive behavior toward attaining short-term goals, whereas *distal motivations* are those that activate goals directed toward becoming a relevant possible self. Both proximal and distal forms of motivation are important to identity development. For example, a novice just starting a new job may be proximally motivated to learn about the day-to-day routines of the team, how the organization operates, and where in the team to make the biggest impact. However, apportioning some time to learn the boss' role and how other divisions in the company operate may also be a distal motivation.

With these two motivations at work simultaneously, we come to the final component of the WSC model shown in Figure 1: Self-development. Our self-development motives can be proximal or distal—yet they are predominantly focused on moving us from our current self to the relevant possible self (in this case: being a leader). Leaders will identify situational cues in each environment, thus driving the form of self-development. Let's return to our novice example. The employee may learn that the manager expects a presentation to be delivered to important clients next week. But perhaps this employee struggles with giving formal talks. So, they seek out advice from peers and then practice giving the presentation in front of them to become confident in mastering the material and enacting a professional delivery. In this example, there was a schematic information assessment regarding the current self, identification of a deficiency—public speaking—and proximal motivations driving preparation for the task ahead. Eventually, that same novice may voluntarily enroll in a part-time MBA program to continue their education and be competitive for future promotions. Knowing that the program will take three years to complete, the WSC activates distal motivations as well.

> **MOTIVATION:**
> The need or reason for doing something. (Cambridge Dictionary)

Activity 2: Motivation to Lead

Some of us are highly motivated to lead but not everyone wants to be a leader. And even those who like to lead may not want to serve in a leadership position habitually. Here's a short questionnaire to gauge how much you want to lead, which was developed by Chan and Drasgow (2001). Specifically, it measures your motivation to take on leadership positions based on your actual enjoyment of being a leader and your ability to see yourself as a leader in relation to who you are as a person.

Instructions: Please read each statement below carefully and choose the answer (using the scale below) that best describes your **level of agreement**.

Scale:

1	2	3	4	5
Strongly Disagree	Disagree	Neutral	Agree	Strongly Agree

	Statement	Response
1	I am definitely not a leader by nature	
2	Most of the time, I prefer being a leader rather than a follower when working in a group	
3	I tend to take charge in most groups or teams that I work in	
4	I am in my element when leading others	
5	I have always thought of myself as a leader	
6	I am the type of person who is not interested in leading others	
7	I believe I can contribute more to a group if I am a follower rather than a leader	
8	I am the type of person who likes to be in charge of others	
9	I see myself succeeding in leadership challenges	
10	I usually want to be the leader in the groups that I work in	
11	I know exactly what it takes to lead others	
12	I am the type who would actively support a leader but prefers not to be appointed as leader	
13	I was born to lead	
14	I am seldom reluctant to be the leader of a group	
15	I have the characteristics that people associate with leadership	

Activity 2: Learning Outcomes

Calculate your scores. Please note this self-assessment includes reverse-scored items, so for items 1, 6, 7, & 12, replace every 5 with a 1; for every 4, replace with a 2; if you scored a 3, keep it the same; for every 2, replace with a 4; for every 1, replace with a 5.

Interpretation: This questionnaire is most often used in research, so it is not a diagnostic measure per se, meaning there are no specific "cutoffs" that delineate those who are highly motivated from those who are not. However, look closely at how you responded. If you responded with mostly 4s or 5s, you are likely highly motivated to serve in leadership positions.

Copyright © 2001 by American Psychological Association. Reproduced with permission. Chan, K.-Y., & Drasgow, F. (2001). Toward a theory of individual differences and leadership: Understanding the motivation to lead. Journal of Applied Psychology, 86 (3), 481–498. https://doi.org/10.1037/0021-9010.86.3.481

The Working Self-Concept and Identity Development

SELF-REGULATION: the ability to control or direct disruptive impulses and moods, and the control to suspend judgement and to think before acting. (Goleman, 2004)

As alluded to throughout this textbook, a key ingredient to identity development is **self-regulation** (Day et al., 2014). Once you can regulate your behavior, you can therefore decide to allocate time and effort toward different goals, such as becoming a leader (or if you already are a leader, then perhaps you can become better and more effective). Possessing self-regulation means you are also able to choose to focus on the task of becoming a leader *over* other undertakings. Importantly, the working self-concept is the framework you use to make this decision (and others). There is typically a gulf between how people see themselves in the present (the current self) versus who they want to be (the possible self). Your WSC activates knowledge (schemas) and behavioral patterns (scripts) related to both (current vs. self) as they move from one context to another. While individuals set developmental goals to help move them closer to their ideal possible self, the environment also presents cues. This causes a re-prioritization of behavioral goals to meet proximal demands related to the job or the people with whom they work. Thus, some temporarily choose to satisfy proximal motivations over distal ones, especially with developmental motivations. If you have ever heard the organizational cliché "building the airplane as it is flying," just know that the same can be said about the connection between the WSC, identity, and self-development. That aside, we caution against sidelining distal motivation toward identity development too much because doing so risks stagnation. In short, you must *choose* to make self-development relevant in your life—within your *self*.

Activity 3: Describing Your Working Self-Concept

How would you describe your working self-concept as a leader? If you can describe it, chances are you can either work towards shaping and developing it, or you can use your description to see how you might want to change it. How much emphasis (weight) do you place on each component?

For example, do you find yourself expending more effort on attaining your current/proximal goals, or are you more oriented towards working to become that possible self we described earlier in the chapter?

Take a few moments to fill out the boxes below.

	Description	Weighting (1-10)
Self-views as a leader	How do you *see* yourself as a leader today? • • •	1-10: _____
Current goals as a leader	What are your *current goals* as a leader? • • •	1-10: _____
Proximal motivations as a leader today	What motivates you to serve as a leader *today*? • • •	1-10: _____
Possible selves as a leader	What *kind* of leader do you want to become? • • •	1-10: _____
Distal motivations as a leader	What are the *people, things, or beliefs* motivating you to *become* the leader you want to be in the future? • • •	1-10: _____

	Description	Weighting (1-10)
Self-development	What are you *doing now* to move towards becoming the leader you want to be in the future? • • •	1-10: _____

Activity 3: Learning Outcomes

Once you have completed the prompts, reflect on the following question: How well does what I wrote reflect what I want to be now and in the future? If you find it challenging to complete a specific section, you may need more reflection on that area. If you find it difficult to envision your possible selves, you may need to set aside time to research potential careers or speak with possible mentors to articulate a plan for your future.

This chapter thus far has largely focused on the self through the individual lens (so, all about *you*). But because identity is also a social phenomenon, the complexity grows significantly when we layer in interpersonal and collective views of the self. The next portion of this chapter is devoted to understanding how identity and self-development change when relationships and connections with others, groups, and organizations are considered.

Complexity and Identity

LEADER COMPLEXITY: How well a leader is able to differentiate and integrate information about his/herself, the leadership process, and the context. (Hannah & Avolio, 2010)

We have closely examined the WSC and have primarily discussed it in terms of how it operates in different roles. But elsewhere in this textbook, we will describe how, over time and with greater leadership experience, a leader's identity develops to a point where being a leader becomes part of who we are—*leading* becomes part of our identity. Behavioral science research shows that our leader identity is neither monolithic nor simple—after all, humans are never just one "thing"—but rather, it is complex, and the complexity grows as we live (Lord & Brown, 2005). Although complexity often has a negative connotation—let's admit it, we generally prefer simple concepts over complex ones—it has a very positive connotation for leaders. Complexity gives you a very wide, deep pool of knowledge and behaviors to call upon while leading.

© fran_kie/Shutterstock.com

What do we mean by **leader complexity**? A helpful way to think of leader identity complexity is to return to the idea of schemas and scripts. Simplicity turns to complexity as we add more knowledge about and become better able to differentiate the nuances within the topic of leadership. For example, people early in their careers may believe they should take a directive approach to leading (maybe they watched too many movies depicting successful leaders as overly brash and demanding). So, they try to adopt that approach. However, as they gain experience, they learn that such an approach might work in one context but fail miserably in another. As they move through their careers, these leaders continue to add complexity to their views about leadership (e.g., leadership approach A will probably be effective in situations X and Y, but not in situation Z).

Another way to conceptualize leader identity complexity is to think about how the knowledge we have within each of our identity schemas *is* or *is not* interrelated (Hannah et al., 2009). If you refer to Activity 1, you will see there are many different aspects or roles that we have in our lives—mentor, colleague, parent, etc. These roles are generally filled with positive characteristics, though people usually have a few aspects that contain negative characteristics (after all, none of us are perfect). As we build the different aspects of our lives and fill each with schematic knowledge, we begin to learn that many are interconnected (Hammond et al., 2017). For instance, let's assume you are a leader in an organization, and you are hosting a mentorship session with someone who reports to you. Someone with a complex leader identity understands that while all the schematic knowledge held in the mentor role applies to that context (e.g., challenging, supportive, empathetic, etc.), knowledge pulled from the parent role (e.g., caring, ethical) and public speaker role (e.g., persuasive) is also highly applicable to mentoring.

There is little doubt that you have formed close relationships with others throughout your life. People make these attachments for several reasons—relationships provide safety and joy, learning experiences, and they help us find meaning in our lives (Bowlby, 1969). Specifically, our behavioral scripts and schematic information within our WSC will be shaped by the quality and valence (i.e., positive and negative) of the information we receive from others while serving in leadership roles. And in turn, this affects other aspects of the self, such as self-esteem (Brewer & Gardner, 1996). Yet this dynamic is not restricted to receiving feedback from followers, and extensive research shows that a leader's self-views are also shaped by the feedback we receive from friends, family, peers at work, and bosses. For example, leaders at all stages of development—but especially emerging leaders—tend to attach themselves to mentors they respect because they wish to learn from and emulate mentors' behavior (Lester et al., 2011).

© imtmphoto/Shutterstock.com

Efficacy and the Working Self-Concept

We have a very practical reason for describing aspects of the working self-concept in such detail: You can use the WSC to help identify and develop qualities that you believe you lack as a leader. For example, when we ask leadership students to list the characteristics they wish they had more of, confidence is universally listed in the top five. Indeed, a lack of confidence has been shown in leadership research to be one of the biggest barriers to leader emergence (Liu et al., 2019). This makes sense, given that most people will not attempt to do something—in

LEADER EFFICACY: The leader's belief that he or she has the knowledge, skills, and abilities to enact behaviors that will effectively influence other people. (Hannah et al., 2012)

our case, lead—unless they are confident that they will succeed. The confidence to lead is typically referred to as **leader efficacy**, which encompasses a leader's belief that he or she has the knowledge, skills, and abilities to enact behaviors that will effectively influence other people (Kwok et al., 2021; Hannah et al., 2012). Efficacy is one of the most researched phenomena in psychology because it "affect[s] whether individuals think in self-enhancing or self-debilitating ways, how well they motivate themselves and persevere in the face of difficulties" (Bandura & Locke, 2003, p. 87). Breaking this statement into its components, we can easily see how influential efficacy is to leaders' WSC. It shapes how they think about themselves as leaders, what they are motivated to do as leaders, and whether they are willing to stick it out as leaders when the context becomes challenging.

This assertion has been supported by much research. For example, results from a meta-analysis of 114 studies showed that efficacy was significantly related to work performance regardless of the task complexity of the work (Stajkovic & Luthans, 1998). Leading others is certainly a complex task, so it follows that leader efficacy should make a difference in a variety of outcomes. Research supports the link between leader efficacy and motivation to lead (Chan & Drasgow, 2001), leader emergence (McCormick et al., 1999), and leaders' performance as rated by their bosses and followers (Chemers et al., 2000). Leadership scholars also recognize that efficacy comes in different forms and that we should think about it in the parallel streams of a leader's **self-efficacy** and a leader's **means efficacy** (Hannah et al., 2012). While self-efficacy refers to your self-confidence to lead in a specific context, means efficacy is related to feeling confident that you have the tools or resources within your environment to lead successfully. For example, you may be confident in your abilities to influence a group of people to work towards an objective—you have a plan, you are a great communicator, you are well-liked and respected, you have the support of your boss and your followers—but the task may require certain materials or capabilities that are outside of your direct control as a leader. This, in turn, shakes your confidence that the goal can be met. As an emerging leader, you should assess *both* self-efficacy and means efficacy as you step towards taking on leadership roles. Finally, the link between efficacy and leadership is important enough for us to revisit periodically throughout the remainder of the text, especially in Chapter 11. There, we will dedicate a section to developing various aspects of efficacy.

SELF-EFFICACY: As it applies to leadership, one's self-confidence to lead in a specific context. (Hannah et al., 2012)

MEANS EFFICACY: As it applies to leadership, one's confidence that the available tools and resources needed within a leadership context are sufficient. (Hannah et al., 2012)

In Review

This chapter describes the self and the working self-concept (WSC)—the durable representations of ourselves that we habitually call upon to drive thought, motivation, and action. The self is comprised of schemas and scripts that shape expectations and behaviors across domains and situations. The working self-concept permeates how we develop across our lifespan, especially in the case of our identity and our own leadership development. The views we have of ourselves today (current self) interact with current goals, the aspirational views of what we one day want to become (future self), and motivations that change across contexts. At times, these aspects of the WSC are in tension with each other, largely due to a confluence of environmental cues that we face every day. The self is not monolithic—we develop different identities as we take on new roles both in and outside of the workplace.

So as the knowledge we hold in our schemas and behavioral scripts becomes more complex with experience and practice, we become better able to interconnect our various identities into a more integrated life as a leader across contexts.

The first activity is intended to illuminate the schemas you hold and the scripts that are enacted when those schemas are activated. Schemas are memories we have but can also be thought of as the roles we play in different domains. So, our "Partner" schema consists of memories about that role and the expectations that accompany it, and the scripts are the behavioral guides—to be complementary, interdependent, and cooperative. Through the action of cataloging your schemas, you can begin to predict the behaviors you will be likely to enact in different scenarios.

The next sections describe the working self-concept in detail, particularly when related to self-development toward acquiring leadership abilities. Activity 2 assesses your motivation to lead, and 3 integrates your working self-concept into your identity construction process. Both activities should help you uncover your self-views, your current goals, your proximal and distal motivations, and your actions on self-development. Increasing your self-awareness regarding your current feelings on motivation to lead will certainly connect to the actions you are taking in this arena. Gaining insight into how the working self-concept is generated and enacted impacts how intentional you can be as you move through your life stages. Connecting your proximal motivations and actions to your distal motivations in a purposeful manner is the key to any self-development process, leader-focused or not.

As we learn about our working self-concept and integrate our identities, we see how complex leadership interactions can become. Leadership development not only depends on how well we can enact leadership behaviors in specific situations but also is reliant upon the breadth of skills we must deploy based on situational requirements. Effective leaders are constantly adapting to the needs of their followers, other stakeholders, and the general environment.

We strive for the agency to make our own decisions, and we also have the power to take control of our own leadership development and take steps towards building out the personal characteristics we need to lead, such as leader efficacy. Confidence builds from taking on leadership opportunities and learning from missteps. Leaders also thrive when they have the means and resources necessary to be able to take action as intended.

The next chapter explores how your traits, KSAs, and motivations generate your individual-level identity. Learning about these individual-level characteristics will give you insight into how you interact and connect with others in multiple domains.

Learning Objectives

Define and explain the self and the working self-concept

The self is the structure of knowledge that organizes our memories and our behaviors. The way we think about our self drives the actions we take in response to environmental stimuli. We have schemas (our memories tied to the roles we play) and scripts (patterns of actions we take in specific situations) that make up what we know about ourselves and why we act the ways we do. The working self-concept is the activated self that guides our behavior in the moment. The working self-concept includes our current self-views, possible selves, and current goals—all of which are context-specific and embedded within the situation.

Understand how to use the working self-concept to influence leader development

The working self-concept, as noted above, is the activated self that directs our behavior in the moment. It is driven by reactions to the environmental stimuli but also by our internal motivations – those that are proximal or short-term, those that are distal or long-term, and those that are grounded in self-development. If we choose leadership skills as an important part of our self-development, then our current self-views and goals are shaped around that idea. We then construct possible selves as vehicles for that leadership skill development and set short- and long-term objectives accordingly.

Describe how identity relates to leader complexity

As we mature and develop our leadership abilities, we recognize that differentiating and integrating information about the self, the leadership process, and the context is imperative for success. This is leader complexity, being able to act and react in the moment while new information is constantly becoming available. Building a leader identity across domains with a broad pool of skills and deep knowledge about how those skills work in different environments is a major component of any successful leader. The breadth of actions allows the leader to choose the appropriate skill for the specific context; the depth allows the leader to adopt and deliver the skill with ease.

Identify requirements for building leader efficacy

Efficacy is one of the most impactful skills a leader can develop, and the lack of efficacy is one of the biggest barriers to leader emergence. Not only should you have confidence in your leadership abilities (self-efficacy), but you also should recognize the importance of ensuring you have the tools and resources necessary to complete your tasks (means efficacy). You can build your leader self-efficacy by taking on leadership roles in multiple domains.

Key Terms

Self (Pg. 37)

Schemas (Pg. 38)

Scripts (Pg. 38)

Working Self-Concept (Pg. 39)

Motivation (Pg. 43)

Self-Regulation (Pg. 44)

Leader Complexity (Pg. 46)

Leader Efficacy (Pg. 48)

Self-Efficacy (Pg. 48)

Means Efficacy (Pg. 48)

Critical Thinking Questions

1. Think about your resume or job search profile. If resumes and profiles are tools that catalog experience but also present possible selves, what requirements should you add to convince a possible employer of your potential?
2. As a manager, how can you help your teammates discover their working self-concepts? What are some ways you can experiment with proximal and distal motivations while also keeping the team on track?
3. How can you simplify the complexity of leadership for those you mentor, coach, or lead? How do you think one should go about exploring the breadth and depth of their leadership abilities?
4. What are some specific plans you could put into place at your workplace to help others develop their self-efficacy? How can you provide means efficacy to those willing and able to seek out and accept leadership opportunities?

References

Amato, P. R. (2001). Children of divorce in the 1990s: An update of the Amato and Keith (1991) meta-analysis. *Journal of Family Psychology, 15*(3), 355.

American Psychological Association (2022). Definition of primary motivation, secondary motivation, extrinsic motivation, intrinsic motivation. https://dictionary.apa.org/

Bandura, A., & Locke, E. A. (2003). Negative self-efficacy and goal effects revisited. *Journal of Applied Psychology, 88*, 87–99.

Bowlby, J. (1969). *Attachment and loss: Vol. 1. Attachment.* Basic Books.

Brewer, M. B., & Gardner, W. (1996). Who is this" We"? Levels of collective identity and self representations. *Journal of Personality and Social Psychology, 71*(1), 83–93.

Burns, J. M. (2012). *Leadership.* Open Road Media.

Chan, K. Y., & Drasgow, R. (2001). Toward a theory of individual differences and leadership: Understanding the motive-to-lead. *Journal of Applied Psychology, 86*, 481–498.

Chemers, M. M., Watson, C. B., & May, S. T. (2000). Dispositional affect and leadership effectiveness: A comparison of self-esteem, optimism, and efficacy. *Personality and Social Psychology Bulletin, 26*, 267–277.

Day, D. V., Fleenor, J. W., Atwater, L. E., Sturm, R. E., & McKee, R. A. (2014). Advances in leader and leadership development: A review of 25 years of research and theory. *The Leadership Quarterly, 1*(25), 63–82.

Day, D. V., & Harrison, M. M. (2007). A multilevel, identity-based approach to leadership development. *Human Resource Management Review, 17*(4), 360–373.

Fiske, S. T. (1992). Thinking Is for Doing: Portraits of Social Cognition From Daguerreotype to Laserphoto. *Journal of Personality and Social Psychology, 63*(6), 877–889.

Fletcher, K. A., & French, K. A. (2021). Longitudinal effects of transitioning into a first-time leadership position on well-being and self-concept. *Journal of Occupational Health Psychology*.

Goleman, D. (2004). What makes a leader? *Harvard Business Review*, *82*(1), 82–82.

Gottfredson, R. K., Wright, S. L., & Heaphy, E. D. (2020). A critique of the Leader-Member Exchange construct: Back to square one. *The Leadership Quarterly*, *31*(6), 101385.

Hammond, M., Clapp-Smith, R., & Palanski, M. (2017). Beyond (just) the workplace: A theory of leader development across multiple domains. *Academy of Management Review*, *42*(3), 481–498.

Hannah, S. T., & Avolio, B. J. (2010). Ready or not: How do we accelerate the developmental readiness of leaders? *Journal of Organizational Behavior*, *31*(8), 1181–1187.

Hannah, S. T., Avolio, B. J., Walumbwa, F. O., & Chan, A. (2012). Leader self and means efficacy: A multi-component approach. *Organizational Behavior and Human Decision Processes*, *118*(2), 143–161. https://doi.org/10.1016/j.obhdp.2012.03.007.

Hannah, S. T., Woolfolk, R. L., & Lord, R. G. (2009). Leader self-structure: A framework for positive leadership. *Journal of Organizational Behavior: The International Journal of Industrial, Occupational and Organizational Psychology and Behavior*, *30*(2), 269–290.

Kihlstrom, J.F. & Klein, S.B. (1994). The self as a knowledge structure. In R. S. Wyer, Jr. & T. K. Srull (Eds.), *Handbook of social cognition* (2nd ed., pp. 153-208). Lawrence Erlbaum Associates.

Kwok, N., Shen, W., & Brown, D. J. (2021). I can, I am: Differential predictors of leader efficacy and identity trajectories in leader development. *The Leadership Quarterly*, *32*(5), 101422.

Lester, P. B., Hannah, S. T., Harms, P. D., Vogelgesang, G. R., & Avolio, B. J. (2011). Mentoring impact on leader efficacy development: A field experiment. *Academy of Management Learning & Education*, *10*(3), 409–429.

Liu, Z., Riggio, R. E., Day, D. V., Zheng, C., Dai, S., & Bian, Y. (2019). Leader development begins at home: Overparenting harms adolescent leader emergence. *The Journal of Applied Psychology*, *104*(10), 1226–1242.

Locke, E. A., & Latham, G. P. (2006). New directions in goal-setting theory. *Current Directions in Psychological Science*, *15*(5), 265–268.

Lord, R. G., & Brown, D. J. (2004). *Leadership processes and follower self-identity*. Psychology Press.

Lord, R. G., Brown, D. J., & Freiberg, S. J. (1999). Understanding the dynamics of leadership: The role of follower self-concepts in the leader/follower relationship. *Organizational Behavior and Human Decision Processes*, *78*(3), 167–203.

Lord, R. G., & Hall, R. J. (2005). Identity, deep structure and the development of leadership skill. *The Leadership Quarterly*, *16*(4), 591–615.

Markus, H., & Kunda, Z. (1986). Stability and malleability of the self-concept. *Journal of Personality and Social Psychology*, *51*(4), 858–866.

Markus, H., & Nurius, P. (1986). Possible selves. *American Psychologist, 41*(9), 954–969.

Markus, H., & Wurf, E. (1987). The dynamic self-concept: A social psychological perspective. *Annual Review of Psychology, 38*(1), 299–337.

McCormick, M. J., Tanguma, J., & Lopex-Forment, A. S. (2002). Extending self-efficacy theory to leadership: A review and empirical test. *Journal of Leadership Education, 1*(2), 1–15.

Pfeffer, J. (2015). *Leadership BS: Fixing workplaces and careers one truth at a time.* Harper Business.

Stajkovic, A. D., & Luthans, F. (1998). Self-efficacy and work-related performance: A meta-analysis. *Psychological Bulletin, 124*(2), 240–261.

CHAPTER 4

Individual-Level Identity: Character, Traits, and Motivation

CHAPTER OUTCOMES

1. Define and explain the link between traits and leadership
2. Explore and understand the ways in which personality is conceptualized and measured
3. Define the traits that may hinder your ability to lead in an ethical way
4. Describe the components of individual-level motivation as they relate to leadership

Purpose of this Chapter

There are three levels of leader identity: individual, relational, and collective (Brewer & Gardner, 1996). The individual level is what sets your self apart from others, the relational is how we associate with others interpersonally, and the collective level is how we categorize ourselves as members of groups. The next three chapters will focus on how our identity is shaped at these varying levels, but in this chapter, we focus on the individual-level aspects of identity. These are your personal characteristics, including traits such as physical attributes, intelligence, and personality; competencies such as wisdom and judgment; and motivations such as your needs and desires. To differentiate ourselves from others, we must be aware of all the attributes that comprise our individuality. These attributes drive our organizational behaviors and give rise to our self-development goals, including our intentions around leadership emergence. Theories covered in this chapter focus on traits and individual drivers of motivation. We discuss how the constellation of characteristics, personality factors, and motivation can impact how individuals behave in organizations and enact leadership behaviors.

What Is the Individual-Level of Identity?

At the beginning of this text, one of the first exercises asked you to complete "I see myself as…" statements. In this chapter, our focus will be on the aspects of your self that individuate you from others. These factors are grounded in personal characteristics such as your personality, achievements you have made, such as your education, and the desires that motivate your actions. The individual-level of identity is typified by comparisons to others and actions that are in one's self-interest (Brewer & Gardner, 1996). Maintenance of one's self-esteem may be a major motivating factor in the behaviors enacted at this level; there is little self-reflection or feedback from others; these attributes are just how you see your self. If you refer back to your list, you can use "I" to signify which statements describe such individual-level factors, "R" to delineate those based in interpersonal relationships and "C" for those based on membership in social groups. We begin this chapter with a review of attributes that comprise this individual-level identity and discuss the implications for organizational behavior and leadership development.

Traits and Trait Theories

Traits and competencies are part of our individual-level identity, and they warrant a close examination into how they influence our actions. We present a brief historical review about how the thinking on traits and competencies has evolved over the last century. Because research shows that some traits and competencies matter much more than others in regard to organizational behavior and leadership, we narrow our focus to those that have the strongest evidence-based findings.

TRAITS:
Physical and behavioral attributes of individuals that are shaped by both genetic and environmental factors. (APA, 2021)

PERSONALITY:
Consistent patterns of behaviors, emotions, and feelings that make individuals unique. (APA, 2021)

Traits are physical and behavioral attributes of individuals that are shaped by both genetic and environmental factors. Take height, for example. Research shows that our height is approximately 80% attributable to heritability[1]. Yet height is also shaped by environmental factors such as nutrition and the quality of healthcare we receive early in life (Yang et al., 2010). Intelligence—or general cognitive ability—is also highly heritable but can be significantly influenced by environmental factors that can promote or hinder brain functioning (Plomin & Deary, 2015). Behaviorally, traits such as **personality** help describe (and, at times, accurately predict) how one may act across a range of situations (APA, 2021). As we grow older, traits largely stabilize. When they do change, the shifts tend to be small and spread out over a long time, usually decades (Roberts et al., 2008). Generally, traits are difficult to methodically develop, at least genuinely. For example, you cannot take an eight-hour crash course on how to become genuinely extraverted, though you might be able to adopt extraverted behaviors in certain contexts (i.e., faking extraversion at a company party). Thus, it is easy to understand why organizations are enamored with hiring individuals who possess a range of desirable traits. Those characteristics are enduring and cannot be trained efficiently. Thus, the search for a specific catalog of traits that can lead to superlative performance has been a major focus for thousands of years.

People and algorithms love lists. The internet era ushered in the ubiquitous listicle writing style, where authors convey their thoughts by inventorying the Top 3 or Top 10 things one must do to accomplish all forms of tasks. Listicles are pervasive

---

[1] Although heritability and genetics are frequently used interchangeably, it is often done so incorrectly. The common definition of heritability is the personal characteristics which can be inherited from our parents. Statistically, heritability is the variance that can be explained *in a population* due to genetic factors and therefore does not universally apply to an individual. So when we note that 80% of our height is attributed to heritability, that does not mean that 80% of *your* height is related to genetics because the environment in which you grew up in may have promoted or hindered your growth.

in leadership and management literature as well, where bestselling books like *The Seven Habits of Highly Effective People* (Covey, 1989, 2004) and *The Leadership Challenge* (Kouzes & Posner, 1987, 2006) advocate for emerging leaders to adopt a series of behaviors or gain competencies to help them reach their potential. These leadership self-help books are popular—Covey's *Seven Habits* has sold over 25 million copies—and many who purchase them believe they are helpful in part because lists are easy to grasp. After all, wouldn't life be easier if we could simply checklist our way to becoming the leader we want to be, *then* focus on all the other things?

A quick review of texts dating to antiquity (e.g., Plato, Socrates, Marcus Aurelius) reveals students and scholars alike generated listicles long before the internet or the rise of the self-help industry. While we know that traits and competencies matter to many workplace outcomes, scholars have searched in vain for a comprehensive list that can accurately describe the ideal person for any situation. There are hundreds of traits and competencies that might be beneficial to organizational members. The leader-follower influence process is complicated, and context matters greatly—a dominant trait may be highly beneficial in one situation but a hindrance in another.

Interest in the "trait theory of leadership approach" has waxed and waned since the mid-1800s, and empirical support for that view of leadership is somewhat mixed. For example, Carlyle (1869) framed leaders as individuals (from his perspective, usually men) with heroic qualities who stand ready to act and make a difference when warranted. This prevailing view was continuously echoed through the end of World War I, where leaders were believed to differ from followers based on measurable traits and, more specifically, that leaders were imbued from birth with special characteristics—charisma, oratory skills, good looks, a sense of timing, and more (Weber, 1924, Bass & Bass, 2009). Thus, this **"great man"** theory of leadership held that certain people were born leaders who, rather than being molded by contextual forces, did just the opposite. It was the *leaders* who mastered the environment and shaped history.

The application of the scientific method resulted in critical reviews of the great man theory. During the 1940s, leadership scholars such as Stogdill (1948) advocated that situational factors heavily influenced both leader traits and the leadership process, which would counterbalance the perceived weight that heritable traits have on leaders. After Stogdill and Shartle (1948, p. 286) reviewed 128 published studies on leadership, they concluded: "[l]eadership resides in individuals, but only by virtue of their interactions with other persons." Despite what Stogdill and other leadership researchers found about the influence a situation had on leadership development or performance, they still agreed that traits mattered. The more important questions became "How much do traits matter?" and "Under which circumstances do they matter most?" Below, we cover a few traits commonly believed to matter in leadership and discuss the empirical support for each.

GREAT MAN THEORIES: A belief that individuals in every society possess different degrees of intelligence, energy, and moral force, and in whatever direction the masses may be influenced to go, they are always led by the superior few. (Bass, 1990)

Physical Characteristics

Think back to your days in grade school. You may recall that those who emerged as leaders—the captain of a sports team, class president, or those voted "most likely to succeed"—had several things going for them and that they were likely attractive. As described in Chapter 2, we make attributions about leaders beginning early in life. Although we may want to live in a meritocratic world where people are hired and promoted based on their potential, abilities, and performance, many decisions regarding *who gets the opportunity to lead* are based on shallow attributions about one's appearance. In short, physical characteristics matter somewhat, and the empirical evidence supports this notion. Returning to the time when the great man theory of leadership was prominent, several studies from the 1930s suggested that leaders tended to be taller, in better physical shape (thinner, more athletic), and were deemed more attractive (Bass & Bass, 2009). People tend to ascribe a "**halo effect**" to attractive people, in line with the notion that "what is beautiful is good" (Lorenzo et al., 2010). However, there are limits to this perception (Eagly et al., 1991).

HALO EFFECT: A tendency to think about or evaluate a person or thing as generally good based on a single quality rather than assessing them based on a range of qualities. (Thorndike, 1920)

INTELLIGENCE: One's ability to understand and use information, apply thought and reason, adapt to environmental cues, and learn from experience. (APA, 2021)

While making attributions about leaders based on their physical features might seem shallow, more recent research suggests there may be some very good reasons why we do. While humans apply an attractiveness heuristic to attributions about leaders, they may do so because attractiveness serves as an imperfect diagnostic proxy for health (White et al., 2013). These researchers conducted a series of experiments illustrating that while people prefer attractive job candidates in general, their preference grew significantly when study participants were primed with health concerns prior to making their hiring decisions. Selecting leaders is a high-stakes context (i.e., the hiring decision has consequences for the organization), and the study suggests that if there is no other way to determine the health of a candidate, decision-makers may default to a candidate's appearance. This is not to suggest, however, that this group of "beautiful people" is predestined to become or succeed as leaders—far from it. It simply means that while they likely have a slight advantage over others, the advantage can easily be overtaken by more relevant factors, such as intelligence and competencies like wisdom and judgment. Keep in mind that attractiveness is merely one of many leadership traits that matter, but time and again, the evidence shows that other traits matter much more.

© Mikhail_Kayl/Shutterstock.com

Intelligence

© Natanael Ginting/Shutterstock.com

Intelligence is one's ability to understand and use information, apply thought and reason, adapt to environmental cues, and learn from experience (APA, 2021). It is difficult to argue against leaders who possess these qualities, given that when we are in a follower role, we trust leaders to make decisions that hopefully are based on logic, experience, and information. Behavioral scientists have gone to great lengths to tease out the variants of intelligence and associated concepts, such as general intelligence (described above), practical intelligence (commonly referred to as "street smarts," or one's ability to acquire and use tacit knowledge about everyday life), and creative intelligence (one's ability to derive novel solutions or develop ideas) (Bass & Bass, 2009; Rusmore, 1984).

Research consistently shows that various forms of intelligence are predictive of leadership emergence, effectiveness, and performance—but intelligence alone is far from the sole or even deciding factor in those outcomes. For example, while one study found a strong correlation between intelligence and leadership emergence (i.e., intelligent individuals became leaders) (Lord et al.,1984), a comprehensive meta-analysis of 96 studies completed 20 years later found that while intelligence was indeed a factor in who became leaders, the correlation had dropped by more than half (Judge et al., 2004). They also found that intelligence was not particularly helpful to leaders when they were under significant stress because their intellectual abilities are dedicated to dealing with the stressor, not necessarily with the tasks of leading. The authors concluded that, on average, being an intelligent leader only helps you so much. And when you are facing a high-stress environment, intelligence may not matter at all. We discuss the importance of meta-analytic studies in Callout Box 1.

Callout Box: Meta-Analyses, Leadership, and Traits

By now, you've likely noticed this text relies heavily on peer-reviewed empirical research. This is important for several reasons. Unlike hard sciences that have *laws* (e.g., the law of gravity), there are few proven absolutes in behavioral sciences. Instead, we rely heavily on the results of imperfect scientific studies to help us understand human behavior (in this case, leadership). Although we offer our opinions throughout the text, those opinions are informed by scientific work that is heavily scrutinized by other scientists in the field before publication. While this is far from a flawless process—questionable research using weak scientific methods does get published—the process is nevertheless the best we have in terms of creating knowledge that is based on both objective evidence and expert consensus. There is a hierarchy of scientific journals, with some publishing a higher quality/more rigorous product. We cite these for the information included in this text.

One of the best ways to assess what we know about a topic is via meta-analysis, which is a "study of studies." Keep in mind that thousands of studies about psychology, leadership, and management are published every year. Due to the volume and the competing results (i.e., one study concludes "X," while the next study finds the opposite), it becomes difficult to make inferences or see clear trends in results. Meta-analyses are intended to pool research results from all the studies done on a topic and accurately describe key conclusions. Although meta-analyses have their flaws (i.e., if the studies included in the meta-analysis are based on flawed research methods, the meta-analysis will suffer from the "garbage in, garbage out" problem), scientists heavily rely on them to serve as a triangulation point for understanding what we know about a particular topic.

Meta-analyses also help us scope the degree to which a context drives a stereotypical outcome. As outlined previously, the great man theory of leadership left little room for the consideration of women as leaders. And despite evidence to the contrary, this bias against women is still somewhat pervasive even today (e.g., the "Glass Ceiling" and "Glass Cliff"). In the 1990s, Alice Eagly and coauthors (1992) examined this issue closely via a meta-analysis of 61 studies. They found that when female leaders acted in ways stereotypically associated with men (e.g., autocratic and directive), their followers devalued the contributions of the female leaders. Likewise, this sex-based devaluation was more pronounced when the female leaders worked in industries that, at least at that time, were dominated by men. A few years later, Eagly and her coauthors (1995) examined the leadership effectiveness of male and female leaders and, regardless of the context of the study (e.g., done in a laboratory or in real organizations), both men and women were equally effective leaders. However, like their earlier finding, males performed better in industries stereotypically associated with men, while women did better in industries stereotypically associated with women.

Perhaps the greatest strengths of meta-analyses are that they improve the precision of findings across a range of studies, they explain (and at times settle) debates amongst contradictory studies, and they tend to tone down the "noise" inherent across studies (e.g., **heterogeneity** of samples or other contextual factors). We placed this description of meta-analyses in the current chapter about leadership characteristics because the field has published many high-quality meta-analyses about leader traits, leader personality, emotional intelligence, and more. Taken together, we believe in evidence-based leadership education and practices, and there is a lot of evidence out there. Due to the online 24-hour news cycle, leadership research gets even more attention than before. Rarely a day goes by without a media member reporting on a new study that found something interesting, so it is becoming increasingly difficult to discern outliers from trends. Since meta-analyses allow us to see the forest rather than the trees, we recommend you give those studies a closer look.

HETEROGENEITY: Having the quality of diversity within or across groups. (APA 2021)

So, what matters more: what a leader thinks (intelligence) or what a leader does (behaviors)? Not surprisingly, recent research found that leader behaviors—such as communicating a vision and inspiring followers to question the status quo—were far more influential than individual intelligence levels to the objective performance evaluations they received (Cavazotte et al., 2012). Keep in mind, however, that our intelligence is foundational to how and what we think, which in turn shapes our leadership behaviors. As noted, the prevailing view of successful and effective leaders is that they are highly intelligent.

Education

Education—the technical knowledge we gain from formal or informal learning opportunities—is a trait insofar as it is a consistent individual difference that shapes cognition and action. What we learn tends to stick with us, and it is very

© Dolores Bilbao/Shutterstock.com

difficult to "unlearn what we've learned." Education matters in a variety of leadership contexts. It serves as a barrier for entry (i.e., applicants must have an undergraduate degree to be considered for selection to the management training program) and portends to skills and potential one has (i.e., a tech company may only consider those with a computer science degree to lead a team of programmers). Scores of studies in the private sector (Howard & Bray, 1988) and the military (Bass, 1985) show that education is a key ingredient to leader potential and success.

And yet, while getting a proper education may allow you entry into leadership roles within certain professions, education alone is hardly a guarantee of success. As we describe later in this chapter, people who are highly competent at technical tasks are not always suited for leadership roles if they lack communication skills, patience with those less technically astute, or are so arrogant or enamored with their technical abilities that they alienate coworkers (i.e., they're narcissists) (Lombardo et al., 1988).

Likewise, the relevancy of knowledge gained through education and your ability to apply that knowledge at work also matters, as it speaks to your legitimacy as a leader. For example, within the military's aviation community, being a competent pilot is a prerequisite to being allowed to lead other aviators. While being a skilled communicator and having excellent organizational skills might help a pilot lead other pilots, one will likely struggle to be respected by junior pilots if they lack outstanding aviation credentials. The same applies to doctors, engineers, architects, and other highly technical professions. These professions have a few things in common. They are highly technical, and they typically require some form of apprenticeship or residency pipeline in which technical knowledge is transitioned to practice under the watchful eye of seasoned experts. Thus, some fields expect their leaders to be "experts" first, which often begins with attaining an outstanding education in a particular career field.

Wisdom and Judgment

We often consider intelligence as being a heritable measure of how someone processes information, accesses memory and thinks creatively. But there is an additional category of intelligence known as crystallized cognitive ability. This form of intelligence is acquired over a lifetime (Northouse, 2021) and manifests as wisdom and judgment.

Wisdom and judgment are often used interchangeably, but they are distinct—albeit closely related—leader characteristics. Ancient writings on wisdom exist, with Aristotle framing it as one's ability to contemplate what it means to live a good life (Ameriks & Clarke, 2000). Others, such as Rowley (2006, p. 1250), take a more contemporary view of **wisdom** and define it as "the capacity to put into action the most appropriate behavior, taking into account what is known (knowledge) and what does the most good (ethical and social considerations). Taken together, a leader's wisdom serves as both a deliberative (i.e., considering several options) and evaluative function (i.e., deciding which option is the best) related to making a decision.

WISDOM:
The capacity to put into action the most appropriate behavior, taking into account what is known (knowledge) and what does the most good (ethical and social considerations). (Rowley, 2006, p. 1250)

Judgment nests within wisdom as the evaluative function and is largely focused on taking action. Leadership scholars are placing more emphasis on judgment, given its link to decision-making, with some going so far as to say that "[g]ood judgment is the essence of good leadership" (Tichy & Bennis, 2007, p. 7). Judgment is shown by leaders when "making the tough call" between several options, all of which might be suboptimal. For example, despite several preceding US Presidents promising to end the war in Afghanistan, President Joe Biden faced a difficult choice: either end the war or extend it into a third decade. He chose to end the war and faced withering criticism at home and abroad. Herein lies a paradox about leader judgment: In line with the attribution errors discussed in Chapter 2, the effectiveness of one's judgment is typically weighed against the outcome, not the ethicality of the decision or the extensive deliberative process that goes into making the decision. So, leaders who show "good" judgment are often those who make the hard call that ends with a positive outcome. But if things go wrong, a leader's judgment will likely be questioned, regardless of how noble their intentions are or how carefully they think through their decisions.

JUDGMENT:
The ability to make considered decisions or come to sensible conclusions. (Oxford English Dictionary)

Most research agrees that both wisdom and judgment improve with experience (Mumford et al., 2000). Leaders can gain wisdom and judgment by reflecting on past actions, considering what might have led to their decisions, and considering what might work better in the future (Mumford et al., 2017). Beyond thinking through one's own actions, the nexus of leadership, wisdom, and judgment is social interaction—leaders make decisions that affect others. When reflecting on their own actions, leaders tend to cast themselves as the heroes of their own stories. Yet memories are often faulty, self-serving and tend to omit important details that, when brought to light, might help leaders make wiser decisions in the future. If you want to strengthen your wisdom and judgment, do so by receiving input from those around you and by asking them for an honest, objective review of what transpired.

Some organizations, such as the US military, use guided and socially interactive reflection as a cornerstone of leader development. This is referred to as an after-action review (AAR). AARs occur after every training or real-life event, and help leaders come to terms with decisions they made (often under pressure), how those decisions influenced the organization and its members, and how better decisions might be made in the future. Activity 1 will guide you through the AAR process.

Activity 1: After Action Review

Most books about wisdom and judgment tell you that both traits are gained across your lifespan due to a combination of success, failure, observation, and reflection. Leaders can accelerate the development of wisdom and judgment in themselves and others by seeking feedback to foster self-awareness. The AAR process is quite effective, costs little, and can be completed rapidly. While the primary goal of an AAR is to improve organizational performance, they also provide leaders with an unvarnished look at their leadership performance during an event. There are formal and informal formats to the AAR, and the US Army publishes a guide available for your review, found https://pinnacle-leaders.com/wp-content/uploads/2018/02/Leaders_Guide_to_AAR.pdf.

© bangoland/Shutterstock.com

For our purposes in this activity, we will focus on the informal AAR, assuming you are the leader of a group of people trying to accomplish some sort of work task.

- Step 1: Announce to your group members ahead of time that you intend to perform an AAR upon the conclusion of the event (strive to perform the AAR within a few hours of event completion, so details remain fresh).
- Step 2: Select a facilitator (someone other than you) since you will lead the group through the event (you can serve as the facilitator, but that is less effective). Best practices include asking for someone outside of your group who can independently observe what happens within the group as the event unfolds. The facilitator should also be familiar with both the AAR process (i.e., they read the guide ahead of time) and understand the end goals of the event.
- Step 3: Select a notetaker, so the details that emerge from the AAR are not forgotten.
- Step 4: Conduct the task.
- Step 5: After event completion, call the group together and quickly establish that the facilitator will lead the group through the AAR. The facilitator must set the ground rules for the discussion. While ground rules vary, they generally include stating that everyone must participate, that the AAR is not a critique or evaluation of the success or failure per se but rather about improving as a group, and that respectful disagreements are encouraged because they help everyone see things from different angles.

Step 6: **Review what was supposed to occur.** The facilitator and group members come to an agreement regarding what was supposed to happen during the event. This will allow you to gauge how well group members understood your intent and the goals for the event. In most cases, you will likely see some *drift* between what you—the leader—intended to occur and what your group members *thought* you intended to occur. This part of the AAR is also an opportunity for everyone in the group to refamiliarize themselves with performance standards that should have been met during the event. And, by extension, if there are no published performance standards for the event, then perhaps a major learning outcome that can be applied in the future is that standards should be set *before* performing the event.

Step 7: **Establish what *actually* happened.** The facilitator and group members then review what actually occurred during the event. There are several ways to do this, and usually, the facilitator should break this part of the discussion into phases whenever possible (i.e., set up something like a story arc with a beginning, middle, and end). A good facilitator will ask for perspectives from a lot of sources within the group—this is a good time to ensure that everyone is involved.

Step 8: **Determine what was right or wrong with what happened.** The facilitator probes to mesh what actually happened with the performance objectives and the actual performance outcomes. In other words, the facilitator should ask, "Did we meet our goals? Why or why not?" Even if goals are met, the facilitator should also ask, "Did we meet our goals within the published standards?" In other words, the facilitator should not only help the group understand if the goals were met but also help the group determine if the job was done correctly within the established benchmarks. After receiving input from the group, the facilitator should turn to the leader and ask for his or her response to the previous questions. One best practice is to end this phase of the AAR by cataloging the strengths and weaknesses of the group's performance during the event.

Step 9: **Determine what must be done differently in the future.** This phase of the AAR is a bit sobering. The facilitator should ask group members to own up to what they must improve upon before performing the task again in the future, then ask them to commit to doing so. A best practice is for facilitators to announce at the beginning of the AAR that they will be asking for this information from every member of the group at the end. Typically, the AAR ends with the leader describing what and how he or she intends to improve in the future.

Post-AAR reflection. Though the AAR may be over, the real learning for you has only just begun. You just received a significant amount of feedback from your group members about performance during an event, and that performance reflects how well you led them during the event. What did you learn about yourself? What traits or behaviors were activated during the event, and why were they triggered? How well did you communicate during the event? Did your group members really understand what they were supposed to do to accomplish the goals? If things became stressful during the event, did you tend to "take over" or work *through* others during the event? Aside from what you said during the AAR, what *else* would you do differently in the future? What can you do today to help ensure that you do those things differently in the future? Pondering these questions will help you show better judgment and become a wiser leader.

Activity 1: Learning Outcomes

Once the AAR is complete, critique the actual AAR process by answering the following:
- What characteristics did your facilitator have that made him or her more/less effective?
- Did you try to serve as your own facilitator? If so, how effective was that approach?
- Describe the engagement of your group members. Did they take it seriously? Did their body language or comments suggest they took the event seriously?
- Did disagreements emerge? Was professional language used? Did you have to intervene, or did the facilitator handle it?
- What might you try in the future to improve your AAR process?
- What can you do within the group to routinize the AAR process?

What Is Personality?

PERSONALITY:
Consistent patterns of behaviors, emotions, and feelings that make individuals unique. (APA, 2021)

In its simplest form, a person's **personality** is a unique and largely consistent constellation of behavioral and cognitive traits. While our personality does not compel us to think or behave in a particular way in every situation, personality does shape how we *tend* to think or behave in *many* situations. Most people who have taken an introductory psychology course are familiar with the most known personality traits—introversion and extraversion—but as we describe in this section of the chapter, there are several others. Barring trauma or mental illness, the changes that do occur during adulthood are usually incremental across decades (Roberts & Mroczek, 2008; Helson et al., 2002).

We carry our personality with us as we enter the workplace. And while change occurs, those changes are typically too gradual to be readily apparent to us or our coworkers. As we outline below, emphasis on leader personality is amplified in organizations because leadership is a social phenomenon, and power dynamics are a part of this terrain. In the sections that follow, we cover a range of personality facets and conceptualizations that help to shape leader identity, including core self-evaluations, the Big Five personality factors, and HEXACO.

CORE SELF-EVALUATIONS:
A group of traits that include self-esteem, generalized self-efficacy, local of control, and emotional stability; these traits are important to leadership. (Judge et al., 1998)

Core Self-Evaluations

How we fundamentally see ourselves, others, and the world around us is central to our identity, and this "bottom line" appraisal of ourselves is particularly important when it comes to leadership (Judge et al., 1998). These appraisals of ourselves are known as **core self-evaluations** and include self-esteem, generalized self-efficacy, locus of control, and emotional stability (each defined in Table 3.1 below).

Table 1*: Definitions of Core Self-Evaluation Traits

Trait	Definition
Self-esteem	The overall value we place on ourselves as people.
Generalized self-efficacy	Our perception of how well we cope with stress, perform work and succeed at tasks in life.
Locus of control	The amount of control we feel we have over our lives and the environment.
Emotional stability	Our tendency to be confident, secure, and not overly worrisome.

*Adapted from Judge & Bono, 2001

Our core self-evaluations are reflected in many ways, especially in terms of how we perform at work and how we treat others, mainly followers. According to Tim Judge and John Kammeyer-Mueller (2015, p. 332), "[p]eople who have positive core self-evaluations see themselves positively across a variety of situations, and approach the world in a confident, self-assured manner." This makes sense when you consider that people with high self-efficacy feel they are able to do their jobs well, those with high self-esteem likely see themselves in a positive light and will stand up for themselves, those with a high locus of control believe they can shape their environment and have agency to do so, and those with high emotional control will approach problems optimistically and be less likely to be overly worrisome (or make others worry). These traits are not necessarily Pollyannish—those who have high core self-evaluations are neither overly optimistic nor narcissistic per se—but rather, the traits tend to be grounded in reality and informed by one's history and experiences.

Perhaps what also makes core self-evaluations appealing is that the four components combine to form what behavioral scientists call a *higher-order factor*, meaning the combination of the four is more impactful when working together than they would be considered separately. In other words, the whole is greater than the sum of its parts (Judge et al., 2002). This concept is particularly important when it comes to fostering a leader's identity, as a surplus in one core self-evaluation (e.g., self-efficacy) likely will not cover for a significant shortfall in another (e.g., emotional stability). The key is *balance*.

The Big Five

There are countless psychological concepts that arguably make up a person's personality, which is, in part, why the **Big Five** emerged as the dominant way to frame personality within the study of leadership. Perhaps the greatest strength of the Big Five is that research shows the five factors—neuroticism, extraversion, openness to experience, agreeableness, and conscientiousness—are highly predictive of leadership emergence, job satisfaction, and performance. To understand and rank the importance of each of the five factors, researchers have gone to great lengths, but the answer is very opaque: It depends on what and who is being evaluated. For example, the correlations between the Big Five factors and leadership emergence in military or government leaders will look different than the Big Five factors and leadership effectiveness in investment bankers (Bass & Bass, 2009).

BIG FIVE:
The Five Factor Model of Personality, commonly referred to as the Big Five, which includes neuroticism, extraversion, openness to experience, agreeableness, and conscientiousness. (Goldberg, 1992)

© Olivier Le Moal/Shutterstock.com

Table 2*: The "Big Five" Personality Traits, Definitions, and Facets

Factor	Definition	Facets
Neuroticism	The degree to which someone experiences distress, nervousness, or insecurity.	• Anxiety • Hostility • Depression • Self-consciousness • Impulsivity • Vulnerability
Extraversion	The degree to which someone is confident, assertive, enthusiastic, and social.	• Warmth • Gregariousness • Assertiveness • Activity • Excitement-seeking • Positive emotions
Openness to experience	The degree to which someone is imaginative, artistic, sensible, and intellectual.	• Fantasy • Aesthetics • Feelings • Actions • Ideas • Values
Agreeableness	The degree to which a person is sympathetic, trusting, cooperative, warm, loving, and good-natured.	• Trust • Straightforwardness • Altruism • Compliance • Tender-mindedness • Modesty
Conscientiousness	The degree to which someone is dependable, responsible, hardworking, persevering, and organized.	• Competence • Order • Dutifulness • Striving for achievement • Self-disciplined • Deliberative

*Adapted from Bass & Bass (2009)

As reflected in Table 2, each of the five components is made up of six facets for a total of 30. The Big Five offers nuance, better precision, and more detail for leaders to consider about themselves. Take extraversion, for example. The research consistently shows that extraversion is highly predictive of who will emerge as leaders. Generally, higher extraversion scores are better (Judge et al., 2002). What is often glossed over, though, is that certain roles may call for different facets of extraversion. Whereas leading a team of salespeople in a high-pressure context may call for leaders to show extraverted facets of gregariousness and assertiveness, leading a team of hospice nurses may call for extraverted facets of warmth and positivity. As we cover later in this chapter, leaders should try to find opportunities where their dominant personality traits fit well with their job demands.

Chapter 4: Individual-Level Identity: Character, Traits, and Motivation

Activity 2: Assessing Your Big Five Personality Traits

There are several ways to assess your personality, some of which are better than others. For example, while the Myers-Briggs Type Indicator (MBTI) is very popular in corporate America, it is also deeply flawed (Gardner & Martinko, 1996; McCrae & Costa, 1989). We, therefore, avoid using or recommending it because it is not scientifically valid or reliable. On the other hand, the NEO-PI-R (Costa & McCrae, 2008) has extensive research support and is considered a valid measure of personality. Likewise, the IPIP-50 is a very good measure of personality that focuses on the Big Five.

Complete the IPIP-50

The International Personality Item Pool (IPIP) 50-item measure (Goldberg, 1992) assesses each of the Big Five factors of personality described in this chapter. We ***highly*** recommend you complete the online version of the IPIP-50 and save or screenshot your scores. You may complete it <u>here</u> at the openpsychometrics.org website[2]. The online version is anonymous and compares your score against thousands of others who have voluntarily completed the survey online.

Activity 2: Learning Outcomes

Interpreting Your Results

As described previously, the IPIP-50 is interpreted via a normative comparison (your score is compared to the "norms" of other people who completed the survey). For example, if you took the IPIP-50 on the openpsychometrics.org website, your percentile scores are derived from the more than 20,000 other people who completed the survey in the past, giving you a general idea of where your scores fall in the population. You should access in your report your scores along with trait descriptions for each of the five factors. Reflect upon your scores and your agreement or disagreement with the findings.

HEXACO

Although the Big Five has a deep history of empirical evidence and captures much of what most people and organizations care about when assessing personality, it is hardly the only way to frame personality. Although it tends to somewhat overlap the Big Five, the HEXACO personality framework has gained traction. It is particularly appealing because it measures a few areas that the Big Five does not and refines the definitions of some Big Five factors. HEXACO assesses honesty and humility—both highly desirable in leaders—while the Big Five does not.

As shown in Table 3, Ashton and Lee (2007) differentiate the HEXACO framing from the Big Five not only in terms of their similarities but also their differences. For example, whereas the Big Five assesses the degree to which someone may be high or low in a particular factor (e.g., conscientiousness), HEXACO takes this a step further. It not only assesses the degree to which someone might be high or low in one factor but also assesses the degree to which someone might be high or low in the *antithesis* of that factor. Carrying the conscientiousness example forward, an individual could show traits of diligence and care while at the same time show signs of impulsiveness. Therefore, the HEXACO conceptualization of personality leaves room for more nuance in understanding one's personality.

Chapter 4: Individual-Level Identity: Character, Traits, and Motivation

Table 3*: The Six-Factor HEXACO Personality Structure and Facets

Factor	Defining Adjectives	Facets
Honesty-Humility	*Synonyms:* Sincere, honest, faithful/loyal, modest/unassuming, fair-minded *Antonyms:* Sly, greedy, pretentious, hypocritical, boastful, pompous	• Sincerity • Fairness • Greed-avoidance • Modesty
Emotionality	*Synonyms:* Emotional, oversensitive, sentimental, fearful, anxious, vulnerable *Antonyms:* Brace, tough, independent, self-assured, stable	• Fearfulness • Anxiety • Dependence • Sentimentality
Extraversion	*Synonyms:* Outgoing, lively, extraverted, sociable, talkative, cheerful, active *Antonyms:* Shy, passive, withdrawn, introverted, quiet, reserved	• Expressiveness • Social boldness • Sociability • Liveliness
Agreeableness	*Synonyms:* Patient, tolerant, peaceful, mild, agreeable, lenient, gentle *Antonyms:* Ill-tempered, quarrelsome, stubborn, choleric	• Forgiveness • Gentleness • Flexibility • Patience
Conscientiousness	*Synonyms:* Organized, disciplined, diligent, careful, thorough, precise *Antonyms:* Sloppy, negligent, reckless, lazy, irresponsible, absent-minded	• Organization • Diligence • Perfectionism • Prudence
Openness to Experience	*Synonyms:* Intellectual, creative, unconventional, innovative, ironic *Antonyms:* Shallow, unimaginative, conventional	• Aesthetic appreciation • Inquisitiveness • Creativity • Unconventional

*Adapted from Table 2, p. 154 of Ashton & Lee (2007)

Research on HEXACO in the leadership domain remains popular (de Vries, 2018). For example, one study asked followers to rate both their leaders' personalities and leadership styles (de Vries, 2012). The results showed strong relationships between HEXACO factors and supportive, charismatic, ethical, and task-oriented leadership styles. Likewise, recent research examining several studies showed strong relationships between HEXACO factors in leaders and both leader emergence and effectiveness (Blake et al., 2022). The HEXACO model has also been shown to outperform the Big Five when it comes to predicting integrity and ethical business decision-making in leaders (Lee et al., 2008)—a finding that may be particularly useful to organizations wishing to integrate personality assessments into their hiring and selection processes.

© Olivier Le Moal/Shutterstock.com

The Dark Triad

Of course, there are aspects of our personality that can work for or against us when working with or leading others. While this can be said for every personality factor we've described thus far—there are volumes of research on the "too much of a good thing" phenomenon (so, you can be *too agreeable* or *too conscientious* [Pierce & Aguinis, 2013])—the **Dark Triad** especially stands out. Comprised of narcissism, Machiavellianism, and psychopathy, leaders who show a prominent degree of Dark Triad tendencies can cause significant damage to organizations and employees.

© James.Pintar/Shutterstock.com

While we all want a positive self-esteem, **narcissism** is a step too far. According to the American Psychiatric Association, extreme narcissism is a form of mental illness characterized by having a grandiose sense of self-importance, lacking empathy, having a sense of entitlement, and being exploitative and arrogant (APA, 2013). Reading this, you might say, "That sounds like my old boss!" But narcissistic personality disorder is at the extreme spectrum of personality and is uncommon. Rates in the US population range from 0.5% to 5% (Ronningstam, 2013), and because it is a mental illness, it is considered debilitative without medical treatment (i.e., it gets in the way of having a normal life) (Mitra & Fluyau, 2020). What is more common, however, is people—especially leaders—showing narcissistic tendencies, which can hamper effectiveness in many ways. Empirical research has shown that narcissistic leaders place their needs ahead of their employees (Glavin et al., 2010) and treat employees unfairly, resulting in high turnover rates (Resick et al., 2009). Narcissistic leaders also tend to hold back important information from work teams that need it (Nevicka et al., 2011) and devalue the input of others while inflating the importance of their own opinion (Grijalva et al., 2015).

Whereas a narcissist may boast to try to self-enhance their image, Machiavellians are grounded in reality—they know their strengths and weaknesses, and they see context for what it is. But they are also skilled manipulators (Paulhus & Williams, 2002). If you have ever been convinced to do something that is clearly against your self-interest—like when your manager convinced you to take the blame for something you didn't do—then you have run up against a Machiavellian. **Machiavellianism** as a psychological construct is derived from the writings of Niccolò Machiavelli, who wrote extensively in the 1500s about the importance of using deceit and manipulation to further political agendas. The phrase "the ends justify the means" is attributed to Machiavelli, meaning virtually anything is allowed—deceit, manipulation, treachery, crime—for the end goal to be met (Mansfield, 1998).

The third personality factor in the Dark Triad, **psychopathy**, is characterized by a set of behaviors such as lacking remorse, poor impulse control, an unwillingness to accept blame, being superficially charming, and showing no anxiety despite obvious danger (Cleckley, 1941, Patrick et al., 2009, Landay et al., 2018). The notion that senior leaders in organizations (like CEOs) are psychopaths is a popular one (Babiak & Hare, 2006), though "clinical" levels of psychopathy are exceedingly rare in the workforce. Most of the research on psychopathy in leaders instead focuses on "subclinical" levels of psychopathy, meaning leaders may show some sign of psychopathic behaviors but are still able to function and succeed at work.

The Dark Triad in the workplace can obviously have detrimental effects; individuals with these dominant traits are ripe for causing serious damage. But the

DARK TRIAD: A constellation of traits consisting of narcissism, Machiavellianism, and psychopathy. (Furnham, Richards, & Paulhus, 2013)

NARCISSISM: Being excessively egocentric, such as having an inflated interest in oneself. (APA 2021)

MACHIAVELLIANISM: Being excessively cunning, willing to use deceit or unethical manipulation. (Mansfield, 1998)

PSYCHOPATHY: Broadly lacking remorse, having poor impulse control, refusing to accept blame, and showing no anxiety when threatened. (APA 2021)

research is also mixed as to the utility of leaders showing *some* degree of the Dark Triad when the context calls for it. For example, narcissism has repeatedly been shown to predict leader emergence (e.g., narcissists usually do well in job interviews), and leaders are perceived to be more effective if they have a *moderate* amount of narcissism (Grjjalva et al., 2015). Management scholars such as Pfeffer (2015) have long since touted the value of narcissism and Machiavellianism under the right conditions, especially in times when leaders need to make their case while receiving performance evaluations or charting their path up the corporate ladder. Vergauwe and coauthors (2021) were similarly able to provide evidence where psychopathic leader traits combined with boldness resulted in effectiveness. Though much of the leadership literature suggests that "nicer" personality constructs are the ones we hope to have as a leader, we operate in both cooperative and competitive environments. There may be instances when leaders must be more assertive and aggressive, less remorseful, more self-centered, and more manipulative to reach organizational goals. Now, this does not mean you should *prefer* to work for this leader or work in an organization that promotes such a leader—nevertheless, these leaders do exist. And if they realize they have a higher degree of these three tendencies, perhaps they'll become more self-aware and thus better able to control them. Taken together, there's a bit of narcissism, Machiavellianism, and psychopathy in us all. Those traits are a part of our identity, so it is more a question of when, where, and to what ends we activate or restrain them and whether or not we choose to work for individuals who lead foremost with them.

Summary of Leader Traits

We have examined in detail several characteristics and traits, but there are many, many more. While traits are obviously important, they are also only a portion of what constitutes identity (as we discuss elsewhere in this book). The debate about which matters more to leader effectiveness, leader traits or leader behaviors, continues to this day. Scott DeRue and coauthors (2011) conducted a meta-analysis where they pooled the results of 79 studies that assessed the ability of leader traits (gender, intelligence, and the Big Five personality factors) and leader behaviors (initiating structure, transformational behaviors, transactional behaviors, and other "full range" behaviors that will be described later in this text) to predict a range of leader effectiveness benchmarks (leader effectiveness, group performance, follower job satisfaction, and follower satisfaction with their leader). Regarding leader traits, DeRue and his team found that while traits were predictive of the effectiveness benchmarks, they paled in comparison to leader behaviors. For example, the pooled group of leadership traits only accounted for 2% of the variance in how satisfied followers were with their jobs (vs. 51% for leader behaviors); 6% in how satisfied they were with their leaders (vs. 70% for leader behaviors); 14% in group performance (vs. 20% for leader behaviors); and 22% in leader effectiveness (vs. 47% for leader behaviors). Thus, when it comes to gauging leader effectiveness, what leaders *do* matters far more than their traits.

Individual-Level Motivation

While traits are important and give us a foundation for self-awareness, we also need to understand what drives individual actions. The next section will review the general ideas behind motivation and cover the well-known content theories of motivation. As discussed in Chapter 3, motivation provides us with purpose and direction in the behaviors we enact. There are two forms of motivation. **Primary motivations** are typically physiological in nature and tend to focus on basic human needs, such as hunger, sleep, and safety. **Secondary motives** are usually characterized by social and psychological needs, including forming and having friendships, being challenged and rewarded by work, and attaining personal or professional status. While primary motivations are powerful, much of our working life is spent shaping and directing secondary motivations to further the goals of the organizations in which we participate.

PRIMARY MOTIVATIONS: Impulses that drive us toward satisfying basic needs, such as acquiring food, sleep, and physical security. (APA, 2022)

SECONDARY MOTIVES: Impulses that drive us toward attaining social relationships, finding meaningful work, or acquiring social status. (APA, 2022)

While the needs that drive us and the behaviors we enact to satisfy those needs are unique, the motivation *process* is consistent. We all start with some **unsatisfied need** that creates **tension**—either stress or desire that moves us to action. These actions are the **drives** that produce **goal-oriented behaviors.** Once we enact those behaviors, we **achieve our goals** and **satisfy our needs.** This then **reduces** or alleviates the **tension** (Ramlall, 2004).

Let's examine a simple example. Say you are sitting on your couch watching a sporting event, and you get thirsty. There is a physiological tension where you can feel your thirst. You are driven to action by that thirst, which motivates the goal-directed behavior of getting up off the couch to go to your refrigerator to grab the drink—achieving your goal, satisfying your need, and reducing the tension you feel. With primary motivations, the reduction of tension is clear – it is easy to feel when a physiological need has been satisfied. For secondary motivations, it is important to visualize what goal achievement looks like, so you can enjoy the reduction of tension that accompanies need satisfaction.

Activity 3: The Motivation Process

Using the process outlined above, detail the motivation process for one of your unsatisfied secondary needs. Explain every step of the process.

1. Unsatisfied need
2. Tension
3. Drives
4. Goal-oriented behaviors
5. Goal Achievement/Need Satisfaction
6. Tension Reduction

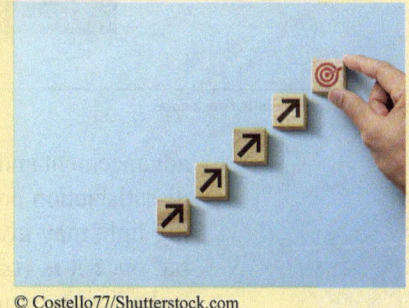
© Costello77/Shutterstock.com

Activity 3: Learning Outcomes

Breaking down the motivation process into discrete steps will help you consider how you tend to approach goals. Being able to recognize the tension that comes from unsatisfied needs and how that translates to the drives that produce goal-oriented behaviors is a key step in building your own approach to self-development. Finally, visualizing the moment that you achieve a goal will help you celebrate your goal achievements.

Chapter 4: Individual-Level Identity: Character, Traits, and Motivation

Figure 1: Maslow's Hierarchy Compared to ERG Theory

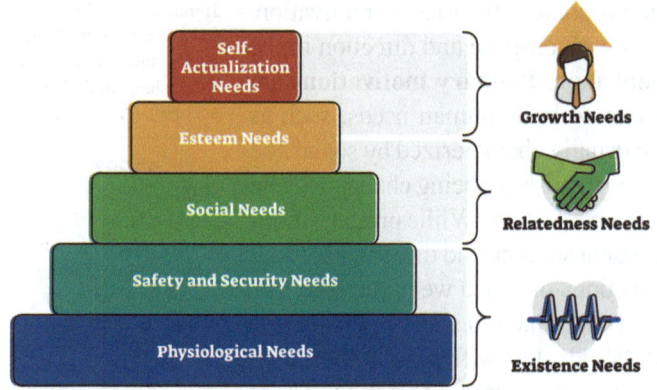

© VectorMine/Shutterstock.com

© Skyline Graphics/Shutterstock.com

Early motivation theories such as Maslow's Hierarchy of Needs (Maslow, 1943, 1954) and Alderfer's ERG theory (Alderfer, 1969) focused on these primary and secondary behavioral drivers. While Maslow envisioned a pyramid, with the primary needs (physiological and safety needs) creating the foundation after which the higher-order needs (social, esteem, and self-actualization needs) were pursued, Alderfer developed an alternative theory depicting the core needs of Existence, Relatedness, and Growth in a non-progressive manner. Figure 1 shows how these two theories relate to one another. The key difference helps explain why and how individuals may seek to satisfy growth or self-actualization needs (pursuing an education) before securing some existence or physiological needs (lacking a steady food or housing supply). Maslow's theory could never quite explain starving artists or introverts seeking a higher calling without satisfying social needs. ERG allows individuals to reflect upon which needs are salient at the time and then pursue them accordingly.

In organizations, encouraging motivation can be as basic as determining which actions are necessities or hygiene factors and which actions can drive performance motivators. Hygiene here does not mean cleanliness. It refers to the practices taken to preserve health—in this context, organizational health. Herzberg and colleagues (Herzberg et al., 1959) examined the environmental factors that help limit dissatisfaction—suitable working conditions and satisfactory wages—compared to the actions that can enhance satisfaction—opportunities for advancement and meaningful work (Herzberg et al., 1959). The constraints that limit dissatisfaction do not tend to motivate superior performance; for example, a flickering light may give you a headache and lead to annoyance with your surroundings, but once it is fixed, a manager would not expect an increased dedication to one's tasks, just a return to normal performance. On the other hand, an opportunity for advancement or new (wanted) responsibilities may lead to increased engagement and higher performance outcomes. Motivating factors often activate the individual needs or desires we have to be successful. Once again, our identity is shaped by these motivations, which can be externally or internally motivated.

Extrinsic motivations are the incentives that drive us towards attaining some sort of tangible reward. For instance, while finding purpose and meaning in work is important, most employees agree to come to work and do a job because it pays

EXTRINSIC MOTIVATIONS: The impulse to attain some sort of tangible reward, such as a college degree, a job promotion, or financial compensation. (APA, 2022)

a salary or a wage, which in turn satisfies other desires (being able to buy food or take care of one's family). Conversely, **intrinsic motivations** are those derived from the benefit of the act itself rather than attaining an external reward. Except for the most talented and accomplished among us, most musicians play music for pure enjoyment and will never be paid for doing so. At a basic level, extrinsic and intrinsic motivations are value neutral (i.e., one is not better than the other), but this can change as the context changes. For example, most people would agree that individuals should be paid based on their performance, so it is perfectly fine for them to be extrinsically motivated to reach performance goals. However, we may view the same individual's extrinsic motivation quite differently if it motivates unethical behavior in pursuit of a performance goal. We might also admire the person who is intrinsically motivated to lead others because of the positive impact on others—but that view likely would change if organizational goals are consistently unmet.

> **INTRINSIC MOTIVATIONS:** The impulse to do those things which we enjoy the most, not because we hope to attain some tangible reward, but rather because we enjoy the process and experience of doing those things. (APA, 2022)

Summary of Individual-Level Motivations

We have presented a few content-driven theories of motivation that relate to individual-level identity. While the content of these theories is important, it is how and why they drive individual behavior that is of interest here. Yes, all humans need food, water, sleep, and shelter to survive, but individuals choose or choose not to pursue those goals over others that seem less related to survival, like working 80-hour+ weeks on a new, innovative idea. Understanding the patterns of one's motivations is another step towards self-awareness. At certain times, social needs may outweigh self-esteem needs; at other times, an extrinsic reward such as higher pay may supersede the need for responsibility at work. When we add in interactions with other individuals and the relational- and collective-level aspects of identity, how and why we pursue the goals we do matters even more.

Your traits as a leader will only take you so far because the individual level of identity is concentrated on comparing and differentiating your self from others and acting in your self-interest. The context, your behaviors, and how you relate to others matters tremendously in terms of leader effectiveness and performance. The drives you have towards satisfying particular motivators can also impact how others perceive your intentions and their willingness to engage with you in pursuit of those goals.

In Review

Chapter 4 pulls together several distinct psychological concepts that are related and serve as cornerstones of the mosaic of leader identity. Each of us has a unique set of traits, personality, and motivations, and any combination may serve to help or hinder our ability as leaders to influence followers.

Further, our understanding of the role that each play in leadership has grown considerably over the last century. The science supporting our modern understanding of leadership has largely dispensed with the "Great Man Theories" of leadership that suggested that select individuals were born with the necessary qualities to lead others. While genetics certainly play an important role in developing certain traits and personality characteristics, we know that the environment matters more. Thus, leadership is less of a made *or* born dichotomy but it is rather more of a complementary made *and* born relationship.

There is a range of traits that are more closely aligned with genetics, such as physical appearance and intelligence. Conversely, there are other traits, such as education, that are more closely associated with environmental/contextual factors. Further, traits can be developed to some degree, but more germane to the leadership domain, traits can be honed with effort. Specifically, an individual may be highly intelligent, yet leaders must learn to effectively employ their intelligence when influencing others.

One set of traits that tend to be most relevant to leader identity is *personality*, which is the behavioral and emotional predispositions we all have. While it is pervasive in nearly every aspect of our lives, personality does not dictate behavior and thus should be viewed as a *tendency* to behave or emotionally respond in each context. Our personalities begin to develop at birth and gradually stabilize in adulthood, although research has shown that personality incrementally changes across our lives. While there is no agreed-upon constellation of personality characteristics that leaders must have, the most widely studied personality frameworks include Core Self-Evaluation Traits, the Big Five, and HEXACO, described in detail in the current chapter. Leaders should understand that since the leadership process is a social one, their personality characteristics are amplified across the organization because leaders are under constant observation by followers.

Lastly, leader identity is also influenced by various types of motivations—the drivers of behavior and emotions—and these motivations may vary widely across different contexts. It is common for emerging leaders to first orient their motivations toward meeting their primary needs, such as job security and a reasonable wage. Yet, as they progress in their career as a leader, the primary motivations often give way to secondary motivations, such as forming high-quality relationships with others, deriving purpose and meaning in work, and organizational stewardship. When influencing others, leaders must keep in mind that since motivations vary across people and contexts, their motivations may not perfectly align with those of their followers. This is not problematic per se, provided that leaders do not dismiss the motivations of others; individualized consideration is warranted, which we cover more closely in Chapter 9.

Learning Objectives

Define and explain the link between traits and leadership

Traits are the physical and behavioral attributes you have that are shaped by both genetic and environmental factors. As we age, traits tend to stabilize and typically only change incrementally. Within the leadership context, the traits that matter more are the ones you can leverage to better help you influence others. There are so many traits that influence the leadership process that a single text likely cannot capture them all, so in this chapter, we linked leadership with *physical characteristics* (e.g., height, attractiveness, etc.), *intelligence*, *wisdom* and *judgment*, and *personality*. The key is to be aware of your unique set of traits and understand how to leverage those traits in a positive way within the leader-follower influence process.

Explore and understand the ways in which personality is conceptualized and measured

Personality is the consistent pattern of behaviors, emotions, and feelings that make individuals unique. Our personality does not force us to behave or feel a certain way, but rather personality is more about a consistent tendency. In other words, an introvert might skip most workplace social functions, but it does not mean that he or she will skip *every* social function. Personality is conceptualized in several ways, and in this chapter, we present three common frameworks: the *Core Self-Evaluation Traits*, the *Big Five*, and *HEXACO*. People tend to assess and categorize personality based on observation—after all, extraverts are usually easy to identify—but personality is typically measured via validated surveys, such as the *IPIP-50* and others.

Define the traits that may hinder your ability to lead in an ethical way

There are parts of our personality that can work against us when trying to lead others ethically. For example, leaders exhibiting high levels of the *Dark Triad*—*narcissism*, *Machiavellianism*, and *psychopathy*—have been shown to cause significant harm to organizations and followers alike. It is important to note that leaders often exhibit some of these characteristics in specific contexts, and there is research suggesting that being a bit narcissistic and Machiavellian can be beneficial for leaders. However, we advise that leaders show restraint and carefully regulate their Dark Triad tendencies, given the negative impact they can have on the leader-follower dynamic when not properly managed.

Describe the components of individual-level motivation as they relate to leadership

Motivations provide us with purpose and direction for our behaviors. There are two broad categories of motivations: *Primary motivations*, which are focused on basic human needs, such as food and safety, and *secondary motivations*, such as forming friendships and attaining goals and status. The chapter describes three broad motivational theories, which include Maslow's *Hierarchy of Needs*, Alderfer's *ERG theory*, and Herzberg's *Two Factor Theory* of workplace motivation. Lastly, we introduced *intrinsic* and *extrinsic* motivations. For leaders, the important takeaways are that followers are motivated in different ways, and thus it is a mistake to discount an individual's motivations if they do not align with those of the leader. Indeed, while a mid-career employee may be motivated by secondary motivations and is striving towards significant achievements in order to meet her esteem needs, a new employee fresh out of college may be heavily focused on primary motivations, such as ensuring he has a salary high enough to pay rent and make student loan payments.

Key Terms

Traits (Pg. 56)	Judgment (Pg. 61)
Great Man Theories (Pg. 57)	Personality (Pg. 56, 64)
Halo Effect (Pg. 58)	Core Self-Evaluations (Pg. 64)
Intelligence (Pg. 58)	Big Five (Pg. 65)
Heterogeneity (Pg. 60)	Dark Triad (Pg. 69)
Wisdom (Pg. 61)	Narcissism (Pg. 69)

Machiavellianism (Pg. 69)
Psychopathy (Pg. 69)
Primary Motivations (Pg. 71)
Secondary Motivations (Pg. 71)
Extrinsic Motivations (Pg. 72)
Intrinsic Motivations (Pg. 73)

Critical Thinking Questions

1. How have your views on leaders being born (i.e., the "Great Man Theory") vs. made (i.e., shaped by context) changed over your life?
2. Although the chapter covers a range of traits, what other traits not described here do you think influence the leadership process?
3. Can you describe a time when you witnessed someone exhibit behaviors related to the *Dark Triad*? What emotions did you feel when you saw this behavior?
4. What are the common themes across the three motivation theories described in this chapter? Those theories include Maslow's *Hierarchy of Needs*, Alderfer's *ERG theory*, and Herzberg's *Two Factor Theory* of workplace motivation.

References

Alderfer, C. P. (1969). An empirical test of a new theory of human needs. *Organizational Behavior and Human Performance, 4*(2), 142–175.

American Psychological Association (2021). Definition of trait, intelligence, personality, heterogeneity, psychopathy, and heritability. https://dictionary.apa.org/

American Psychiatric Association (2013). *Diagnostic and statistical manual of mental disorders: DSM-5*. Arlington, VA.

Ameriks, K., & Clarke, D. M. (2000). *Aristotle: Nicomachean ethics*. Cambridge University Press.

Ashton, M. C., & Lee, K. (2007). Empirical, theoretical, and practical advantages of the HEXACO model of personality structure. *Personality and Social Psychology Review, 11*(2), 150–166.

Babiak, P., & Hare, R. D. (2006). *Snakes in suits: When psychopaths go to work*. Regan Books.

Bass, B. M. (1985). *Leadership and performance beyond expectations*. Collier Macmillan.

Bass, B. M., & Bass, R. (2009). *The Bass handbook of leadership: Theory, research, and managerial applications*. Simon and Schuster.

Blake, A. B., Luu, V. H., Petrenko, O. V., Gardner, W. L., Moergen, K. J., & Ezerins, M. E. (2022). Let's agree about nice leaders: A literature review and meta-analysis of agreeableness and its relationship with leadership outcomes. *The Leadership Quarterly*, 101593.

Carlyle, T. (1869). *Heroes and hero-worship* (Vol. 12). Chapman and Hall.

Cavazotte, F., Moreno, V., & Hickmann, M. (2012). Effects of leader intelligence, personality and emotional intelligence on transformational leadership and managerial performance. *The Leadership Quarterly*, *23*(3), 443–455.

Cleckley, H. (1941). *The mask of sanity: An attempt to reinterpret the so-called psychopathic personality*. The C. V. Mosby Company.

Costa Jr, P. T., & McCrae, R. R. (2008). *The Revised Neo Personality Inventory (neo-pi-r)*. Sage Publications, Inc.

Covey, S. R. (1989; 2004). *The 7 habits of highly effective people*. Simon & Schuster.

Derue, D. S., Nahrgang, J. D., Wellman, N. E. D., & Humphrey, S. E. (2011). Trait and behavioral theories of leadership: An integration and meta-analytic test of their relative validity. *Personnel Psychology*, *64*(1), 7–52.

De Vries, R. E. (2018). Three Nightmare Traits in Leaders. *Frontiers in Psychology*, *9*, 871–871.

De Vries, R. E. (2012). Personality predictors of leadership styles and the self–other agreement problem. *The Leadership Quarterly*, *23*(5), 809–821.

Eagly, A. H., Ashmore, R. D., Makhijani, M. G., & Longo, L. C. (1991). What is beautiful is good, but…: A meta-analytic review of research on the physical attractiveness stereotype. *Psychological Bulletin*, *110*(1), 109–128.

Eagly, A. H., Karau, S. J., & Makhijani, M. G. (1995). Gender and the effectiveness of leaders: a meta-analysis. *Psychological Bulletin*, *117*(1), 125–145.

Eagly, A. H., Makhijani, M. G., & Klonsky, B. G. (1992). Gender and the Evaluation of Leaders: A Meta-Analysis. *Psychological Bulletin*, *111*(1), 3–22.

Fiske, S. T. (1992). Thinking Is for Doing: Portraits of Social Cognition From Daguerreotype to Laserphoto. *Journal of Personality and Social Psychology*, *63*(6), 877–889.

Furnham, A., Richards, S. C., & Paulhus, D. L. (2013). The Dark Triad of personality: A 10 year review. *Social and Personality Psychology Compass*, *7*(3), 199–216.

Galvin B.M., Waldman D.A., & Balthazard P. (2010). Visionary communication qualities as mediators of the relationship between narcissism and attributions of leader charisma. *Personnel Psychology, 63*, 509–537.

Gardner, W. & Martinko, M. (1996). Using the Myers-Briggs Type Indicator to study managers: A literature review and research agenda. *Journal of Management, 22*, 45–83.

Goldberg, L. R. (1992). The development of markers for the big-five factor structure. *Psychological Assessment*, *4*(1), 26–42.

Goleman, D. (2004). What makes a leader?. *Harvard Business Review*, *82*(1), 82–82.

Grant, A. (2014). The dark side of emotional intelligence. *The Atlantic, 2*.

Grijalva, E., Harms, P. D., Newman, D. A., Gaddis, B. H., & Fraley, R. C. (2015). Narcissism and leadership: A meta-analytic review of linear and nonlinear relationships. *Personnel Psychology*, *68*(1), 1–47.

Harms, P. D., & Credé, M. (2010a). Emotional intelligence and transformational and transactional leadership: A meta-analysis. *Journal of Leadership & Organizational Studies*, *17*(1), 5–17.

Harms, P. D., & Credé, M. (2010b). Remaining issues in emotional intelligence research: Construct overlap, method artifacts, and lack of incremental validity. *Industrial and Organizational Psychology*, *3*(2), 154–158.

Helson, R., Jones, C., & Kwan, V. S. (2002). Personality change over 40 years of adulthood: Hierarchical linear modeling analyses of two longitudinal samples. *Journal of Personality and Social Psychology*, *83*(3), 752–766.

Herzberg, F. (1968). *One more time: How do you motivate employees* (Vol. 65). Harvard Business Review.

Herzberg, F., Mausner, B., & Snyderman, B. (1959). *The motivation to work*. Wiley.

Howard, A., & Bray, D. W. (1988). *Managerial lives in transition: Advancing age and changing times*. Guilford Press.

Joseph, D. L., & Newman, D. A. (2010). Emotional intelligence: An integrative meta-analysis and cascading model. *Journal of Applied Psychology*, *95*(1), 54–78.

Judge, T. A., & Bono, J. E. (2001). Relationship of core self-evaluations traits—self-esteem, generalized self-efficacy, locus of control, and emotional stability—with job satisfaction and job performance: A meta-analysis. *Journal of Applied Psychology*, *86*(1), 80–92.

Judge, T. A., Bono, J. E., Ilies, R., & Gerhardt, M. W. (2002). Personality and leadership: A qualitative and quantitative review. *Journal of Applied Psychology*, *87*(4), 765–780.

Judge, T. A., Colbert, A. E., & Ilies, R. (2004). Intelligence and leadership: A quantitative review and test of theoretical propositions. *Journal of Applied Psychology*, *89*(3), 542–552.

Judge, T. A., Erez, A., Bono, J. E., & Thoresen, C. J. (2002). Are measures of self-esteem, neuroticism, locus of control, and generalized self-efficacy indicators of a common core construct?. *Journal of Personality and Social Psychology*, *83*(3), 693–710.

Judge, T. A., & Kammeyer-Mueller, J. D. (2011). Implications of core self-evaluations for a changing organizational context. *Human Resource Management Review*, *21*(4), 331–341.

Judge, T. A., Locke, E. A., Durham, C. C., & Kluger, A. N. (1998). Dispositional effects on job and life satisfaction: The role of core evaluations. *Journal of Applied Psychology*, *83*(1), 17–34.

Kouzes, J. M., & Posner, B. Z. (1987; 2006). *The leadership challenge*. John Wiley & Sons.

Landay, K., Harms, P. D., & Credé, M. (2019). Shall we serve the dark lords? A meta-analytic review of psychopathy and leadership. *The Journal of Applied Psychology*, *104*(1), 183–196.

Lee, K., Ashton, M. C., Morrison, D. L., Cordery, J., & Dunlop, P. D. (2008). Predicting integrity with the HEXACO personality model: Use of self-and observer reports. *Journal of Occupational and Organizational Psychology*, *81*(1), 147–167.

Locke, E. A. (2005). Why emotional intelligence is an invalid concept. *Journal of Organizational Behavior*, *26*(4), 425–431.

Lombardo, M. M., Ruderman, M. N., & McCauley, C. D. (1988). Explanations of success and derailment in upper-level management positions. *Journal of Business and Psychology*, *2*(3), 199–216.

Lord, R. G., Foti, R. J., & De Vader, C. L. (1984). A test of leadership categorization theory: Internal structure, information processing, and leadership perceptions. *Organizational Behavior and Human Performance*, *34*(3), 343–378.

Lorenzo, G. L., Biesanz, J. C., & Human, L. J. (2010). What is beautiful is good and more accurately understood: Physical attractiveness and accuracy in first impressions of personality. *Psychological Science*, *21*(12), 1777–1782.

Mansfield, H. C. (1998). *Machiavelli's virtue*. University of Chicago Press.

Maslow, A. H. (1943). A theory of human motivation. *Psychological Review, 50*(4), 370–396. https://doi.org/10.1037/h0054346

Maslow, A. H. (1954). Abraham Maslow's Hierarchy of needs motivational model. Harper and Row.

McCrae, R. & Costa, P. (1989). Reinterpreting the Myers-Briggs Type Indicator from the perspective of the five-factor model of personality. *Journal of Personality,* 57, 17–40.

Mitra, P., & Fluyau, D. (2020). Narcissistic Personality Disorder. *StatPearls*. https://www.ncbi.nlm.nih.gov/books/NBK556001/

Mumford, M. D., Marks, M. A., Connelly, M. S., Zaccaro, S. J., & Reiter-Palmon, R. (2000). Development of leadership skills: Experience and timing. *The Leadership Quarterly*, *11*(1), 87–114.

Mumford, M. D., Todd, E. M., Higgs, C., & McIntosh, T. (2017). Cognitive skills and leadership performance: The nine critical skills. *The Leadership Quarterly*, *28*(1), 24–39.

Nevicka, B., Ten Velden, F.S., De Hoogh, A.H.B., & Van Vianen, A.E.M. (2011). Reality at odds with perceptions: Narcissistic leaders and group performance. *Psychological Science, 22*, 1259–1264.

Northouse, P. G. (2021). *Leadership: Theory and practice*. Sage publications.

Patrick, C. J., Fowles, D. C., & Krueger, R. F. (2009). Triarchic conceptualization of psychopathy: Developmental origins of disinhibition, boldness, and meanness. *Development and Psychopathology, 21*, 913–938.

Paulhus, D. L., & Williams, K. M. (2002). The dark triad of personality: Narcissism, Machiavellianism, and psychopathy. *Journal of Research in Personality*, *36*(6), 556–563.

Pfeffer, J. (2015). *Leadership BS: Fixing workplaces and careers one truth at a time*. HarperCollins.

Pierce, J. R., & Aguinis, H. (2013). The too-much-of-a-good-thing effect in management. *Journal of Management*, *39*(2), 313–338.

Plomin, R., & Deary, I. J. (2015). Genetics and intelligence differences: Five special findings. *Molecular Psychiatry*, *20*(1), 98–108.

Ramlall, S. (2004). A review of employee motivation theories and their implications for employee retention within organizations. *Journal of American Academy of Business, 5*(1/2), 52–63.

Resick C.J., Whitman D.S., Weingarden S.M., & Hiller N.J. (2009). The bright-side and the dark-side of CEO personality: Examining core self-evaluations, narcissism, transformational leadership, and strategic influence. *Journal of Applied Psychology, 94,* 1365–1381.

Roberts, B. W., & Mroczek, D. (2008). Personality trait change in adulthood. *Current Directions in Psychological Science, 17*(1), 31-35.

Roberts, B. W., Wood, D., & Caspi, A. (2008). The development of personality traits in adulthood. In O. P. John, R. W. Robins, & L. A. Pervin (Eds.), *Handbook of personality: Theory and research* (pp. 375–398). The Guilford Press.

Ronningstam, E. (2013). An update on narcissistic personality disorder. *Current Opinion in Psychiatry, 26*(1), 102–106.

Rowley, J. (2006). What do we need to know about wisdom? *Management Decision, 44*(9), 1246–1257.

Rusmore, J. T. (1984). *Executive performance and intellectual ability in organizational levels.* Advanced Human Systems Institution, San Jose State University.

Stogdill, R. M. (1948). Personal factors associated with leadership: A survey of the literature. *The Journal of Psychology, 25*(1), 35–71.

Stogdill, R. M., & Shartle, C. L. (1948). Methods for determining patterns of leadership behavior in relation to organization structure and objectives. *Journal of Applied Psychology, 32*(3), 286–291.

Thorndike, E. L. (1920). A constant error in psychological ratings. *Journal of Applied Psychology, 4*(1), 25–29. doi:https://doi.org/10.1037/h0071663

Tichy, N. M., & Bennis, W. G. (2007). *Judgment: How winning leaders make great calls.* Penguin.

Vergauwe, J., Hofmans, J., Wille, B., Decuyper, M., & De Fruyt, F. (2021). Psychopathy and leadership effectiveness: Conceptualizing and testing three models of successful psychopathy. *The Leadership Quarterly*, 1–20.

Weber, M. (1924). Gesammelte Aufsätze zur Soziologie und Sozialpolitik. J.C.B. Mohr (Paul Siebeck).

White, A. E., Kenrick, D. T., & Neuberg, S. L. (2013). Beauty at the ballot box: Disease threats predict preferences for physically attractive leaders. *Psychological Science, 24*(12), 2429–2436.

Yang, J., Benyamin, B., McEvoy, B. P., Gordon, S., Henders, A. K., Nyholt, D. R., Madden, P. A., Heath, A. C., Martin, N.G., Montgomery, G. W., ... & Visscher, P. M. (2010). Common SNPs explain a large proportion of the heritability for human height. *Nature Genetics, 42*(7), 565–569.

Zaccaro, S. J., Gilbert, J. A., Thor, K. K., & Mumford, M. D. (1991). Leadership and social intelligence: Linking social perspectives and behavioral flexibility to leader effectiveness. *The Leadership Quarterly, 2*(4), 317–342.

CHAPTER 5
Relational-Level Characteristics and Influence Processes

CHAPTER OUTCOMES

1. Assess relational-level leadership as part of your current leader identity
2. Appraise situations and choose the appropriate leadership style in Situational Leadership Theory
3. Identify behaviors to build your relational-level leader identity
4. Debate the pros and cons of follower orientations focused on co-production versus passivity

Purpose of This Chapter

In this chapter, we explore theories that focus on the relational-level of identity. For developing leaders, our **relational identity**—how we connect with others and see ourselves interacting with those we lead—becomes especially important for two reasons. First, because leading others is an influence process, leaders *must* form some type of relationship with followers (close, distant, positive, transactional, etc.). Second, how we view ourselves as leaders is heavily influenced by the responses, criticisms, advice, and opinions we receive from those we lead. When exploring levels of identity, the goal is to uncover the root of the behavior and how it is enacted in relation to other people. Theories covered in this section draw upon relationships between leaders and followers that require an interpersonal influence process. While the concepts covered in Chapter 4 focus on the individual- or leader-level, the concepts covered here focus on interactions between leaders and followers, and on how we develop our social identity. These interactions historically focused on how leaders motivate followers (task- or relationship-focused), but they more recently entail several different influence processes including leadership development and succession planning. We explore situational leadership theory, leader-member exchange, and path-goal theory. We discuss how the leader-follower relationship motivates organizational outcomes and performance.

RELATIONAL IDENTITY: How we connect with others and see ourselves interacting with those we lead. (Brewer & Gardner, 1996)

What is the Relational-Level of Identity?

In Chapter 4, you revisited the "I see myself as…" statements regarding the levels of your identity as part of the Twenty Statements Test (Kuhn & McPartland, 1954). In this chapter, we will cover the relational or interpersonal aspects of your leader and organization identity and how different motivation processes arise from those connections. Please refer back to your statements and identify those that are relational in nature, where your interactions are based on actions and reactions that construct the relationship. These behaviors are based in strong relationships such as a leader-follower dyad or a partnership between spouses or parents. They may also arise from a small and cohesive team. These are typified by a reciprocal-role relationship—where one party's actions continue to affect the others until the relationship concludes. Thus, the leader does not "own" the behaviors, and all parties recognize the commingled and reciprocated aspect of the relationship. In these types of relationships, maintaining the interpersonal connection is the foremost motivation (Sluss & Ashforth, 2007). We drive forward based on family obligations and expectations, work hard due to our relationship with our manager, or adapt our leadership styles because of ties to our followers. These attachments make us think beyond our own self and include others in our working self-concept. Many of the theories covered here as relational-level or interpersonal leadership theories focus on interpersonal influence, particularly in regard to motivating performance.

THE OHIO STATE STUDIES: The Ohio State Leadership Studies were conceived as an interdisciplinary research program at the end of World War II, a program that would enable a large-scale attack on an important area (leadership) and would maintain a clear focus and unity of purpose … It was clearly guided and focused on a single objective—to advance knowledge of leadership phenomena. (Schriesheim & Bird, 1979)

Consideration and Initiating Structure— The Ohio State Studies

Early studies conducted by researchers at **The Ohio State University** moved beyond the trait approaches. They focused on two separate dimensions of leader behaviors: consideration and initiating structure.

Consideration focuses on behaviors that build mutual trust, allow for respect, and take into account followers' feelings. **Initiating Structure** behaviors are role-focused and drive goal achievement. The behaviors were often measured using the *Leader Behavior Description Questionnaire* (LBDQ)—the most widely used leadership questionnaire (Rodriguez, 2013). Thousands of participants have completed this survey to determine their proficiency in consideration or initiating structure behaviors. While we will cover these studies in more detail in Chapter 7, we present the measurement scale here.

© Sergey Nivens/Shutterstock.com

Chapter 5: Relational-Level Characteristics and Influence Processes

Activity 1: Complete the LBDQ

The LBDQ provides insight into your preference for both or either task-focused or people-focused behaviors. Recognizing your attitude towards motivating followers will help you incorporate interpersonal influence into your leadership and work styles. Subsequent theories explored how the characteristics of followers create the mutual recognition required for a successful and thriving relationship.

For the following items, please answer on a Likert scale: 0 (Never), 1 (Seldom), 2 (Occasionally), 3 (Often), 4 (Always)

My supervisor…

1. does personal favors for group members.
2. makes attitudes clear to the group
3. does little things to make it pleasant to be a member of the group.
4. tries out new ideas with the group.
5. is easy to understand.
6. rules with an iron hand.
7. finds time to listen to group members.
8. criticizes poor work.
9. speaks in a manner not to be questioned.
10. keeps to themself (R). *
11. looks out for the personal welfare of individual group members.
12. assigns group members to particular tasks.
13. schedules the work to be done.
14. maintains definite standards of performance.
15. refuses to explain actions (R). *
16. acts without consulting the group (R). *
17. backs up the members in their actions.
18. emphasizes the meeting of deadlines
19. treats all group members as equals.
20. encourages the use of uniform procedures.
21. is willing to make changes.
22. makes sure that is part in the organization is understood by all group members.
23. is friendly and approachable.
24. asks that group members follow standard rules and regulations.
25. makes group members feel at ease when talking with them.
26. lets group members know what is expected of them.
27. puts suggestions made by the group into operation.
28. sees to it that group members are working up to capacity.
29. gets group approval on important matters before going ahead.
30. sees to it that the work of group members is coordinated.

SCORING KEY FOR CONSIDERATION (Items 1, 3, 5, 7, 10 (R), 11, 15, 16, 17 (R), 19 (R)). For reverse-coded items, please swap 0 for 4, 1 for 3, 3 for 1, and 4 for 0.

SCORING KEY FOR INITIATING STRUCTURE (Items 2, 4, 6, 8, 9, 12, 13, 14, 18, 20, 22, 24, 25, 28, 30)

> ### Activity 1: Learning Outcomes
> The maximum score for each dimension is 60. Typically, a score of 45 or above on these dimensions indicates these skills are used often. If one dimension is scored high and the other low, your supervisor may have either a tendency to initiate structure or have consideration for people, but not both. If the scores are high on both dimensions, your supervisor may be able to deploy the behaviors as needed for the followers and the context. If the scores are low across the board, then your supervisor may be disengaged or choosing to use a different leadership approach. If this is the case, write down some examples of your supervisor's behaviors and discuss.

Situational Leadership Theory

SITUATIONAL LEADERSHIP THEORY: An optimal style of supervision can be prescribed for given levels of subordinate maturity. (Hersey & Blanchard, 1972; 1982)

Situational Leadership Theory (SLT) proposes that there is an optimal style of supervision that depends on follower maturity (Hersey & Blanchard, 1972; 1982). In a departure from earlier studies and approaches to leadership, this theory centers on the relationship and task-oriented behaviors leaders choose *in response to* follower characteristics like maturity, commitment, and motivation. At its core, this theory exists within the relational-level, as the leadership approach will differ for each unique leader-follower relationship. Thus, the leader seeks the appropriate motivation and supervisory style for each unique follower needed to achieve maximum success. This theory is prescriptive in nature—the leader estimates the followers' abilities and enthusiasm, and then chooses which leadership behaviors to deploy.

As depicted in Figure 1, for followers with low levels of maturity and enthusiasm levels, the leader should **tell** the follower how to complete the tasks, what the goals are, and the roles the follower must play. It is task-forward. For those who are willing to perform the work, but don't know how, the leader should **sell**

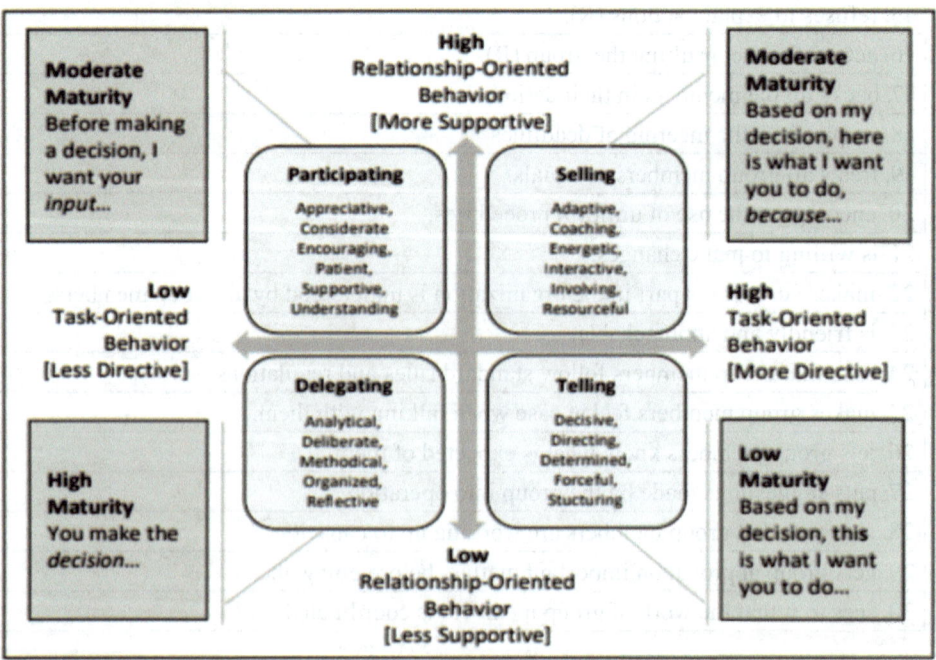

Figure 1: The Situational Leadership Model

Source: (Arora & Baronikian, 2013).

the follower. The leader must support the existing enthusiasm while simultaneously guiding the follower through the work to increase their abilities. In this role, the leader is there both to guide followers through the assigned tasks and to create a positive relationship to ensure the follower does not become discouraged. For followers who have the abilities but may be unenthusiastic about the work, the leader should seek opportunities for the follower to **participate**. Participation can increase one's feelings of responsibility and increase their intrinsic motivation to complete the assigned work. Finally, for followers of the highest levels of maturity—the types capable and willing to complete the work—the leader should **delegate** tasks and seek to empower the followers.

SLT gives the leader clear directions regarding effective leader behaviors based on different situations. However, there are some challenges in using this theory. Although it has been adopted across many corporate training programs (Blanchard, Zigarmi, & Nelson, 1993), the impacts from a research standpoint have not always been easy to quantify. The outcomes are unclear for a few different reasons. First, it is difficult to quantify follower maturity and commitment, particularly across different types of positions. Second, published empirical studies show that the frequency of matching between leader style, follower commitment, and follower readiness or follower maturity is low. And finally, the questionnaire used in the research has been criticized (Fernandez & Vecchio, 1997). To get a sense of the tool used in this training, you can take your own self-assessment of your situational leadership acumen.

Activity 2: Situational Leadership Activity

Step 1: Please read the following scenarios and choose the answer that makes the most sense given your approach to leadership, the abilities of the followers, and the task requirements.

Situation	Do you:
1. You normally have a collegial relationship with your team. Recently, your low-key approach and interest in their lives is being disregarded, and you notice issues with their performance.	A. Turn your focus towards processes and policies? B. Remind the team you are available for all questions, but limit your daily conversation? C. Sit down with each team member to enact goal-setting activities? D. Make an effort to keep your distance?
2. Your team's performance is improving due to your focus on task assignments, expectations, and individual responsibilities.	A. Make sure you interact with each team member in a welcoming and warm way, while also reminding team members of the performance standards? B. Avoid changing your current behaviors? C. Emphasize the group's inclusiveness and each member's importance? D. Focus on the deliverables and work product?
3. Your team has a problem for which they cannot find a solution. Typically, you allow them to address their own challenges without intervention. So far, they have been effective and relate well with one another.	A. Intervene and work directly with the team to generate solutions together? B. Allow them to address the challenge on their own? C. Jump in immediately to fix the problem? D. Give the team the resources they need to in their problem-solving approaches and give them support as they meet the challenge?

4.	You want to create some healthy disruption in your team, although they have a consistent track record of accomplishing their tasks. They do understand change may be necessary.	A. Encourage team interaction while disrupting typical processes, but limit your directive behaviors? B. Tell the team what the changes are and carefully inspect their adoption of the new procedures? C. Empower the team to redesign their procedures? D. Allow the team to make recommendations, but in the end, decide on the new procedures?
5.	Your team's effectiveness is decreasing over time. It seems like the team members are unconcerned with deadlines and task completion. When this happened before, you refocused on task requirements and role definition. You are constantly reminding them about deadlines to finalize deliverables.	A. Allow the group to figure things out on their own? B. Allow the team to make recommendations, but in the end, decide on the new procedures? C. Continue to refocus on task requirements and role definition? D. Encourage team interactions regarding roles and responsibilities while limiting your directive behaviors?
6.	You are new to a very high functioning team. The former team leader was very autocratic and micro-managed the team. You want to maintain the current performance but be less directive and you want to create interpersonal relationships with the team members.	A. Focus your behaviors on highlighting how well the team is performing? B. Focus on deadlines and deliverables? C. Allow the team to run independently? D. Encourage team participation in problem-solving, but ensure the deliverables are completed on time?
7.	Your team may need a new design. Individual team members have submitted ideas to you. They have been performing at a high level and are quite adaptable.	A. Reveal the new design and ensure they adopt it correctly? B. Encourage team participation in the design change, and allow the team to implement the new approaches? C. Adapt to team member's ideas, but ensure the implementation is working as you intended? D. Encourage team interactions regarding roles and responsibilities while limiting your directive behaviors?
8.	Your team is doing great. Everyone gets along and performance is high. You feel a little disconnected and indecisive about your role.	A. Allow the team to keep working as it is without getting involved? B. Address your indecisiveness with the group and make any requested changes? C. Create new goals and tasks and then oversee their adoption closely? D. Solicit goal-setting ideas in a laid-back manner?
9.	You take a leadership position in a team that is behind on adopting new procedures. Many of the team members are absent from team meetings. Those that do show up are more interested in socializing than working. You believe they have the ability to do their work effectively, but their motivation to work is low.	A. Leave it up to the team to figure it out? B. Solicit ideas from the team and ensure they meet their responsibilities? C. Focus on deadlines and deliverables with close supervision? D. Solicit goal-setting ideas in a laid-back manner?
10.	Your team has been effective at meeting challenges in the past, but currently is not adapting to their new task requirements. One integral team member recently moved to a new position and left the team.	A. Solicit ideas from the team to address and issue but leave it up to them to adapt? B. Focus on deadlines and deliverables with close supervision? C. Leave them alone? D. Solicit ideas from the team, but also ensure they meet their responsibilities?

Chapter 5: Relational-Level Characteristics and Influence Processes

11. You just got promoted! The previous team leader was very involved at both a personal and professional level with the team. The team works well together, and their performance is quite effective.	A. Direct the group and ensure their tasks and responsibilities are clearly defined? B. Use participative leadership while problem-solving and highlight the team's excellent performance? C. Review past performance and explore new procedures for approaching the work? D. Leave them alone?
12. You have noticed some interpersonal conflict between team members, but the team is still on track for completing its long-term objectives. In the past, the team has been very effective and worked well together. Each team member has the knowledge, skills, and abilities to complete their roles effectively.	A. Come up with a solution and change the team processes? B. Leave it to the group to address the conflict? C. Intervene and address the conflict and refocus on team processes? D. Give the team the resources they need to participate in problem-solving approaches and give them support as they meet the challenge?

Step 2: Review your answers to see if there is a theme to your answers in relation to the situational leadership model. Are most of your answers telling, selling, participating, or delegating? Does your approach change based on the experience level of the team? Is it more task or relationship-oriented?

Step 3: Work with your classmates to identity areas where you disagree on the "correct" approach. Discuss the reasons why one classmate may choose one approach compared to another.

Source: Gretchen Vogelgesang Lester and Paul Lester

Activity 2: Learning Outcomes

This activity gives you the opportunity to review different types of scenarios you may encounter as a leader. While you may tend to use task or relationship behaviors (or a combination of the two) based upon your temperament and current skill set, you may find your followers require a different approach in some circumstances. An effective leader will adapt their behaviors to meet their followers and support their needs towards continuous improvement.

Once you have completed the activity, discuss your answers with a classmate. Where did you take a similar approach? When did your approaches differ? In a corporate training scenario, you would work with a coach to standardize the responses for your unique workforce.

Perhaps the best takeaway from this theory is the focus on followers and awareness of their needs for motivation and direction. Another important consideration from this theory is the idea that job level may be a better category to focus on versus follower maturity or readiness—some jobs require more *telling* due to their entry-level nature, while others may allow for more *delegating* due to their professional nature. As a leader, adopting the mindset that each follower needs a unique approach to their skill development and tapping into the appropriate motivational style is a great benefit. Leaders who view followers through a Theory Y lens (as discussed in Chapter 2) believe in the abilities of their followers and should seek to develop those abilities to fulfill their potential.

Path-Goal Theory

Path-Goal Theory factors followers' motivations into the behaviors a leader will exhibit. Like situational leadership theory, path-goal centers on the relationship between leaders and followers. House defined the theory as follows: "The

PATH-GOAL THEORY: The motivational function of the leader consists of increasing personal payoffs to subordinates for work-goal attainment and making the path to these payoffs easier to travel by clarifying it, reducing roadblocks and pitfalls, and increasing the opportunities for personal satisfaction en route. (House, 1971, p. 324)

motivational function of the leader consists of increasing personal payoffs to subordinates for work-goal attainment and making the path to these payoffs easier to travel by clarifying it, reducing roadblocks and pitfalls, and increasing the opportunities for personal satisfaction en route." (House, 1971, p. 324). Thus, followers' expectations regarding the ability to perform duties in the pursuit of a specific work goal (along with the potential rewards for their actions) create a strong motivation to perform. The leader sets the rewards for goal attainment and provides support for the follower in the pursuit of the goal (House, 1971). Leaders offer behaviors that create structure for followers and clarify role ambiguity. In return, they should see increased follower performance and satisfaction. Much like a mountain guide setting out a course for mountain climbers, the leader can create the most optimal path for the follower, set intermediate goals, and seek to reduce potential challenges—providing conditions to successfully complete the goals.

A key tenet of the path-goal theory is the understanding that the amount of clarification needed by followers regarding tasks and directions will impact the relationship between initiating structure-type tasks and follower satisfaction. So, followers who need more direction and structure will welcome those behaviors and be more satisfied. Meanwhile, those who prefer to be empowered to choose their own approach to their work will be less satisfied if the leader attempts to provide structure.

Now, let's expand on the framework outlined in the Ohio State studies (initiating structure and consideration). There are four categories of leader behaviors that can be deployed as part of path-goal theory:

Table 1: Path-Goal Theory Behaviors

Directive path-goal clarifying behavior: • Explain job duties • Schedule and coordinate work • Clarify polices, rules, procedures	**Participative behavior:** • Encourage followers to influence decision-making • Consult with followers • Take opinions and suggestions into account when making decisions
Supportive behavior: • Satisfy follower needs and preferences • Display concern for welfare • Create friendly and supportive work environment	**Achievement-oriented behavior:** • Encourage performance excellence • Set challenging goals • Seek improvement • Show confidence in followers' abilities

Source: Gretchen V. Lester, adapted from House, 1996

Activity 3: Path-Goal Reflection

Think about a particular goal you had that required the assistance of a leader, mentor, coach, or relative.

- What was your starting point? What was the end goal?
- Break up the goal into smaller targets and barriers you encountered along the way.
- Describe the behaviors the other person enacted to help or encourage your progress.
- If you can, sort the behaviors into one of the categories in Table 1.

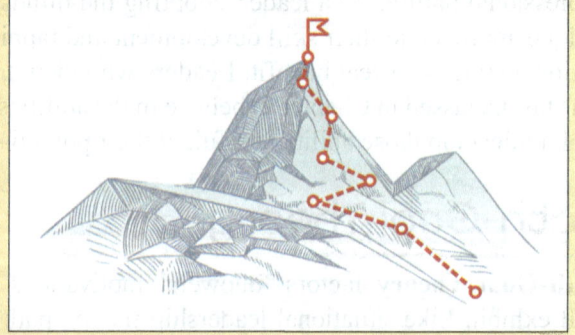

© Net Vector/Shutterstock.com

Activity 3: Learning Outcomes

After reflecting upon a time you worked interactively with a leader to achieve a goal, you may realize how important a partner is in your pursuit of success. If you can enlist others' help in your current goals, you may find it helpful to create interim steps, seek out support when needed, and recognize the types of behaviors that are most beneficial to you as you embark on new goals.

Initial path-goal theory and subsequent research findings show evidence that leaders who reduce barriers for followers who are striving toward goal attainment generate higher levels of satisfaction. However, a major limitation of path-goal theory is the continued use of the initiating structure/consideration lens and the suggestion that leader behavior can be reduced to a short list of acceptable actions. In Activity 3, you may have come up with leader-enacted behaviors that did not fit into any of the categories presented in Table 1. Perhaps some of the behaviors fit neatly into one category, while others could map onto more than one dimension. Therefore, a more practical way to think about the theory is two-fold. First, focus on clarifying the job tasks, the process of goal attainment, and ensuring the rewards systems are attractive to the followers. And second, motivate strong performance through the process of personal accomplishment and by removing potential barriers to goal attainment.

Vertical Dyad-Linkage

Continuing with the idea that there are unique leader-follower relationships, a theory that began as "**vertical dyad-Linkage**" (VDL) evolved into the "leader-member exchange" (LMX) theory. Vertical dyad-linkage—theorized by Dansereau and colleagues (1975)—described the differences between leader-follower relationships. In this approach, a set of followers or subordinates is not described as a collective group all exhibiting the same level of maturity (or with the same needs requiring direction as in situational leadership theory), but rather as a group of unique individuals, each requiring and exhibiting a different relationship with the leader. As workforces continue to diversify, approaching followers as a uniform group no longer makes practical sense.

Vertical Dyad-Linkage:
A theory that explores the individual dyadic relationships formed between leaders and their subordinates or followers. (Dansereau, Graen, & Haga, 1975)

Now, let's take a moment. Think about a few of the relationships you have had with a group leader. Were the relationships between the leader and your fellow group members all the same? Did the leader activate the same leadership behaviors with you as they did with the other members? Most likely not. As you grew your abilities, engaged in different settings, and interacted with peers, teammates, or community members, your interactions with your leader(s) were likely quite different. The research provides evidence that leaders and followers *together* create these unique dyadic relationships (Dansereau, Graen, & Haga, 1975). The images in Figure 2a and 2b illustrate the difference between the two approaches. In Figure 2a, the leader communicates to all followers at once and in the same manner. In Figure 2b, representing vertical dyad-linkage, the leader and follower co-communicate in varying styles.

Figure 2a: Average Leadership Style

Figure 2b: Vertical Dyad-Linkage

Leader-Member Exchange

LEADER-MEMBER EXCHANGE (LMX): The general phenomenon of how leaders' and followers' exchanges serve to clarify followers' roles within their organizations. (Gottfredson et al., 2020)

Viewing the leadership relationship as a dyadic exchange moves beyond a leader imposing behaviors via an employment contract. Instead, it emphasizes an interpersonal influence process where each party adapts their behaviors to positively influence the working relationship (Dansereau et al., 1975). The initial exploration of **leader-member exchanges** found that they could be categorized into in-groups and out-groups, and that as the relationship between the leader-follower in-group dyads matured, the members received more attention and support from the leaders. On the other hand, the out-groups experienced more job issues, turnover, and negative attitudes towards their work.

As the research continued to focus on these in-groups and out-groups, the quality of the dyadic exchanges between leaders and followers arose as the main driver of the outcomes. Thus, researchers began to theorize and test these leader-member exchanges (LMX). These dyadic interactions contributed to mature or high-quality relationships, and organizations saw positive outcomes such as mutual trust, fondness, devotion, and esteem between members (Cogliser, Schriesheim, Scandura, & Gardner, 2009). These attractive outcomes impacted the leader, the follower, work groups, and the organization.

More recent work has focused on the "leadership making" aspect of the LMX theory (Graen & Uhl-Bien, 1995). The central question of "How can leaders help co-create high quality relationships?" is nested in interpersonal influence. If the out-groups see negative outcomes, leaders should absolutely seek to minimize outgroups and find ways to create high-quality relationships with all followers. Communication between members is extremely important, making up "social transactions" that serve as the basis for the relationship as it matures towards partnerships.

© mills21/Shutterstock.com

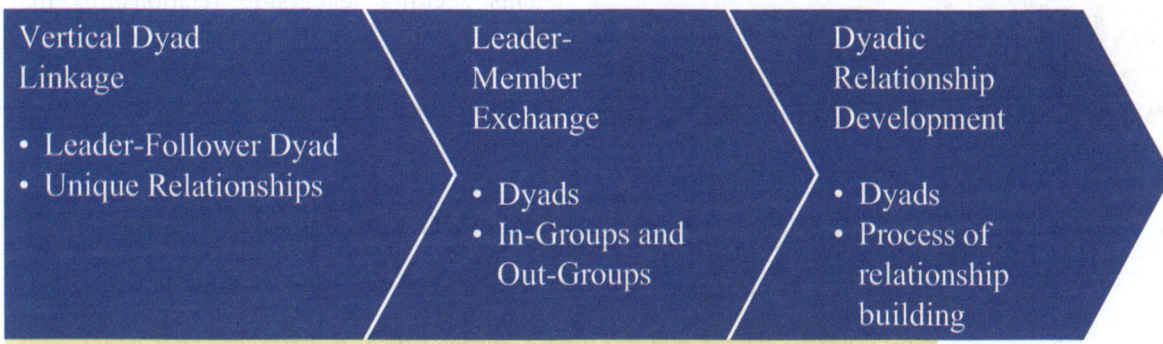

Figure 3: The Development from VDL to LMX to Leadership-Making

Source: Gretchen Vogelgesang Lester and Paul Lester

While these theories focus on the relationship between leaders and followers and seek to explore the dyad as the unit of observation, a recent stream of research has focused on follower needs and expectations and how they influence the relationship.

Followership Theories

For much of the history of leadership and organizational behavior, the follower or subordinate was a secondary referent. Although situational leadership theory, path-goal, and LMX include follower attributes as an important component of the dyad, the impetus for many of these theories still focused on the leader's actions.

Chapter 5: Relational-Level Characteristics and Influence Processes

FOLLOWERSHIP: A role played by individuals occupying a formal or informal position or rank (e.g., a subordinate in a hierarchical "manager—subordinate" relationship; a follower in a "leader—follower" relationship); a relational interaction through which leadership is co-created in combined acts of leading and following. (DeRue & Ashford, 2010; Fairhurst & Uhl-Bien, 2012; Shamir, 2012)

Followership theories take the opposite perspective and focus on the actions followers can take to create the leadership relationship. A leader without followers is not truly a leader.

Followership is defined as "a role played by individuals occupying a formal or informal position or rank (e.g., a subordinate in a hierarchical 'manager-subordinate' relationship; a follower in a 'leader-follower' relationship)", or "as a relational interaction through which leadership is co-created in combined acts of leading and following" (DeRue & Ashford, 2010; Fairhurst & Uhl-Bien, 2012; Shamir, 2012; Uhl-Bien et al., 2014). As the leadership *process* is one co-constructed by actors interacting towards the pursuit of an outcome, it is important to examine that process from multiple perspectives. The role of the actor in the follower position is to allow for interpersonal influence—in essence, to commit to working with the leader (Uhl-Bien et al., 2014). The follower identity can be constructed in a similar way to the leader identity. We could use the drawing activity in Chapter 2, but change the referent—drawing an effective follower. Such an illustration may be a representation of our "Implicit Follower Theory." One's working self-concept can also include "follower" as a role within a group. In all of these approaches, followers are active agents seeking leadership relationships that coalesce with their needs, knowledge, skills, and abilities. Please take the following questionnaire for insight into your own views on followership.

© Pictrider/Shutterstock.com

Activity 4: Complete the Followership Questionnaire

Followership Role Orientation Scale

The questions below will assess your beliefs about followers' roles in relation to leaders in an organizational setting. When we say "follower," we are referring to an employee who is working with leaders to achieve desired outcomes. In answering the following questions, please think generally about followers and their interactions with leaders or "higher-ups" in organizations. Please indicate the extent to which you agree with the following statements.

1	2	3	4	5	6
Strongly Disagree	Disagree	Somewhat Disagree	Somewhat Agree	Agree	Strongly Agree

1. Followers should be on the lookout for suggestions they can offer to superiors. _____
2. Followers should proactively identify problems that could affect the organization. _____
3. As part of their role, followers must be willing to challenge superiors' assumptions. _____
4. Followers should be proactive in thinking about things that could go wrong. _____
5. Followers should communicate their opinions, even when they know leaders may disagree. _____

Chapter 5: Relational-Level Characteristics and Influence Processes

6. At the end of the day, followers cannot be held accountable for the performance of a unit. _____
7. Being a follower means you don't have to think about changing the way work gets done. _____
8. Followers do not have to take on much responsibility for thinking about how things get done. _____
9. Because one is a follower, s/he does not have to worry about being involved in decision making. _____

Activity 4: Learning Outcomes

Please use the scoring instructions provided to determine your views on followers as co-producers or passive members of a leadership dyad. Insight into this tendency increases the visibility of the follower role and may change how you view others as you seek to co-construct a leadership-followership relationship with others.

Scoring:
- Items 1-5 = co-production orientation. Add your sum out of 30 possible points. Higher scores indicate stronger beliefs on this dimension.
- Items 6-9 = passive orientation, Add your sum out of 24 possible points. Higher scores indicate stronger beliefs on this dimension.

Citation:

Melissa K Carsten, Mary Uhl-Bien, Lei Huang, *Leadership*, vol. 14, issue 6, pp. 731-756, copyright © 2017 by SAGE Publications. Reprinted by Permission of SAGE Publications.

Followership should be a position that individuals claim in a relationship. Followership is not a default state—there are specific behaviors one must enact to be a follower. While Kelley (1992) proposed five followership styles ranging from passive to active and dependent to independent, followers in a functioning leadership relationship should ideally be active, contributing members.

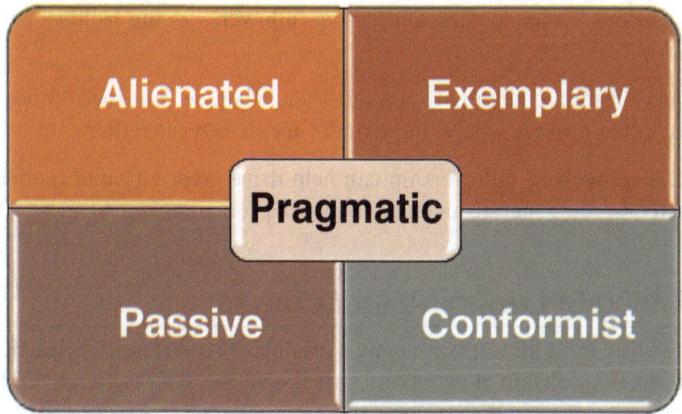

Source: Gretchen Vogelgesang Lester and Paul Lester

Alienated followers are often cynical and have distrust for the organization. They have the ability to perform, but may choose not to because of their skepticism. They are independent yet passive. **Passive followers** look to others for guidance. They are dependent upon their leaders for constant direction. **Conformist followers** are dependent upon the rule structure of the organization. They will take action on the orders given from their leaders. **Exemplary followers** are independent and active. They are willing to question their orders, innovate new approaches to work, and motivate stronger performance by working well with others. Finally, **pragmatic followers** draw from each of the other four styles, depending upon the situational constraints. (Bjustad, Thach, Thompson, & Morris, 2006; Kelley, 1992). Individuals may have a dominant followership style, but can certainly adapt to different leaders, contexts, and organizations.

Organizations should recognize the importance of engaged, active followers. Healthy organizations value the follower role and create trusting followership relationships; one longitudinal research study highlights the positive shareholder return of 108% over three years when trust was high between leaders and followers (Froggatt, 2001). Strong organizations understand the relational influence process co-created by leaders and followers and foster those relationships to achieve performance beyond expectations.

Activity 5: Tango: The Dance of the Leader and the Follower

Consider two people dancing. The "follower" does not just get dragged around the dance floor by the leader–each takes an active role to ensure the dance goes smoothly.

Please view the video at https://www.youtube.com/watch?v=Cswrnc1dggg. There is a short introductory sequence with two dancers, Sharna and Isaac, performing the tango.

As noted in the brief introduction, there is first a short clip illustrating graceful followership. The video then highlights a number of different follower types:

- Weak, passive followership: Sharna does nothing and Isaac forces the movement. The heaviness Isaac notes transcends dance; when a leader has to force a follower to engage, the process can be sluggish and unfulfilling.
- Self-serving followership; a show-off: Sharna creates her own moves without input from her leader. The uselessness Isaac notes applies in many situations; when a leader does not have the opportunity to co-create with the follower, the leader disengages.
- Actively resisting followership: Sharna pushes Isaac into changing the course of the dance and throws him off-balance. This pushiness can cause a leader to seek alternative followers, as the rigidity becomes too combative for a working relationship.
- Stable followership: Here, Sharna is a resource helping to support Isaac when he is unsure of the next steps. This type of followership is a co-created process where the partners are stronger together.

In conclusion, Sharna notes that stable, involved followership can help drive creativity and innovation. The leader and follower complement each other to generate an engaging work product.

Activity 5: Learning Outcomes

This video activity illustrates how leaders and followers co-create a product. The different styles clearly show the impact the follower can have on the relationship, a viewpoint that is often underrepresented in leadership and organizational behavior research.

In Review

This chapter describes relational-level theories, interpersonal processes where individuals interact with others to generate our social identity. As we note, relational-level behaviors are grounded in strong relationships with others.

Thus, relational-level identities are motivated by concern for the interests of others. Part of your leader identity includes your enacted behaviors and the reactions to those behaviors by others. The activities and self-report assessments in this chapter are provided to help you increase your self-awareness of your preferences regarding others. For example, the LBDQ will highlight whether your concern and care for others will be more or less salient than the attention and motivation to complete tasks. Likewise, the followership survey will highlight your ease with taking on a follower role in certain interactions. The more you can understand your preferences as they exist and what they may become, the more you will learn how you relate to others interpersonally. Understanding how you make and foster attachments with others will help you choose the appropriate leadership behaviors in your continued interactions.

The LBDQ activity highlights your preference for initiating structure or consideration behaviors. This may be important as you consider the types of careers and positions you will eventually hold. The items will also allow you to see alternative approaches to managing and leading others. Your preferences for task or relational behaviors can have an impact in organizations, so you must be sure to use explore the situational and personal needs of followers in conjunction with the personal ease or inclinations towards these behaviors.

We also should recognize the impact of the situation. Situational Leadership Theory focuses on assessing the maturity and commitment of followers before recommending leadership behaviors. A leader can choose to tell, sell, participate, or delegate to inspire the followers' performance. Activity 2 is designed to walk you through the decision-making process where you respond to a specific scenario. When comparing to classmates, you may find divergent opinions as to the correct response. You may also find some reactions are widely shared across your classmates. While this theory is prescriptive in nature and recommends specific leadership behaviors in response to the follower conditions, the research findings have been mixed. These varied findings may be due to the complexity of defining follower maturity and commitment in relation to specific situations.

The next section details the path-goal theory, which delves into how leaders can motivate followers towards specific achievements. The leader's role in these interactions is to help define the follower's goals and to eliminate potential barriers towards goal attainment. The leader may enact directive, participative, supportive, or achievement-oriented behaviors, depending on the needs of the follower. Activity 3 asks for you to reflect upon a time when you worked towards a goal interactively with a leader. Understanding the role that others can play in the goal-setting process will allow you to request such support in future goal-related activities. Working in conjunction with another person to clarify the tasks necessary and the rewards available for goal-attainment while anticipating and avoiding potential barriers will help increase your chances of success.

The vertical dyad-linkage (VDL) and leader-member exchange (LMX) theories describe the unique individual relationships leaders create together with their followers. These theories both emphasize the interpersonal influence process occurring within the dyads which lead to positive working relationships. LMX research expanded to describe the in-groups and out-groups that naturally formed due to these relationships and the positive (attention and support for the in-groups) and negative outcomes (turnover and negative attitudes for the out-groups) that resulted from them. Later research addressed the negative impacts of out-group membership and provided more prescriptive actions for leaders and followers to take to develop strong and beneficial relationships.

The final concept in this chapter addresses the follower roles in these interpersonal relationships. Followership is an act of co-construction, where the follower acts with agency to seek out and shape the leadership process. Activity 4 presents the followership role orientation scale and will make you aware of your tendency to view followers as co-producers or passive members. It can also generate reflection on leader-follower relationships that have been either successful or unsuccessful. The final video activity uses the Tango as a metaphor for leader-follower co-production.

The next chapter explores your collective-level identity and how you work in teams. Learning about your social identity will provide insight into leading teams, working together to generate positive team outcomes, and how to use certain leader behaviors to motivate others towards action.

Learning Objectives

Assess relational-level leadership as part of your current leader identity

The relational-level of identity is based on interpersonal relationships. You can review your "I see myself as…" statements for examples of these interactions. Throughout the chapter, the self-assessments highlight your preferences for initiating structure versus consideration, how you can motivate others towards specific goals, and your views on the follower role. As your leadership skills mature, you will notice yourself exhibiting more interpersonal influence as compared to actions grounded in self-interest.

Appraise situations and choose the appropriate leadership style in Situational Leadership Theory

Figure 1 presents the Situational Leadership Theory model. The leader must first determine if the level of follower maturity and commitment, and then enact the behaviors that are more or less supportive. Activity 2 allows you to choose a leader behavior based on a scenario; comparing those results with others will make you aware of your preference for delegating, participating, selling, or telling actions and how responsive you are to the followers' needs.

Identify behaviors to build your relational-level leader identity

Situational Leadership Theory (SLT), Path-Goal Theory, Leader-Member Exchange, and your approaches to followership all include behaviors that strengthen a relational-level identity. With SLT, behaviors that allow followers to participate (considering others' ideas, encouraging participation, etc.) or those that are intended to motivate followers (coaching behaviors and offering resources) help strengthen and support the relationship. Path-goal theory focuses on removing barriers and helping followers articulate clear but challenging goals. LMX builds high quality relationships, and a followership orientation focused on co-production and cooperation all serve to enhance your abilities to maintain strong interpersonal relationships.

Debate the pros and cons of follower orientations focused on co-production versus passivity

The history of leadership research is focused on the leader enacting behaviors towards passive followers. The thinking was that a good leader can motivate strong performance from any follower. Recent research suggests that followers who are active partners in the leadership process are exemplary followers who act independently to innovate new approaches to their work. Overall, the benefits of treating followers as co-producers are greater than forcing followers to conform or act only on the leader's direction.

Key Terms

Relational Identity (Pg. 81)

The Ohio State Studies (Pg. 82)

Situational Leadership Theory (Pg. 84)

Path-Goal Theory (Pg. 87)

vertical dyad-Linkage (Pg.89)

Leader-Member Exchange (Pg. 90)

Followership (Pg. 92)

Critical Thinking Questions

1. In your own words, describe the attribution processes. Give an example of a time you have used the self-serving bias or fundamental attribution error.
2. As a manager, how can you help your employees discover their implicit leadership theories? How can you compare prototypes within your organization?
3. Why do you think individuals romanticize leadership? Why is this important to recognize? Can leaders use romance of leadership in a positive manner?
4. What are the potential outcomes of self-fulfilling prophecies for organizations? As a manager, why should you be concerned about the positive or negative outcomes associated with these processes?

Conclusion

In this chapter, we covered leadership and motivation theories that arise due to a reciprocal-role relationship. These theories employ relational-level interpersonal skills. The first studies that explored this approach were collectively named "The Ohio State Studies". They defined leadership behaviors along two dimensions: initiating structure and consideration. Some critiques of these theories pointed out the situational influences that could require different enacted behaviors, which was encompassed by situational leadership theory. We also covered path-goal leadership, leader-member exchange, and followership theories.

References

Bjugstad, K., Thach, E. C., Thompson, K. J., & Morris, A. (2006). A fresh look at followership: A model for matching followership and leadership styles. *Journal of Behavioral and Applied Management, 7*(3), 304–319.

Blanchard, K. H., Zigarmi, D., & Nelson, R. B. (1993). Situational Leadership® after 25 years: a retrospective. *Journal of Leadership Studies*, *1*(1), 21–36.

Cogliser, C. C., Schriesheim, C. A., Scandura, T. A., & Gardner, W. L. (2009). Balance in leader and follower perceptions of leader—member exchange: relationships with performance and work attitudes. *The Leadership Quarterly*, *20*(3), 452–465.

Dansereau Jr, F., Graen, G., & Haga, W. J. (1975). A vertical dyad linkage approach to leadership within formal organizations: a longitudinal investigation of the role making process. *Organizational Behavior and Human Performance*, *13*(1), 46–78.

DeRue, D. S., & Ashford, S. J. (2010). Who will lead and who will follow? A social process of leadership identity construction in organizations. *Academy of Management Review*, *35*(4), 627–647.

Fairhurst, G. T., & Uhl-Bien, M. (2012). Organizational discourse analysis (ODA): examining leadership as a relational process. *The Leadership Quarterly*, *23*(6), 1043–1062.

Fernandez, C. F., & Vecchio, R. P. (1997). Situational leadership theory revisited: a test of an across-jobs perspective. *The Leadership Quarterly*, *8*(1), 67–84.

Froggatt, C.C. (2001). *Work Naked*. San Francisco: Jossey-Bass Publishers.

Gottfredson, R. K., Wright, S. L., & Heaphy, E. D. (2020). A critique of the Leader-Member Exchange construct: Back to square one. *The Leadership Quarterly, 31*(6), 101385.

Graen, G. B., & Uhl-Bien, M. (1995). Relationship-based approach to leadership: development of leader-member exchange (LMX) theory of leadership over 25 years: applying a multi-level multi-domain perspective. *The Leadership Quarterly*, *6*(2), 219–247.

Hersey, P., & Blanchard, K. H. (1972). The management of change: I. Change and the use of power. *Training & Development Journal*, *26*(1), 6–10.

Hersey, P., & Blanchard, K. H. (1982). Leadership style: attitudes and behaviors. *Training & Development Journal, 36*(5), 50–52.

House, R. J. (1971). A path goal theory of leader effectiveness. *Administrative Science Quarterly*, 321–339.

Kelley R. (1992). *The Power of Followership*. New York: Doubleday

Kuhn, M. H., & McPartland, T. S. (1954). Twenty Statements Test. *American Sociological Review*.

Shamir, B. (2012). Leadership in context and context in leadership studies. *The Oxford Handbook of Leadership*.

Sluss, D. M., & Ashforth, B. E. (2007). Relational identity and identification: defining ourselves through work relationships. *Academy of Management Review*, *32*(1), 9–32.

Uhl-Bien, M., Riggio, R. E., Lowe, K. B., & Carsten, M. K. (2014). Followership theory: A review and research agenda. *The Leadership Quarterly*, *25*(1), 83–104.

CHAPTER 6
Collective-Level Leadership and Teams

CHAPTER OUTCOMES

1. Summarize collective identity
2. Explain social identity theory
3. Construct a team mental model
4. Explore charismatic leadership as a social phenomenon
5. Evaluate servant leadership

Purpose of This Chapter

Leader identities shift based on social settings. This chapter focuses on the collective-level or settings where identity is derived from group membership (Epitropaki et al., 2017). This *level* draws on social categorization and achieving collective goals, *not* on motivating others towards individual goals (as covered in Chapter 5). In our daily lives, individuals become members of collectives like work teams, organizations, fandoms, etc. Rather than use traits or interpersonal influence to enact leadership behaviors, leaders of collectives will adopt the group prototype and motivate performance by comparing to/competing with other groups. Leadership behaviors that focus on visioning and group goals activate the collective-level, which enhances social identification and membership as part of the team. Research in this area explores the different impacts of relational and collective outcomes, providing evidence that leaders who focus on the team as a whole can increase collective efficacy, identification with the group, and group performance (Kark et al., 2003). Theories covered in this chapter explain how we generate social identities, how we work together in teams, and how charisma and servant leadership can motivate group performance. We discuss how the social identity galvanizes individual members to act in a collective approach.

What Is Collective-Level Identity?

A collective identity comes from one's thinking of oneself as a member of a group. When people come together to identify as group members instead of simply individuals, they are more likely to perform work that benefits the collective as a whole, driving up performance and morale (Reicher et al., 2005). These collectives can include businesses or companies where we have jobs, volunteer organizations, sports clubs, or religious groups. Leaders develop a **collective identity** (how we see ourselves leading within an organization and taking on qualities valued by that organization) over time as they align their current and future selves and associated goals with those of the organization. In developmental terms, leaders with a strong collective identity expend more effort working towards leading in ways that are acceptable and to the benefit of the organization. This is not to suggest that individual- and relational-level identities no longer matter, just that those two identities may take a back seat to the primacy of the leader's collective identity. For example, research shows that in times of great crisis, leaders with significant charisma can shift followers' identities to focus on the needs of the collective—this is especially common within the military during wartime (Burns, 2012). This phenomenon is also common in some religions, where members often pause their education or leave their jobs to contribute to the collective by performing lengthy mission trips to foreign countries.

When an individual feels they are a member of a group, they are likely to be motivated to assist other group members (Brewer & Gardner, 1996). Sometimes, identities at either the individual, relational, or collective levels can be active concurrently. To illustrate, please refer to the "I see myself as..." statements you completed in Chapter 1. Review your listed identities and denote the level each is at with an (I), an (R), or a (C). Perhaps you have a few identities that are at multiple levels, such as membership in a student-run organization. Many students may initially join the group to further their self-interest because they want to gain individual accolades or add a line on their resume or job-search profile (I), but then take on training roles to help initiate new members (R) and eventually become an alumni member concerned with the continued success of the organization (C). Other students may join the group because they feel strongly about creating camaraderie with others who share similar lived experiences (R) or because they wish to give back to the larger institution by creating programs geared towards success (C). Either way, membership in the collective is what will allow the organization to flourish after they graduate. The collective identity is what carries an organization or group forward—even as participating individuals may change. Strong collective identities can result in enhanced skills dealing with stress and commitment to the organization (Ashforth & Mael, 1989; Haslam & Reicher, 2006). Please complete Activity 1 to measure the extent to which you have a collective identity.

A further example of collective identity is the fandom surrounding sports teams. You might see fans spend their time rooting for the team, going to team games, buying and wearing team merchandise, organizing watch parties for games, and taking action to promote the team. This team support can lead to new relationships that arise because individuals share common fandom with one another. One's role in fandom can also offer leadership development opportunities

---

COLLECTIVE IDENTITY:
How we see ourselves leading within an organization and taking on qualities valued by that organization. (Brewer & Gardner, 1996)

Activity 1: Collective Identity Inventory

Step 1: In this activity, complete the following items on a scale of 1 (not at all true) to 7 (totally true) to get a sense of the strength of your collective identity.

Collective Identity
1. The groups I belong to are an important reflection of who I am.
2. When I am in a group, it often feels to me like that group is an important part of who I am.
3. I usually feel a strong sense of pride when a group I belong to has an important accomplishment.
4. I think one of the most important parts of who I am can be captured by looking at the groups I belong to and understanding who they are.
5. When I think of myself, I often think of groups I belong to as well.
6. In general, the groups I belong to are an important part of my self-image.
7. Overall, the groups I belong to are unimportant to my sense of what kind of person I am. (reverse scored)
8. If a person insults a group I belong to, I feel personally insulted myself.
9. My sense of pride comes from knowing I belong to groups.
10. When I join a group, I usually develop a strong sense of identification with that group.

Step 2: Calculate your score by adding the items together. Scores will range from 10-70. A score above 50 indicates a stronger collective identity, while scores lower than 30 indicate a weaker collective identity.

Adapted from: Gabriel, S., & Gardner, W. L. (1999).

Activity 1: Learning Outcomes

Those with stronger collective identities will consistently seek out groups to join; those with lower scores may have a stronger desire to individuate themselves from others. Those with strong social needs are motivated to create connections with like others and derive utility from the group's purpose and meaning. While there is no optimal score for collective identity, it is important to be aware of the extremes—too little collective identity may lead you to miss out on opportunities for support and friendship; too much collective identity may lead you to put your group's needs above your own to your personal detriment.

like managing a fantasy league or planning local events. Membership in a fandom collective can also create dislike for fans of other teams based on nothing more than the team individuals adopt. Collective identities can offer positive interactions, opportunities for leadership emergence, and relationship-building. But they can also create negative effects for out-groups. Before we discuss how leaders can harness the energy of these collectives to motivate performance and productivity, we will cover social identity theory, which describes why humans are drawn to membership in groups.

© Jacob Lund/Shutterstock.com

Social Identity Theory

SOCIAL IDENTITY THEORY:
A person's sense of who they are based upon group memberships. (Tajfel, 1979)

In the 1970s, social psychology researchers conceived **social identity theory** to help explain how and why people interact in groups. Typically, people join groups to satisfy socialization needs—humans are social creatures who enjoy interacting with others. By seeking positive affirmation from our groups, we strengthen our belief in the "in-group" and use comparisons to separate ourselves from other "out-groups." It is well documented that we tend to feel the groups we belong to are better than other groups and that we set distinctions from others in order to separate groups (Brown, 2000; Tajfel et al., 1971). In-group members also experience more positive feelings after discriminating against other groups (Lemyre & Smith, 1985; Oakes & Turner, 1980). Once a part of these social groups, humans tend to categorize people for ease of cognitive processing—it is more efficient for our brains to create a group

Callout Box: The Identity-Motivation Paradox

Our framing of leader identity levels may leave you with the impression that the collective-level identity is the "highest" form or perhaps the most noble form of identity that a leader can have. In a sense, this is true: leaders with a developed collective identity tend to be more focused on the organization's needs and convey a sense of "we-ness" in their communications. For these leaders, their reason for leading is much less about themselves or the individual relationships they develop (although those may also be important). Instead, their reasons include embodying the organization's values (i.e., leadership by example) and steering the organization toward reaching its true potential. However, there are important and sobering caveats that should be considered—especially in light of how powerful conflicting motivations are on our individual actions.

For example, the CEO is typically the head of the company, who largely focuses on organizational strategy and resource allocation. Most effective CEOs habitually activate their collective leader identity because that is exactly what the CEO job calls for. But as Stanford Professor Jeffrey Pfeffer (2015) so astutely points out, CEOs are quick to activate their individual-level identity at important times, especially when it comes to fighting for high financial compensation. A 2020 study by the Economic Policy Institute backs up this thought, as it shows that CEO compensation has grown over 1300% in the last 25 years and that the average CEO compensation in the largest US companies was more than 350 times that of those companies' average employee (Mishel & Kanda, 2021). Even the least cynical among us would wonder, "Where's the 'we-ness' in that?" Clearly, this disparity lays bare a festering paradox.

There are a lot of reasons why CEO compensation is so inflated. The root cause is not *solely* greed, although it would be disingenuous to downplay the importance of greed. Consider also that there is an arms race for talent in the largest corporations, CEO compensation is public record in publicly traded companies (so, making a "Keeping up with the Jones" argument is easy), and consulting companies have created a cottage industry that supports compensation recommendations to company boards of directors. Absent government or board regulation, the scales tip towards CEOs seeking higher and higher compensation.

It is also worth noting that while senior leaders may habitually activate their collective-level WSC, there are times when the proximal motivations of the individual-level WSC take precedence. Negotiating compensation is almost certainly one of those times, regardless of whether the negotiator is a CEO or a job candidate just graduating from college. While the college job candidate may be naïve and give in to emotional appeals to accept a lower salary ("be part of the team" or "join something bigger than yourself"), most CEOs are seasoned enough to see through those enticements.

Returning to the theme of greed, there is one more way to frame this paradox. While many senior leaders habitually activate their collective-level leader identity, and while they may also aspire to a future self that is a widely admired and respected leader, there are also other versions of the future self in play: Being and staying wealthy.

prototype to explain behavior than it is to slow our cognitive function and analyze each member's behavior. However, this **"stereotyping"** can create several challenges. When we do things efficiently, we may make errors and attribute behaviors to individuals based on group membership rather than individual behavior.

While a thorough review of social identity theory, stereotyping, and discrimination between groups is not the intent of this chapter, the main points to consider are as follows:

1. People gain positive emotions from group membership.
2. The strength of group identification increases based on separation from others.
3. In-group biases can prevent controlled mental processing that evaluates individuals separately from the groups in which they have been categorized.

Yes, we are social creatures who derive purpose and meaning from group belongingness. Organizations have also realized the performance gains that arise from group environments (Delarue et al., 2008), which is why our workplaces, communities, and education systems prioritize working together. The next section will explore how individuals can come together to work in effective groups.

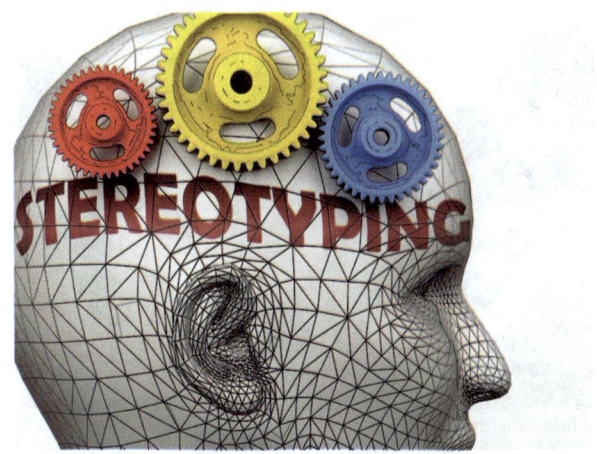
© GoodIdeas/Shutterstock.com

STEREOTYPING: a standardized mental picture that is held in common by members of a group and that represents an oversimplified opinion, prejudiced attitude, or uncritical judgment. (Merriam-Webster)

Group Prototypes

Much like the leader prototypes we discussed in our coverage of implicit leadership theories in Chapter 2, **group prototypes** are attributes like beliefs or practices that sum up a group's similarities (Hogg, van Knippenberg, & Rast, 2012). The group prototype deindividuates the members and sets them apart from others, enhancing the similarities between members and maximizing the differences and distance from separate groups. Reinforcing the prototype incentivizes group norms, creating the standards for behavior required for group membership. Look back to the "I see myself as…" statements exercise and review your collective-level identities. Are any of those collectives governed by a group prototype? Perhaps you are part of a community organization, and the group prototype is one of aid, assistance, and support to the community. The group norms might determine that members spend one day per weekend preparing materials to help the community. If something comes up that supersedes your attendance, your group may feel you are violating norms and may question your commitment.

We learn group norms through "norm talk"—a way of communicating in which group members discuss their group norms (Hogg, Van Knippenberg, & Rast, 2012). Typically, a new member seeks to fit in and quickly learn the norms. Some groups may also use imagery and metaphors to communicate and reinforce their norms. One area in which you can practice developing and communicating group norms is in student teams. Most management courses require student teams. Employers expect college graduates to be able to work in diverse, inclusive teams. One activity that can

GROUP PROTOTYPES: prototype is an individual's cognitive representation of what he or she believes to be the normative properties of the group. (e.g., Hogg & Smith, 2007; Turner 1991; Turner et al., 1987)

© fizkes/Shutterstock.com

help quickly develop group norms is the creation of a team charter, described as a "formal document written by team members at the outset of a team's lifecycle that specifies acceptable behaviors in the team." (Courtwright, McCormick, Mistry, & Wang, 2017 p. 1462). Most team charters include scheduling information, roles each member will take, assignment schedules, and other norms team members may find important. Team charters have been used in student groups across the world—they are a component of accelerating the team formation process and improving communication within the team (Aaron et al., 2014; Johnson et al., 2021).

Activity 2: Creating a Team Charter

Team charters can help teams that are in the forming stage generate norms and instill positive communication processes. Several team charters have been published as part of research studies, and they consistently include the following:

1. Goals and expectations.
    a. What are your shared learning goals for this team?
    b. What are your shared performance goals for this team?
    c. How will you track your progress toward these goals?
    d. What does success look like for your team?

2. Communication tools and technology—please be specific as to the modality with which you will communicate.
    a. How often will you communicate?
    b. What does a reasonable response time look like?
    c. Where will you save your work in progress?

3. Roles and workload distribution for each team member.
    a. How will tasks be completed?
    b. Will roles change? How will you handle communication regarding role changes?
    c. What are everyone's knowledge, skills, and abilities?
    d. What level of effort is each member willing and able to give to this team?

4. Scheduling and deadline reinforcement for course deliverables.
    a. What does your timeline look like for your project?
    b. Who will remind team members of the deadlines?
    c. What actions will you take if deadlines are missed?

5. Dealing with problems and emergency situations.
    a. What feedback processes will you use?
    b. How will you handle conflict within the team?
    c. What actions will you take if performance is not up to standard?

Used with permission of Academy of Management (NY), from *Academy of Management Learning & Education*, vol. 21, no. 2, William H.A. Johnson, David S. Baker, Longzhu Dong, Vas Taras, Charles Wankel© 2002; permission conveyed through Copyright Clearance Center, Inc.

Activity 2: Learning Outcomes

Team charters are one way to set out norms and work through initial disagreements that can hamper teamwork. It is one way to gauge the motivation of the individuals on the team and to recognize preferences for different approaches to work. They can also serve as an inventory of different skill sets. They are most effective at getting the team to start working together quickly and can also serve as a reminder of the commitments the members made to the team.

While team charters help teams quickly share responsibilities and communicate effectively using shared leadership, the impact on actual performance is mixed. A deeper approach to team development is the generation of a team mental model, which can elevate group membership beyond a collective identity towards a working environment where individuals can anticipate the needs and actions of fellow group members.

Team Mental Models

Researchers observing effective teams noted the following: As individuals worked together, a shared understanding arose that allowed members to coordinate quickly and effectively (DeChurch & Mesmer-Magnus, 2010; Klimoski & Mohammed, 1994; Mathieu et al., 2000). This understanding might include relevant knowledge and the ability to predict and anticipate members' behaviors. These "**team mental models**" consisting of shared knowledge were a main driver of effectiveness and performance (Mathieu et al., 2000).

© janews/Shutterstock.com

TEAM MENTAL MODEL: Team mental models are team members' shared, organized understanding and mental representation of knowledge about key elements of the team's relevant environment. (Klimoski & Mohammed, 1994)

Mental models reach beyond the collective identity of a group. They seek to describe how understanding the ways your teammates think and take action can create common expectations regarding tasks and allow for prediction of and coordination between behaviors (DeChurch & Mesmer-Magnus, 2010). To envision this in action, think of a sports team that practices set plays or actors who rehearse their lines and emotional responses. Even when something unexpected happens, this practice or rehearsal still allows the team to coordinate and regroup quickly when communication is not possible. The performance of a team depends on both the similarity and accuracy of the shared mental models (Lim & Klein, 2005).

A leader can help create shared mental models by building a set of processes through which individuals learn and observe each other's behaviors. This step solidifies the processes and reinforces the behaviors to the point where communication is no longer required. These processes also serve to motivate teammates to continue their actions, so the operation continues to generate positive performance. The leader must enact strategic communications regarding the team's mission, the impact of the deliverables or outcomes, and discussions regarding team challenges or problems (an After-Action Review, or AAR [covered in Chapter 4], is an excellent way to reinforce shared mental models). (Murase et al., 2014). In smaller teams, team

Activity 3: Team Mental Models

If you are currently in a group for school or work, you can use a concept mapping tool to explore how similar and accurate your team's mental models are across individuals. Using a concept mapping software like gitmind (gitmind.com), xmind (xmind.net), or any other free concept mapping tool, create a concept map that includes the team tasks, equipment, procedures, working conditions, resources, individual team member responsibilities, strengths, weaknesses, knowledge, skills, and actions you can take to get the team back on track. Once each team member has created their concept map, review them to see how similar they are in capturing all the aspects of your team's work. Then run the maps by the team leader or project manager to ensure the concepts captured are accurate.

© Nattapol_Sritongcom/Shutterstock.com

Activity 3: Learning Outcomes

The articulation of a team mental model can illustrate the complexity that arises from individuals creating a shared understanding. This activity will also allow you to identify misconceptions that can create barriers to team performance.

mental models can arise without an individual stepping into the leadership position. But in more complex teams and situations where time is a factor, a leader will likely have more influence over bringing the shared mental model into existence.

Team charters can help shape a collective identity by creating group norms and generating a group prototype. Team mental models systemize the group norms into a team state where the members efficiently anticipate and regulate actions. While there are many positive impacts of strong collective identity that come from group prototypes and team mental models—such as greater cooperation and effort, higher participation, decisions focused on organizational effectiveness, increased information sharing, and coordinated action (Ashforth, Harrison, & Corley, 2008)—recognizing the existence of these social structures is the first step in overcoming some of the negative impacts of strong group identification. Among these negative impacts are behaviors from "other" marginalized groups, the incorporation of a negative evaluation of the group into individual members' self-concepts (self-stigmatization), unequal distribution of resources that favor in-groups, and unrealistic expectations that may create feelings of inadequacy for a group member (i.e., being categorized as a "brain" early in one's education).

While some work to address these issues resides at the individual level (exploring how a particular label created challenges or barriers), leaders are often called upon to help organizations overcome the other negative impacts. One way leaders can bridge the gaps and overcome distrust between in-groups and out-groups is by creating diverse groups with a higher level of identification (for example: addressing interdepartmental fighting over budgets by activating concern for overall organizational health and performance). Leaders can also help groups recognize organizational boundaries and work across those boundaries with processes that improve communication and create bonding (Day & Harrison, 2007). Creating shared goals for members of all in-groups and out-groups can help build a more cohesive entity. Thus, it is important to explore the roles leaders play in social identity.

Social Identity Theory of Leadership

As we have discussed, individuals can gain a sense of self from their membership in a group. Research suggests that as followers strengthen their identity within the group, they evaluate the group leader's behavior based on whether it agrees with or violates group norms. Thus, the group prototype becomes the measure of leader effectiveness, which might conflict with an individual's implicit leadership theory (Hogg et al., 1998). For example, if you believe that leaders should generally be understanding and supportive of followers, but your weekend soccer league is highly competitive and willing to win at any cost (including cheating), you will evaluate your team captain on their willingness to break the rules to aid your team, not on how they console the team after a loss. This can create conflict across levels, as effective leaders must keep in mind the group prototype to further engage and motivate followers (Steffens, Haslam, & Reicher, 2014). This is true even when followers and leaders do not ever encounter each other—the leader's perceived effectiveness is wrapped up in the follower's belief in the collective (Steffens et al., 2014). Returning to the earlier example of fandom—fans will likely never meet the coach/players in person in any meaningful way, but as long as the coach and the players exhibit the group prototype, fans will remain supportive.

The social identity theory of leadership addresses how individuals can assume leadership positions by strengthening the collective identity of the group (Brewer & Gardner, 1996). By using "norm talk", adopting language that evokes the image of the group prototype, and activating group membership, the leader elevates the "we" and depersonalizes the "I" in a group. Activating this group membership can be achieved merely by using "we" and "us" when describing the challenges facing the group. Leaders that exhibit the group prototype have higher levels of support and trust and are perceived as more effective by the group members (Hogg, Van Knippenberg, & Rast, 2012). In the following sections, we discuss how charismatic leadership and servant leadership embody different approaches to leading those with a collective identity.

Charismatic Leadership

Charisma is a personality characteristic of interest that dates back to ancient times. It was originally viewed as a special attribute gifted by a higher power to an individual meant for greatness (Weber, 1947). Historically speaking, charisma was attributed to leaders who were able to enact great changes in society through their persuasive talents. Charisma was a driving force behind the "Great Man" Theories discussed in Chapter 4, which cemented the idea that these attributes were reserved for the elite and divinely blessed. However, charisma is also nested in the relationships between the leader and their followers, where the followers' beliefs in the leader legitimize the leader and further motivate the leader to continue the pursuit of transcendence (Dow, 1969).

Decades of research into **charismatic leadership** show that it is possible to adopt behaviors that create the perception of charisma. Charisma is not a talent bestowed at birth but rather something that can be taught (Antonakis, Fenley, Liechti, 2011). This leadership approach is quite effective at the collective level,

CHARISMATIC LEADERSHIP: Charismatic leadership is the ability to transmit information in a symbolic, value-based emotional manner. (Antonakis, 2016)

as a charismatic leader can adopt the group prototype, embody the expectations of the collective followers, and use language associated with a strong collective identity (Haslam et al., 2001). The charismatic leader is able to define the social categories of the in-groups and out-groups and mobilize group members toward attaining the group's goals. Charismatic leaders also serve to generate the collective identity by using lore, traditions, rites, branding, and symbolism to further institute a specific culture in an organization (Waldman & Yammarino, 1999).

There is evidence that some individuals are born with a natural ability to wield charisma. Perhaps they are an eloquent and spellbinding orator, or an extrovert instantly at ease in front of a crowd. Those not born with charisma can work to

© Andrew Rybalko/Shutterstock.com

develop it by practicing their speaking skills and using evocative language that elicits emotional responses from followers. Charismatic leaders have high self-confidence, enjoy influencing others, and are quite social. They also use symbolic language to communicate their visions, challenge their followers with great expectations, and use role modeling to illustrate their values (Howell & Shamir, 2005). Charismatic speech has a positive relationship with work output and the contributions individuals make

Activity 4: Charismatic Leadership Scale

Please use a 5-point scale (1 = not at all; 5 = frequently, if not always) to evaluate the extent to which you observe these behaviors in your leader:

1. I am ready to trust him/her to overcome any obstacle.
2. In my mind, he/she is a symbol of success and accomplishment.
3. I'm proud to be associated with him/her.
4. I think of him/her as my role model.
5. I have complete confidence in him/her.
6. He/she is a dynamic, magnetic leader.

A score of 26-30 indicates you perceive your leader as exhibiting high levels of charisma; a score lower than 15 suggests you perceive your leader as lacking charisma.

Used with permission of Sage Publications Inc. Journals, from Adding to Contingent-Reward Behavior: The Augmenting Effect of Charismatic Leadership, David A. Waldman, Bernard M. Bass, Francis J. Yammarino, vol. 15, issue 4 © 1991; permission conveyed through Copyright Clearance Center, Inc.

**While surveys are a common method for evaluating charismatic leadership, a more rigorous approach is to observe or record your leader to evaluate their charismatic leadership tactics. This is discussed below.

Activity 4: Learning Outcomes

The survey scores will highlight the extent to which you feel a leader serves as a figurehead, attracts followers to the cause, and from which you derive positive feelings. Charismatic leaders often give their followers confidence in their abilities to achieve goals and create strong social identities that foster pride. You can evaluate your scores further by evaluating whether the leader is using natural traits and abilities versus those developed over time.

Chapter 6: Collective-Level Leadership and Teams   109

to the public (Antonakis, d'Adde, Weber, Zehner, 2021). The figure highlights the 12 tactics (9 verbal, 3 non-verbal) charismatic leaders use to enhance their motivation of followers.

Charisma is a powerful tool that leaders can wield to create movements—some of which benefit followers, others of which can be manipulative and exploit followers. When discussing charisma, it is appealing to think in terms of "good" or bad." But charisma is a device many leaders use. It is not inherently good or bad. Instead, it is important to think about the reasons behind a leader's use of charisma to motivate groups toward an end goal and to evaluate the goal

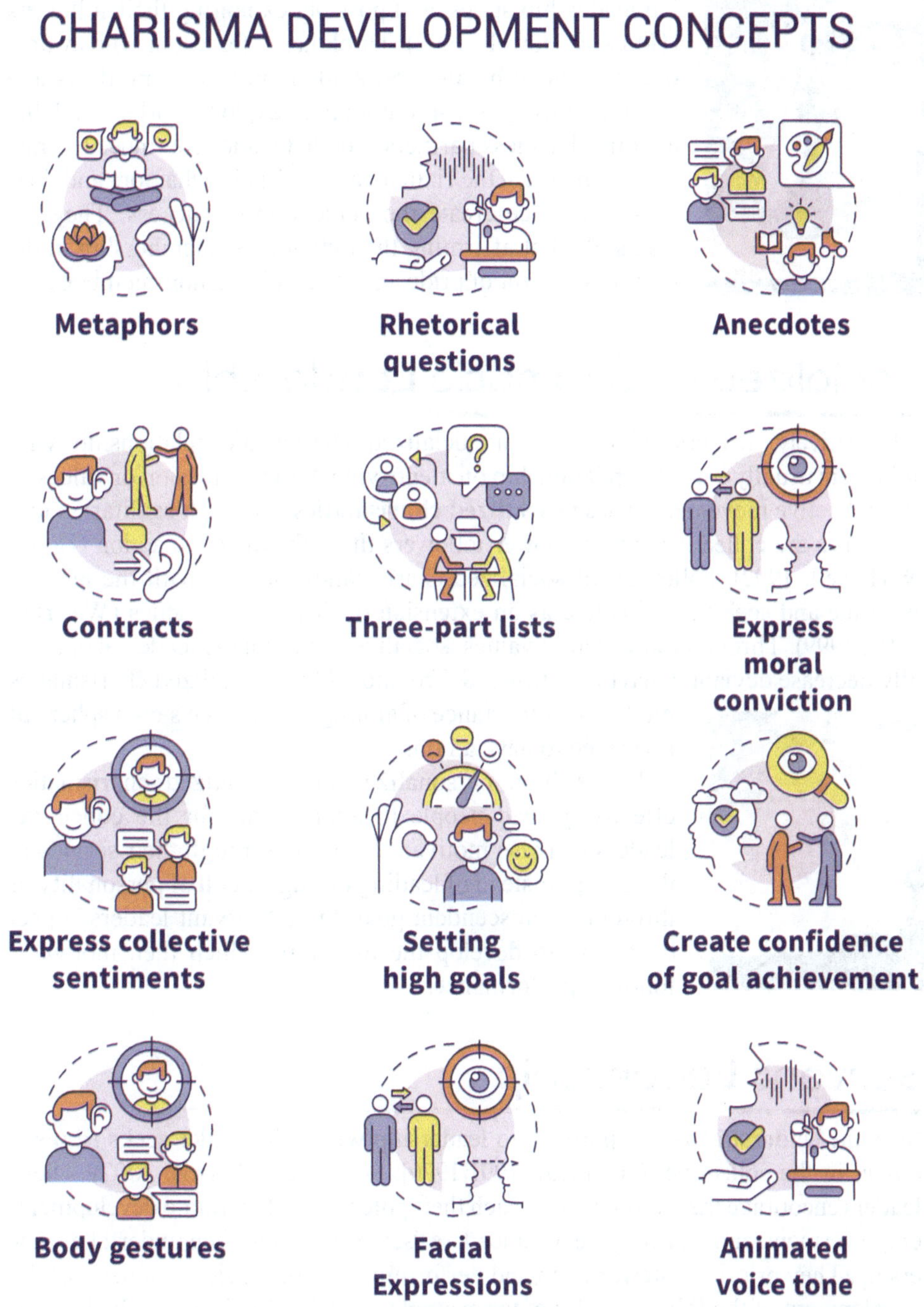

CHARISMA DEVELOPMENT CONCEPTS

Metaphors **Rhetorical questions** **Anecdotes**

Contracts **Three-part lists** **Express moral conviction**

Express collective sentiments **Setting high goals** **Create confidence of goal achievement**

Body gestures **Facial Expressions** **Animated voice tone**

© bsd studio/Shutterstock.com

PERSONALIZED CHARISMATIC LEADERS: (a) is based on personal dominance and authoritarian behavior, (b) serves the self-interest of the leader, and is self-aggrandizing and (c) is exploitive of others. (House & Howell, 1992)

on its merits. To explore this further, we can observe the difference between personalized and socialized charismatics.

Personalized Charismatic Leadership

Leaders who create a personalized charismatic relationship with followers usually base that relationship on identifying with the leader themselves—*not* on the mission or the message. These **personalized charismatics** lead by dominating others, putting their own self-interest to the forefront, using authoritarian leadership styles, and possibly exploiting their followers (House & Howell, 1992). Think here of a leader who awards oneself a huge bonus, draws attention to new products and services through self-promotion, or exploits workers and disappoints business partners. Yet that leader continues to draw interest because the flamboyancy of their behaviors and their self-confidence create the perception of success. They are also skilled at affirming the individuals' membership in the group as a point of pride and at criticizing non-members.

© Prazis Images/Shutterstock.com

SOCIALIZED CHARISMATIC LEADERS: (a) is based on egalitarian behavior, (b) serves collective interests, and is not driven by the self-interest of the leader and (c) develops and empowers others. (House & Howell, 1992/5

Socialized Charismatic Leadership

Alternatively, leaders who create a socialized charismatic relationship with followers usually base that relationship on identifying with the mission or values of the collective movement. These **socialized charismatics** lead with egalitarian ideals, serve the collective, and empower followers through collective action (House & Howell, 1992). Followers of socialized charismatics identify with the leader's message and seek the collective as an extension of their innate values (Weierter, 1997, 1999). Through these shared values, socialized charismatic leaders can actually decrease deviant behaviors (Brown & Trevino, 2006). Socialized charismatics model the importance of aiming beyond one's own sphere of influence to have an impact.

While both personalized and socialized charismatics effectively lead people to attain goals for the collective, leaders can also motivate followers through their service *to* the group. Instead of leading through a cult of personality or through a transcendent goal, these "servant leaders" enact behaviors to develop the followers, which then motivates follower performance.

© Banana Oil/Shutterstock.com

SERVANT LEADERSHIP: Servant-leaders empower and develop people; they show humility, are authentic, accept people for who they are, provide direction, and are stewards who work for the good of the whole. (van Dierendonck, 2011)

Servant Leadership

Servant leadership is an approach to leadership where the leader seeks *to serve others* in the collective (Greenleaf, 1991[1970]; Sendjaya & Sarros, 2002). These leaders encourage their followers to reach their potential and facilitate development, empowerment, and learning. Servant leaders "serve first" and then undertake leadership. They prioritize stewardship and performing acts of service in pursuit of the development of the followers. Take, for example, a CEO who foresees challenging business conditions in the near future. There is a need to quickly reduce operational costs, perhaps by executing layoffs. However, a servant leader may choose instead to reduce their own pay and ask for voluntary pay cuts amongst staff to weather the difficult times. This act of service provides employees with a solid foundation and focuses on the well-being of the community by keeping it intact. This example illustrates servant leadership—the focus is on the leader making decisions that target followers' needs (maintaining employment for all staff).

Servant leaders typically see positive follower outcomes such as increased personal growth, enhanced organizational citizenship behaviors (OCBs, the positive actions employees take to make organizations better places to work), higher engagement, and more collaboration (van Dierendonck, 2011). Servant leaders reap these positive outcomes by building high-quality leader-member exchanges (see LMX, Chapter 5) through persuasive communication. Servant leaders' greatness is nested within their total commitment to serve their followers—either through the organizational mission or the development of those followers. Servant leaders evoke follower commitment through emotional healing, creating community value, conceptual skills, empowering followers, helping followers develop, serving followers first, and behaving ethically (Liden et al., 2008).

The model In Figure 1 shows the antecedents to servant leadership, the characteristics servant leaders exhibit, and the mechanisms through which servant leadership works to generate outcomes such as self-actualization, follower job attitudes, individual performance, and organizational attributes.

Research conducted on servant leadership provides evidence that this type of leader impacts their followers' self-efficacy, job performance, engagement,

Figure 1: A Conceptual Model of Servant Leadership

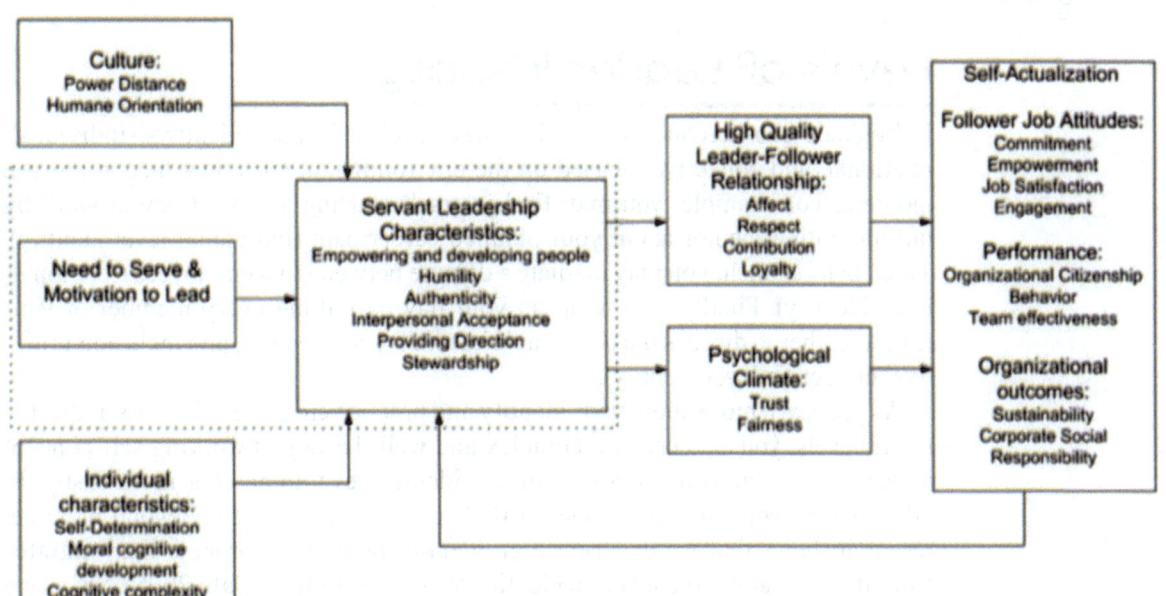

Dirk van Dierendonck, *Journal of Management*, vol. 37, no. 4, pp. 1228-1261, copyright © 2010 by SAGE Publications. Reprinted by Permission of SAGE Publications.

organizational and community citizenship behaviors, commitment, creativity, and turnover intentions. Servant leaders also significantly relate to teams in a positive way—relationships with team performance, team OCBs, and organizational performance are seen (Liden et al., 2015)

Activity 5: Servant Leadership Scale

On a scale of 1 (strongly disagree) to 9 (strongly agree), please evaluate the following servant leadership behaviors you seek in a leader:

1. My leader can tell if something work-related is going wrong.
2. My leader makes my career development a priority.
3. I would seek help from my leader if I had a personal problem.
4. My leader emphasizes the importance of giving back to the community.
5. My leader puts my best interests ahead of his/her own.
6. My leader gives me the freedom to handle difficult situations in the way that I feel is best.
7. My leader would NOT compromise ethical principles in order to achieve success.

Reprinted from Liden, R., Wayne, S., Meuser, J., Hu, J., Wu, J., & Liao, C. (2015). Servant leadership: Validation of a short form of the SL-28. *The Leadership Quarterly, 26*(2), 254–269. With permission from Elsevier

Activity 5: Learning Outcomes

This scale will give you an idea as to whether you work for a servant leader. The highest score is 63, and scores around 50 or more suggest your leader is a steward of your own development. Lower scores may suggest your leader is not as invested in your personal growth and development or may not have a close relationship with you. If you are someone who thrives on the type of support a servant leader can provide, you should seek out leaders you trust, with whom you feel comfortable sharing personal challenges, and those that model servitude by giving back.

Levels of Leader Identity

Individuals can activate any of the three levels of leader identity—individual, relational, and collective—based on the environmental cues they face at a given moment. For example, you may find yourself starting a typical day at work by talking with a mentor about your planned career path (individual-level identity). Then, before lunch, you may mediate a dispute between two employees (relational-level identity). Finally, you wrap up your day by pulling every member of your team together to discuss the company's latest diversity, equity, and inclusion initiative (collective-level identity).

As you learn more about your identity and practice enacting behaviors at the different levels, you also create a complex and well-developed working self-concept which allows you to transition from one identity level to another more easily. In other words, you can make these shifts because you practiced. Beyond practice, research shows that we experience an identity maturation process that migrates from the individual to collective identity over time (Lord & Hall, 2005). So, as we gain more experience, our identity as a leader is much more interwoven with the collective (i.e., promoting the best interests of the group, upholding the company's values) and somewhat less focused on their relational (i.e., being liked as a leader by followers) or individual identity (i.e., personal development or goal attainment).

In Review

This chapter describes collective-level theories, where the social identity exists at the group level. As we note, collective-level behaviors are based on group memberships, and the stronger one identifies with the group, the more likely they are to take on group characteristics. Thus, collective-level identities are motivated by the group's needs. Part of your leader identity includes your enacted behaviors as part of this collective—perhaps to ensure the group's survival or to assist with group performance. The activities and self-report assessments in this chapter are provided to help you increase your self-awareness of your preferences regarding your social identity. For example, the collective identity scale will highlight the importance you place on group membership. The more you can understand your preferences as they exist and what they may become, the more you will learn how your identity adapts to social situations. Understanding how you make and foster attachments in groups will help you identify the groups in which you feel most comfortable enacting leadership behaviors.

The team charter and team mental model activities allow you to practice building team norms and to work with others to recognize each member's skill sets and preferences. This may be important as you work on both educational and professional teams. Being able to begin work quickly with a team and anticipate what members need and how they will act can help with productivity and performance.

We also should recognize the impact a leader can have on generating shared mental models. Building in observation processes and using strategic communication to ensure an understanding of team goals and the overall mission can also help create a team mental model. Leaders must also ensure that the team avoids becoming too cohesive and too insular. A team mental model that systemizes the work and incentivizes coordinated action is ideal; one that marginalizes other groups or leads to disruptive and destructive competition must be avoided. Leaders can avoid too much group cohesion by reminding the team that they are part of a larger organization and reminding teammates of each person's individuality.

The next section details the social identity theories of leadership, which explains how group leaders take on the group prototype and offer a sense of belonging to followers. The leader's role in these interactions is to strengthen the group identity. The leader may use specific types of speech to reinforce the "we-ness" of the group and rites and rituals that generate enthusiasm for the group. Understanding how leaders can create strong group identities is important for moving groups toward action.

Charismatic leadership theory describes the ability of leaders to communicate information in a symbolic and persuasive manner. Originally thought of as a unique and innate trait, recent research provides evidence that charisma can be a learned skill. Charismatic leadership research expanded to highlight the differences between more self-interested or personalized charismatics and those who promote the public good or socialized charismatics. Activity 4 measures the amount of charisma you perceive in a leader. Charisma can often be transmitted to followers through specific language tools, sharing moral convictions, and using goal-setting language to animate followers.

The final concept in this chapter presents the model of servant leadership, where the leader's focus is on developing the follower to their full potential. Activity 5 allows you to rate a leader on several items that connote servant leadership. Servant leaders promote a variety of positive outcomes in followers, including engagement, commitment, organizational citizenship behaviors, decreased turnover, and creativity.

These last three chapters have focused on the three levels of identity: individual, relational, and collective. Each level requires different skills and results in different outcomes. At the individual level, one uses traits and individual abilities to differentiate oneself from others. Relational-level interactions require interpersonal influence and a shared commitment to both parties' goals. The collective-level relies upon social identity and the extent to which individuals can adopt the group prototype while responding to charismatic or servant leadership behaviors.

The next chapter explores your strength of leader identity and how you enact claiming and granting behaviors in both leader and follower roles. Learning about your identity strength will provide insight into your current behavioral preferences and how you can practice those behaviors to become a more effective leader or manager.

Learning Objectives

Summarize collective identity

The collective-level of identity is based on group membership. You can review your "I see myself as…" statements for examples of these interactions. The collective identity self-assessment highlights your preferences for group membership related to your identity. The greater your collective identity, the more you take on the attributes of the group, feel a commitment to the group, but also may view other groups differently. The drives present at the collective-level of identity motivate goal-directed behaviors focused on furthering the group's advancement. Collective identities can create cohesion within groups but also may create dislike for out-groups.

Explain social identity theory

Social identity theory explains how and why people behave in groups. Individuals gain positive emotions from group membership, and the strength of their social identity can create distance and separation from others. Cognitively, our membership in groups allows for the automatic categorization of others, which may result in stereotyping individuals based on group membership. While we benefit from group membership and derive purpose and satisfaction from these social relationships, we also must make the effort to enact more effortful cognitive processing to avoid stereotyping errors.

Construct a team mental model

A team mental model is a shared understanding that allows members to coordinate quickly and effectively. When a team has a common belief system, members can anticipate others' behaviors, which leads to higher performance. The prediction and coordination between members generate a smooth system that can recover from unexpected disturbances. Activity 5 asks you to create your own team mental model to practice illustrating these complex relationships.

Explore charismatic leadership as a social phenomenon

Charismatic leaders thrive in group settings, as the members legitimize the leader's tactics with their beliefs. Charismatic leaders use language to engage the collective identities of followers, define the groups, and use inspirational language to move the group towards actions. Charismatic individuals thrive on influencing others and acting in social settings. Personalized charismatics may exploit followers to achieve their own self-interests, while socialized charismatic leaders work towards fulfilling the mission of the organization by empowering followers to act.

Evaluate servant leadership

Servant leaders focus their behaviors on encouraging others to reach their potential as acts of service and stewardship. Servant leadership is positively related to follower personal growth, organizational citizenship behaviors, higher follower engagement, and increased collaboration. In addition, those who follow servant leaders report higher self-efficacy, job performance, creativity, and lower turnover intentions.

Key Terms

Collective Identity (Pg. 100)

Social Identity Theory (Pg. 102)

Stereotyping (Pg. 103)

Group Prototypes (Pg. 103)

Team Mental Model (Pg. 105)

Charismatic Leadership (Pg. 107)

Personalized Charismatic Leaders (Pg. 110)

Socialized Charismatic Leaders (Pg. 110)

Servant Leadership (Pg. 110)

Critical Thinking Questions

1. In your own words, describe the collective-level of identity. Give an example of a time you have been part of a collective and either motivated the group toward a specific outcome or helped the group achieve an objective. What types of behaviors did you enact as part of the collective?

2. As a manager, how can you help your employees develop their collective-level leadership abilities? How can you help them foster the social identity of the group members? How can you help them avoid stereotyping members of the out-groups?

3. How can you determine if a charismatic leader is using a personalized versus socialized approach to goal achievement? How should you alter your own behaviors for each situation?
4. How can you balance a servant leadership approach while also ensuring your team meets its organizational goals? How do you create opportunities for your followers while also enhancing your own leadership status?

References

Aaron, J. R., McDowell, W. C., & Herdman, A. O. (2014). The effects of a team charter on student team behaviors. *Journal of Education for Business*, *89*(2), 90–97.

Antonakis, J., d'Adda, G., Weber, R. A., & Zehnder, C. (2021). "Just words? Just speeches?" On the economic value of charismatic leadership. *Management Science*. https://doi.org/10.1287/mnsc.2021.4219

Antonakis, J., Fenley, M., & Liechti, S. (2011). Can charisma be taught? Tests of two interventions. *Academy of Management Learning & Education*, *10*(3), 374–396.

Ashforth, B. E., Harrison, S. H., & Corley, K. G. (2008). Identification in organizations: An examination of four fundamental questions. *Journal of Management*, *34*(3), 325–374.

Ashforth, B. E., & Mael, F. (1989). Social identity theory and the organization. *Academy of Management Review*, *14*(1), 20–39.

Brewer, M. B., & Gardner, W. (1996). Who is this" We"? Levels of collective identity and self-representations. *Journal of Personality and Social Psychology*, *71*(1), 83.

Brown, R. (2000). Social identity theory: Past achievements, current problems and future challenges. *European Journal of Social Psychology*, *30*(6), 745–778.

Brown, M. E., & Trevino, L. K. (2006). Socialized charismatic leadership, values congruence, and deviance in work groups. *Journal of Applied Psychology*, *91*(4), 954.

Courtright, S. H., McCormick, B. W., Mistry, S., & Wang, J. (2017). Quality charters or quality members? A control theory perspective on team charters and team performance. *Journal of Applied Psychology*, *102*(10), 1462.

Day, D. V., & Harrison, M. M. (2007). A multilevel, identity-based approach to leadership development. *Human Resource Management Review*, *17*(4), 360–373.

DeChurch, L. A., & Mesmer-Magnus, J. R. (2010). The cognitive underpinnings of effective teamwork: a meta-analysis. *Journal of Applied Psychology*, *95*(1), 32.

Delarue, A., Van Hootegem, G., Procter, S., & Burridge, M. (2008). Teamworking and organizational performance: a review of survey-based research. *International Journal of Management Reviews*, *10*(2), 127–148.

Dow Jr, T. E. (1969). The theory of charisma. *The Sociological Quarterly*, *10*(3), 306–318.

Epitropaki, O., Kark, R., Mainemelis, C., & Lord, R. G. (2017). Leadership and followership identity processes: A multilevel review. *The Leadership Quarterly*, *28*(1), 104–129.

Greenleaf, R.K. (1991). The servant as leader. The Robert K. Greenleaf Center. (Originally published in 1970, by Robert K. Greenleaf).

Haslam, S. A., Platow, M. J., Turner, J. C., Reynolds, K. J., McGarty, C., Oakes, Johnson, S., Ryan, M. K., P. J., ... & Veenstra, K. (2001). Social identity and the romance of leadership: The importance of being seen to be 'doing it for us'. *Group Processes & Intergroup Relations*, *4*(3), 191–205.

Haslam, S. A., & Reicher, S. D. (2006). Stressing the group: Social identity and the unfolding dynamics of stress. *Journal of Applied Psychology*, 91, 1037–1052.

Hogg, M. A., Hains, S. C., & Mason, I. (1998). Identification and leadership in small groups: Salience, frame of reference, and leader stereotypicality effects on leader evaluations. *Journal of Personality and Social Psychology*, *75*(5), 1248.

Hogg, M. A., Van Knippenberg, D., & Rast III, D. E. (2012). Intergroup leadership in organizations: Leading across group and organizational boundaries. *Academy of Management Review*, *37*(2), 232–255.

Howell, J. M., & Shamir, B. (2005). The role of followers in the charismatic leadership process: Relationships and their consequences. *Academy of Management Review*, *30*(1), 96–112.

Johnson, W. H., Baker, D., Dong, L., Taras, V., & Wankel, C. (2021). Do Team Charters Help Team-Based Projects? The Effects of Team Charters on Performance and Satisfaction in Global Virtual Teams. *Academy of Management Learning & Education*, (ja). https://doi.org/10.5465/amle.2020.0332

Kark, R., Shamir, B., & Chen, G. (2003). The two faces of transformational leadership: Empowerment and dependency. *Journal of Applied Psychology*, *88*(2), 246.

Klimoski R. & Mohammed S. (1994). Team mental model: Construct or metaphor? *Journal of Management*, 20, 403–437.

Lemyre, L., & Smith, P. M. (1985). Intergroup discrimination and self-esteem in the minimal group paradigm. *Journal of Personality and Social Psychology*, *49*(3), 660–670.

Liden, R. C., Wayne, S. J., Meuser, J. D., Hu, J., Wu, J., & Liao, C. (2015). Servant leadership: Validation of a short form of the SL-28. *The Leadership Quarterly*, *26*(2), 254–269.

Liden, R. C., Wayne, S. J., Zhao, H., & Henderson, D. (2008). Servant leadership: Development of a multidimensional measure and multi-level assessment. *The Leadership Quarterly*, *19*(2), 161–177.

Lim, B. C., & Klein, K. J. (2006). Team mental models and team performance: A field study of the effects of team mental model similarity and accuracy. *Journal of Organizational Behavior: The International Journal of Industrial, Occupational and Organizational Psychology and Behavior*, *27*(4), 403–418.

Mathieu, J. E., Heffner, T. S., Goodwin, G. F., Salas, E., & Cannon-Bowers, J. A. (2000). The influence of shared mental models on team process and performance. *Journal of Applied Psychology*, 85, 273–283.

Mathieu, J. E., & Rapp, T. L. (2009). Laying the foundation for successful team performance trajectories: The roles of team charters and performance strategies. *Journal of Applied Psychology*, *94*(1), 90.

Mohammed, S., & Dumville, B. C. (2001). Team mental models in a team knowledge framework: Expanding theory and measurement across disciplinary boundaries. *Journal of Organizational Behavior: The International Journal of Industrial, Occupational and Organizational Psychology and Behavior*, *22*(2), 89–106.

Murase, T., Carter, D. R., DeChurch, L. A., & Marks, M. A. (2014). Mind the gap: The role of leadership in multiteam system collective cognition. *The Leadership Quarterly*, *25*(5), 972–986.

Oakes, P. J., & Turner, J. C. (1980). Social categorization and intergroup behaviour: Does minimal intergroup discrimination make social identity more positive? *European Journal of Social Psychology*. 10*(3)*, 295–301.

Rehbock, S. K., Hubner, S. V., Knipfer, K., & Peus, C. V.(2022). What kind of leader am I? An exploration of professionals' leader identity construal. *Applied Psychology*. https://doi.org/10.1111/apps.12389

Reicher, S., Haslam, S. A., & Hopkins, N. (2005). Social identity and the dynamics of leadership: Leaders and followers as collaborative agents in the transformation of social reality. *The Leadership Quarterly*, *16*(4), 547–568.

Sendjaya, S., & Sarros, J. C. (2002). Servant leadership: Its origin, development, and application in organizations. *Journal of Leadership & Organizational Studies*, *9*(2), 57–64.

Steffens, N. K., Haslam, S. A., & Reicher, S. D. (2014). Up close and personal: Evidence that shared social identity is a basis for the 'special' relationship that binds followers to leaders. *The Leadership Quarterly*, *25*(2), 296–313.

Tajfel, H., Billig, M. G., Bundy, R. P., & Flament, C. (1971). Social categorization and intergroup behaviour. *European Journal of Social Psychology*, *1*(2), 149–178.

Van Dierendonck, D. (2011). Servant leadership: A review and synthesis. *Journal of Management*, *37*(4), 1228–1261.

Waldman, D. A., & Yammarino, F. J. (1999). CEO charismatic leadership: Levels-of-management and levels-of-analysis effects. *Academy of Management Review*, *24*(2), 266–285.

Weber, M. (1947). *The Theory of Social and Economic Organizations*. Free Press.

Weierter, S. J. (1997). Who wants to play "follow the leader?" A theory of charismatic relationships based on routinized charisma and follower characteristics. *The Leadership Quarterly*, *8*(2), 171–193.

Weierter, S. J. (1999). The role of self-awareness and self-monitoring in charismatic relationships. *Journal of Applied Social Psychology*, *29*(6), 1246–1262.

CHAPTER 7

Behavioral Theories

CHAPTER OUTCOMES

1. Determine the strength of your leader identity
2. Summarize claiming and granting behaviors
3. Evaluate classical leader behavior studies
4. Describe the Blake and Mouton Managerial Grid™
5. Measure your leader behaviors

Purpose of This Chapter

This chapter begins with an in-depth discussion of leader identity strength (i.e., the extent to which you feel like a leader). Leader identity strength relates to your meaning of leadership and also the levels at which you lead. The more you embody the elements of your leadership meaning and enact leadership from the individual, relational, and collective levels, the stronger your leader identity will become. That strength is reinforced through behaviors that signal your leadership standing and the way followers respond to your actions. We will discuss "claiming and granting" activities that serve to build leadership strength. We also refer to the classic behavioral studies of leadership and the Blake and Mouton Leadership Grid. We end the chapter by discussing behaviors that enable leading change.

Activity 1: Leader Meter

You can gauge the strength of your leader identity by completing the Leader Meter.

Step 1: Shade in the meter to illustrate the extent to which you see yourself as a leader. You may want to complete this in your work or school domain first, then with friends and family, and finally, in a community domain.

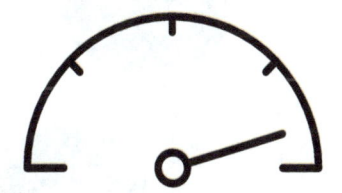
© mike_green/Shutterstock.com

Step 2: Brainstorm the knowledge/skills/abilities you could practice that would generate a higher rating on the meter. Is there a disconnect between aspects included in your definitions of leadership (from the drawing exercise) and the extent to which you see yourself as a leader?

Please keep this leader meter available. We will return to it throughout the chapter.

Activity 1a: Learning Outcomes

Reflect on and discuss with your peers the behaviors you use in the shaded areas that contribute to your leader identity strength. People who see themselves as a leader have a strong identity, while those who defer or resist being called a leader have a weak leader identity. If you only shaded in 25% or less of the meter in Activity 1, you most likely have a weaker leader identity. If you shaded in about half, you possess a moderate leader identity. And if you shaded in 75% or more, you probably have a stronger leader identity.

What Is Leader Identity Strength?

LEADER IDENTITY STRENGTH:
"The extent to which individuals view themselves as leaders" (Clapp-Smith, Hammond, Vogelgesang Lester, & Palanski, 2018; pp. 5)

Leader identity strength captures how much you identify with the idea of being a leader (Hammond et al., 2018). You may want to compare your leader meter with the Motivation to Lead survey you completed in Chapter 3—usually, those who have a strong motivation to lead will also depict a strong leader identity. You can develop your leader identity strength by seeking out and taking on challenges. As you accept leadership opportunities and experience success, you may find your leader identity getting stronger. At the same time, threats or disappointments can diminish your leader identity and perhaps make you rethink your self-concept around leading.

One can strengthen their leader identity by seeking opportunities to practice different leadership skills (Miscenko et al., 2017). Research describes how executives accumulate leadership skills as part of their work experience, leading to enhanced strategic thinking (Dragoni et al., 2011). As discussed in Chapter 3, the motivation to lead may incentivize individuals to adopt provisional leader identities, which they can retain, discard, or revise as necessary to hone their leader self-concept as part of a learning curve. Studies in the fields of adult learning and leader development depict this learning curve as

Figure 1: The J-Shaped Development Curve

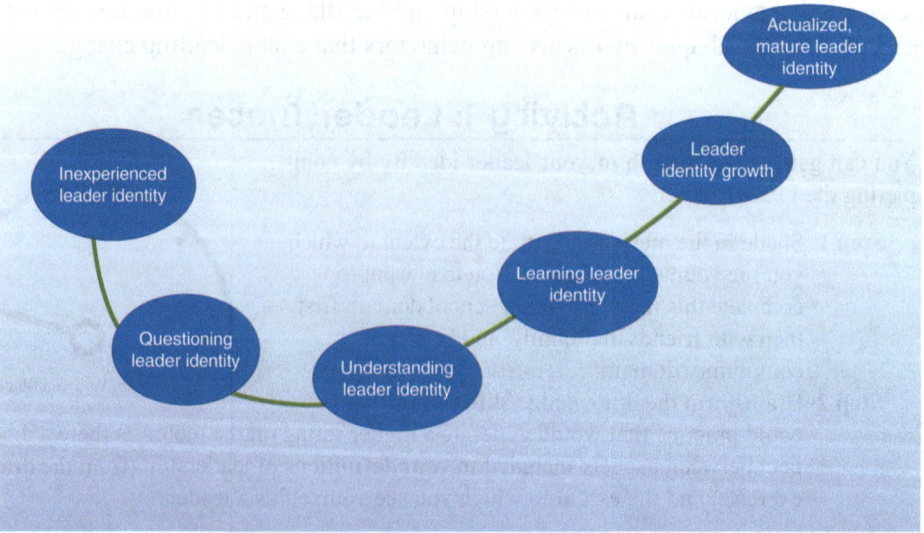

Source: Gretchen Vogelgesang Lester and Paul Lester

having a J-shape (see Figure 1), where a medium or high level of leader strength may actually *dip* when one begins a focused leadership development plan before strengthening their leader identity over time. As leaders learn more about effective/ineffective leadership approaches, they confront their ILTs and perhaps deconstruct beliefs about leader behaviors, then reshape them as part of their learning experience. While this deconstruction process can initially lower identity strength, continued leader identity work will rebuild the leader's self-perception over time. To illustrate this concept, think of a time when you felt your leader identity strength was particularly high—perhaps in high school when you occupied a senior or leadership role on a council, athletic team, or arts club. Now, compare that to the strength of your leader identity when you first started attending your college classes and exploring different clubs offered by your university. Perhaps the unfamiliar environment challenged your expectations and reduced your leader identity strength. But over time, your understanding of the group processes and appropriate leadership behaviors increased, and your leader identity strength hopefully increased as well. Adult development is a series of these changes, and the development process continues to trend upwards in a staggered fashion.

To strengthen a weak leader identity, commitment to a developmental program is required. This is more than feasible. Initial studies show a strengthening leader identity relates to positive outcomes such as goal orientation and motivation to lead. (Day & Sin, 2009; Kragt & Guenter, 2018; Skinner, 2020). We often strengthen our leader identity when there is a discrepancy between our meaning of leader identity and the external standard. In such cases, it is important to reevaluate our implicit leadership theories, draw from our relationships, and redefine our meaning in order to align our approach to leading within our organizations.

© Watcom/Shutterstock.com

A very strong leader identity can also pose hazards. Recent research has found that if you strongly identify as a leader, you might too often set aside your needs to support the group (Lanaj et al., 2020). While this can increase your task performance and impact on the social group, it can also be a type of self-sacrifice where resource depletion and increased work-family conflict are resulting issues. For those who tend to suffer from workaholism or those who are compulsive about their work, these negative effects are even stronger. Ideally, aiming for about 75-80% on the leader identity meter is the optimal balance. This number allows space for new skills and opportunities, creates harmony between your life domains, and instills confidence in you to be able to take on leadership challenges.

We will discuss how you can continue your own leadership development in great detail in Chapter 11. It is a process of continually forming and reforming, replenishing, maintaining, and strengthening your leader identity over time and through different experiences and challenges (Zheng & Muir, 2015). We will also discuss the impact of mentorship programs, executive coaching, and self-directed development. But in this chapter, we focus more on the behavioral building blocks of leader identity strength and the co-construction of a leader-follower relationship through the process of enacting and receiving claiming and granting behaviors (Lanka et al., 2019).

CLAIMING:
Verbal and nonverbal acts that individuals use to assert leadership or followership roles. (DeRue & Ashford, 2010)

GRANTING:
Behaviors that others in a social interaction engage in to recognize a person's leadership or followership role. (DeRue & Ashford, 2010)

The next section describes claiming and granting behaviors and how asserting or bestowing a leadership or followership role can reinforce leader identity.

Claiming and Granting

As noted above, a leader identity can be generated through a process of **claiming** and/or **granting** behaviors, which are enacted in different domains and circumstances. There are behaviors an individual can adopt to cement the leader or follower identity, and there are actions by those around us that can be catalysts or hindrances to leader or follower emergence (Lanka, et al., 2019). Figure 2 illustrates the claiming and granting process:

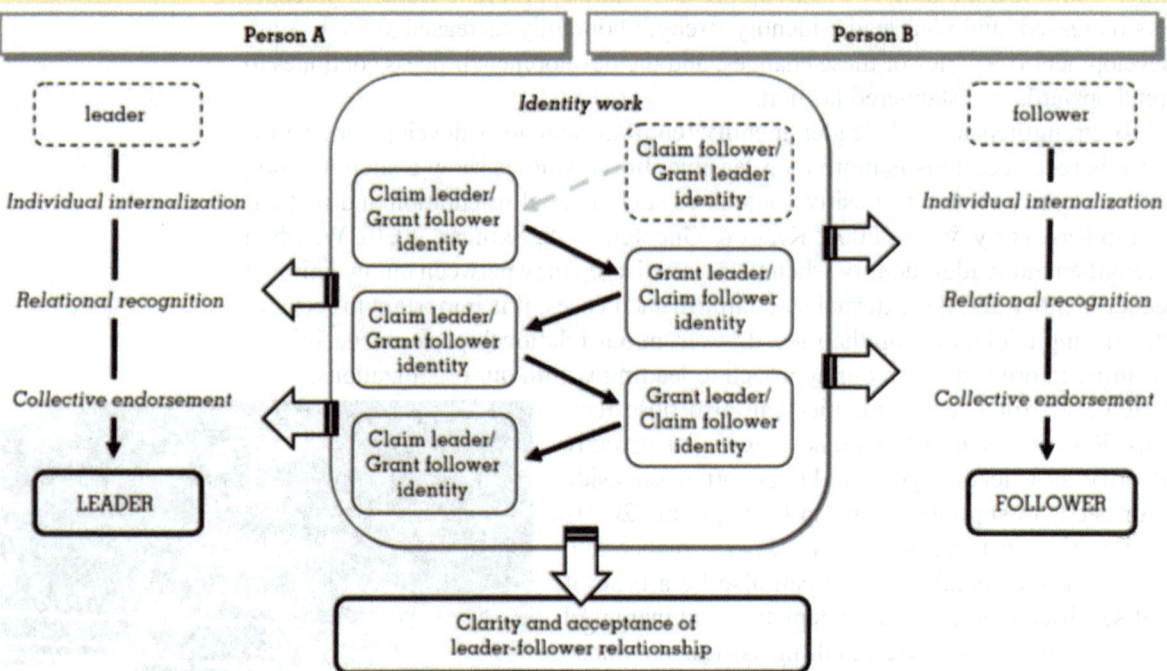

Figure 2: Leadership Identity Construction Process

Used with permission of Academy of Management, from *The Academy of Management Review*, D.S. Derue, S.J. Ashford, vol. 35, no. 4, © 2010; permission conveyed through Copyright Clearance Center, Inc.

Claiming behaviors are those that assert a leader or follower identity while granting behaviors are those that bestow a leader or follower identity (DeRue & Ashford, 2010). To complete the claiming or granting process, others must affirm and support the original action. An example of a claiming behavior from a leader might be announcing, "I am in charge of this project," or even the act of taking a prominent seat in a conference room. The process is confirmed with the rest of the team claiming various follower roles by responding, "Yes, you are in charge," taking less prominent seats, or even skipping the meeting. An example of a leader using granting behavior might be a peer delegating the leadership role or saving a seat for the leader (this concludes with the acceptance of the role or seat). During this process, the potential leader/follower must internalize the leader/follower identity, others must recognize the person as a leader/follower, and the organization or collective group must endorse the leadership/followership role.

Activity 2: Claiming and Granting Activity

Claiming and granting behaviors are signals we use to communicate our interest in pursuing leader or follower roles or bestowing those roles on others. Think back to a time when you took on a leadership or followership role. Next, categorize the behaviors you enacted and those enacted by others.

You can include both assigned and emergent leadership opportunities. Note which actions were verbal vs. non-verbal and those that were direct vs. indirect. Once you complete this chart, compare your experiences with a co-worker, friend, or classmate.

"Whomever pulls the sword from the stone will lead this project."

© Cartoon Resource/Shutterstock.com

Role	Leader	Follower
Claim		
Grant		

Activity 2: Learning Outcomes

Recognizing examples of both leader and follower claiming and granting behaviors will allow you to notice and enact these behaviors in the moment. For those seeking opportunities to lead, you may more quickly display the leader-claiming behaviors to solidify your position, while those seeking opportunities to follow may step back to observe leaders or may choose an active follower-claiming behavior to ensure they do not get drafted into a leadership role against their preference.

Leader emergence is often about timing, so building a repertoire of both leader and follower claiming and granting behaviors will help you choose your opportunities in a strategic fashion.

Researchers have found that an individual's leader identity strength may make the difference between leadership training activities being effective or not (Kragt & Guenter, 2018) and the ability for certain leadership competencies to develop in those pursuing leadership opportunities (Kragt & Day, 2020). Thus, enhancing one's leader identity strength is an important component for any emerging leader, especially as they seek to incorporate new knowledge, skills, abilities, and competencies into their leadership toolbox.

Classic Leadership Behavioral Studies

Claiming and granting approaches to leader identity have their root in behavioral theories of leadership. As research into trait theories dwindled (due to the lack of convergence of a particular set of traits that could predict leader effectiveness), researchers began exploring clusters of specific leadership behaviors to predict positive outcomes like productivity and employee satisfaction. The first of these studies categorized leadership behaviors as authoritarian, democratic, or laissez-faire. Future research programs explored task versus people dimensions. The goal of these programs was to gather enough evidence to create a prescriptive behavioral model that could consistently deliver positive results. While this approach was ultimately unsuccessful (there is no list of effective leadership behaviors that will always work regardless of circumstance), behavioral studies still offer instructive findings regarding generally effective behaviors. In the next section, we will describe the different behavioral categories under study and then highlight the applicable aspects of each, as they may be appropriate for your leader identity development.

Lewin, Lippitt, & White (1939) Studies

© Sirisak_baokaew/Shutterstock.com

AUTHORITARIAN:
A leader who is impersonal and dictates the group's activities and eschews participation. (Lewin, Lippett, & White, 1939)

DEMOCRATIC:
A leader who invokes group planning, encourages individual decision making, and fosters an informal and friendly group climate. (Lewin, Lippett, & White, 1939)

LAISSEZ-FAIRE:
A leader who takes a passive stance, leaves all decisions to the group and offers technical advice on request. (Lewin, Lippett, & White, 1939)

One of the first studies to explore the outcomes of leader behavior on group outcomes was conducted by Lewin, Lippitt, & White (1939) (Scheidlinger, 1993). The researchers observed scouts as they worked in groups on crafts. Different types of leaders were assigned to the groups. The scouts encountered all three types of leaders during the experiment, so comparisons were made both between the groups (authoritarian vs. democratic vs. laissez-faire) and within the groups (the same group of scouts but under the authoritarian, democratic, and laissez-faire leaders). The **authoritarian** leader was impersonal, specified how activities were to be done, and discouraged collaboration among the participants. The **democratic** leader encouraged members of the group to help plan how to complete the tasks, invited the members to use their decision-making skills, and created a welcoming and relaxed environment. The **laissez-faire** leader was indifferent and only available to give advice if specifically asked about technical aspects of the activity. Within each group of scouts, a different social climate emerged. The laissez-faire group was significantly less productive than the other groups, while work only continued in the authoritarian group when the leader was present (work ceased when the leader left the room). The authoritarian group members were also either submissive or aggressive towards the authoritarian leader. This was the only group where status differentials and scapegoating activities occurred between the scouts. The democratic group was the most cohesive and preferred group for the scouts. To this day, researchers continue to explore outcomes derived by democratic or participative leaders versus authoritarian leaders, and the findings continue to support the conclusion that individuals seek leaders who will encourage healthy debate amongst group members and enact behaviors they perceive as democratic and fair-minded.

Ohio State and Michigan Studies

As detailed in Chapter 5, the set of studies that generated *behavioral* theories of leadership proposed that leadership behaviors fell into two broad categories: initiating structure and consideration (Ohio State Studies) or employee orientation and production orientation (Michigan Studies). Both sets of studies cataloged the types of behaviors leaders could exhibit in pursuit of productivity and were outgrowths of the authoritarian versus democratic archetypes from the Lewin, Lippitt, and White (1939) studies. Please refer back to your LDBQ results from Chapter 5 to refresh your memory regarding your use of task-focused or employee-focused behaviors.

In general, task-focused behaviors require planning, clarification of expectations, and controlling behaviors (i.e., monitoring how things are proceeding). Employee-focused or relation-based behaviors are centered on providing encouragement, finding support, recognizing effective performance, and empowering individuals to make their own decisions. While these dimensions are often thought of as independent, the research clearly shows that both types of behaviors have a positive relationship with follower outcomes, and there is no clear "winner" between one type or the other. Interestingly, recent research into the differences between *management* and *leadership* seems to suggest that task-focused behaviors like organizing and supervising are perceived as management activities while motivating and coaching are associated more strongly with leadership (Kniffin et al., 2020). Enacting behaviors from both categories is integral to the success of an organization. However, "leadership" behaviors are overwhelmingly desired more by followers, which leads to preferences in hiring individuals with leadership skill sets, even when the job description requires more management skills. In a follow-up study, researchers were able to overcome this problem by requiring the participants to engage in forced deliberation. This slowed down their decision-making, and in turn, a preference for management-focused behaviors increased. (Kniffin et al., 2020).

We should keep in mind the breadth of behaviors required for successful organizational outcomes and seek to reward individuals who have experience deploying a range of behaviors, not just those that focus on leadership activities. It may take extra effort to recognize which positions require management skills and to evaluate candidates on these less flashy behaviors, but the overall success of the organization is worth these steps. Once again, we should acknowledge the tendency for individuals to romanticize leadership. We should also recognize the extra effort needed to avoid this perceptual error, particularly when a combination of task- and people-oriented behaviors are required.

While the instruments and studies of the behavioral approaches have often been faulted for ignoring the context in which leaders operate, the findings do (with some caveats) generally show positive connections with follower satisfaction and performance, specifically between leaders high in both initiating structure and consideration behaviors (Kerr et al., 1974). Further studies provide evidence of a similar pattern. Leaders who combined employee- and production-oriented behaviors generally oversaw greater productivity in their organizations (Kahn, 1956; Katz et al., 1950; Likert, 1979) and higher follower satisfaction (Morse & Reimer, 1956). More specific findings focus on tension as an important moderator between initiating structure and satisfaction—when time is a factor, followers are more likely to be satisfied with a leader focused on tasks; when time is not a stressor, followers perform better for a more considerate leader. Another important aspect to consider is the nature of the work. If the work is rewarding (the follower feels intrinsically satisfied), the leader's consideration is less important because the follower will self-motivate. As the findings continued to suggest that the strongest performance outcomes were generated by expertise in both task- and people-focused behaviors, Blake and Mouton devised the Managerial Grid™ as a prescriptive approach to leadership development.

Blake and Mouton's Managerial Grid™

Research into the separate dimensions based on tasks/production versus employee focus peaked with the generation of the Managerial Grid™ (Blake & Mouton, 1964; Cai, Fink, & Walker, 2019). As with the prior research, task vs. people behaviors are set on an axis and then graphed according to the extent the behaviors are enacted. Behaviors include the team approach, produce-or-perish management, country club management, middle-of-the-road management, and impoverished management. As depicted in Figure 3, the amount of concern for results and/or people will guide the deployment of leadership behaviors. *Team Management* includes behaviors that incentivize members to work together as a unit to reach maximum productivity. *Produce-or-Perish Management* is focused solely on production and strictly enforces rules and deadlines. *Impoverished Management* reflects disengagement and avoidance of any leadership tasks. *Country-Club Management* focuses on the well-being and enjoyment of the employees to the detriment of production. Finally, *Middle-of-the-Road Management* provides structures focused on productivity and completing tasks—but only at a middling level—and some managerial support for employees.

Figure 3: Blake and Mouton Managerial Grid

Blake and Mouton Managerial Grid

- Country Club Management (high concern for people, low task concern)
- Team Management (high concern for people, high task concern)
- Middle of The Road
- Impoverished Management (low concern for people, low task concern)
- Produce-or-Perish Management (low concern for people, high task concern)

Axes: *Concern for people* (Low to High, vertical); *Task Concern* (Low to High, horizontal)

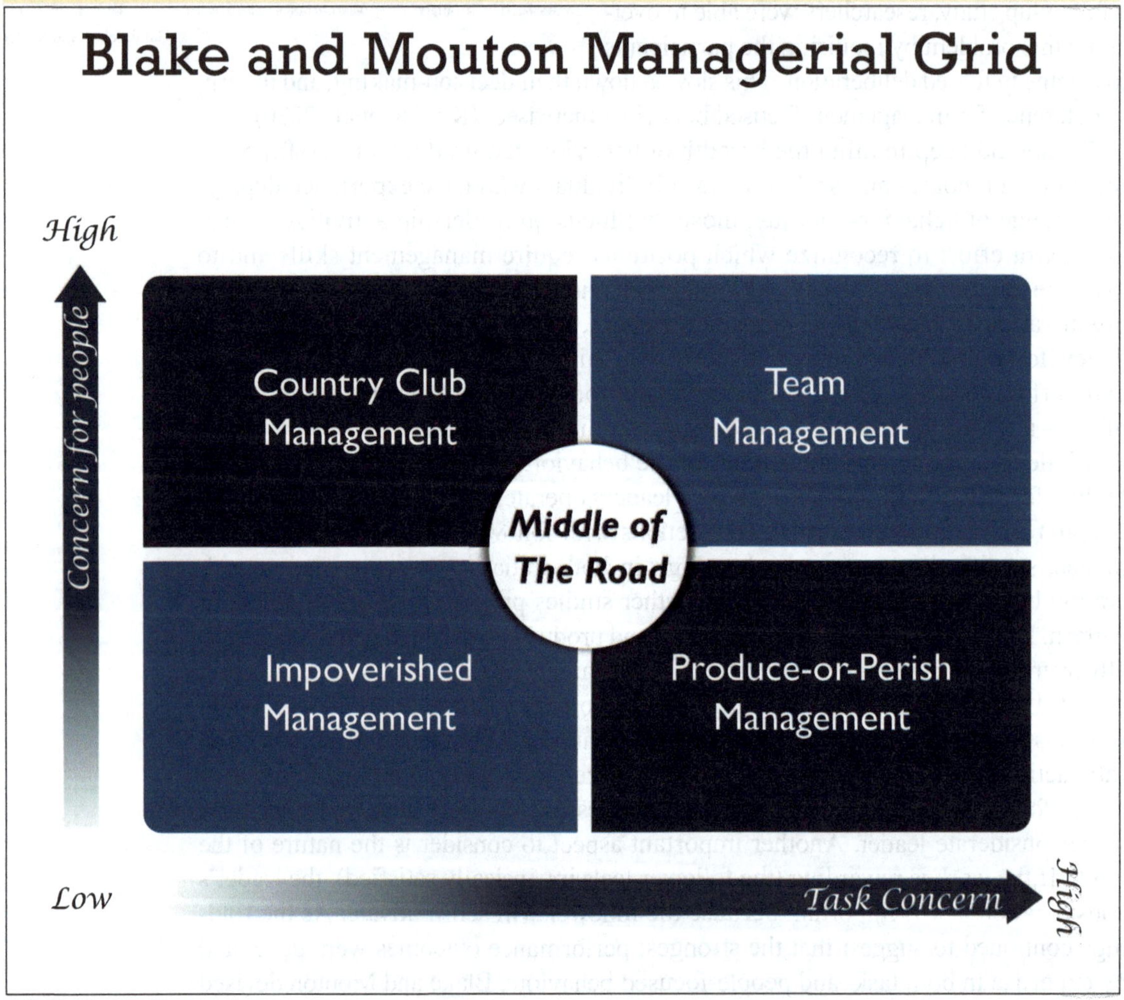

© Skyline Graphics/Shutterstock.com

Activity 3: Managerial Grid Examples

Working together with your peers, find fictional examples of each of these behavioral types. You can use movies, television shows, comedy sketches, books, or other media to illustrate how each archetype might behave. Take 10 minutes to present the example, then discuss it with your classmates to ensure each pattern has a concrete depiction.

Behavioral Types	Examples
Impoverished	
Authority-Compliance	
Country-Club	
Middle of the Road	
Team Leadership	

Activity 3: Learning Outcomes

This activity should give you memorable examples of the managerial behavior approaches highlighted in the grid. While these are prototypes and certainly do not represent all managers who lead with such behaviors, they can give you a sense of how followers respond and what situations may be more appropriate for these approaches.

The simultaneous interrelationships between concern for results and concern for people are the crux of the argument that team management is the "one best way" to lead. However, while the Managerial Grid™ was used extensively in consulting and coaching circumstances, and researchers hypothesized that a team management approach would result in positive outcomes such as increased morale and job satisfaction (Blake & Mouton, 1981), the empirical evidence for the effectiveness of the "one best way to lead" is quite limited. And while the focus for decades centered around the dimensions of task and people, another aspect of leadership behavior that is gaining recognition is the concept of leading change. While an employee or productivity focus is crucial to the success of an organization, it suggests long-term stability. Therefore, recent research expanded the behavioral categories to capture actions required in disrupted or challenging circumstances, acknowledging that certain behaviors are situationally bound.

Leading Change Behaviors

Change-oriented leadership behaviors are enacted in the pursuit of internal and external forces, which demand different approaches to organizational processes. At a time of disruption in traditional business operations, researchers highlighted leadership behaviors that could spark innovation, confront a crisis, or address turmoil (Yukl et al., 2002). The behaviors enacted as part of the "**change-oriented leadership**" grouping included experimentation with new approaches, risk-taking, and fostering creative and innovative thinking. In the initial studies, subordinates rated the leader as more competent when exhibiting change behaviors (Ekvall & Arvonen, 1991). Further studies generated evidence that change-oriented behaviors are necessary for leaders and that these behaviors relate to positive outcomes such

CHANGE-ORIENTED LEADERSHIP: Behaviors focused on innovation of new approaches, risk-taking, and fostering creative and innovative thinking. (Ekvall & Arvonen, 1991)

as organizational commitment and follower satisfaction. Complete the adapted scale in Activity 4 (which includes the change-oriented leadership behaviors along with task-oriented and people-oriented ones).

Activity 4: Complete the Self-Survey

On a scale from 1 (not at all) to 5 (to a great extent), indicate how you use the leader behaviors. Compare your results to the LBDQ that you completed in Chapter 5.

Figure 4: Task-, Relation-, and Change-Oriented Leadership Scale

Behaviour Item and Primary Category

Task-oriented behaviour:
14. Plans in detail how to accomplish an important task or project.
1. Provides a clear explanation of your responsibilities with regard to a task or project.
12. Clearly explains what results are expected for a task or project.
54. Determines what resources are needed to carry out a project.
4. Determines how to organize and co-ordinate work activities to avoid delays, duplication of effort, and wasted resources.
34. Checks work progress against plans to see if it is on target.

Relations-oriented behaviour:
20. Provides encouragement and support when you have a difficult or stressful task.
72. Backs you up and supports you in a difficult situation.
42. Gives you credit for helpful ideas and suggestions
6. Consults with you to get your reactions and suggestions before making a decision that affects you.
22. Provides opportunities to develop your skills and show what you can do.
9. Expresses confidence in your ability to carry out a difficult task.

Change-oriented behaviour:
28. Proposes new and creative ideas for improving products, services, or processes.
52. Is confident and optimistic when proposing a major change.
43. Takes a long-term perspective on problems and opportunities facing the organization.
3. Describes a clear, appealing vision of what the organization can accomplish or become.
35. Negotiates persuasively with people outside the work unit to get agreements or approvals necessary to implement a major change.
32. Studies the products and activities of competitors to get ideas for improving things in his/her organizational unit.

From *European Journal of Work and Organizational Psychology*, VOL. 8, NO. 1 by G. Yukl. Copyright © 1999 by Taylor & Francis. Reprinted by permission. Please note that these items were pulled from a larger scale; thus, the item numbers can be confusing. Please ignore the numbering and complete and score the items per the dimension.

> ### Activity 4: Learning Outcomes
> The adapted leader behavior scale will highlight any change-oriented behaviors you observe in addition to the task vs. people dimensions. Each dimension on the scale has a maximum score of 30. Review the pattern of your scores on the dimensions to increase your self-awareness regarding your usage of these behaviors in your current role.

In Review

This chapter describes your strength of leader identity and the behaviors that you use in leadership opportunities. As we note, your strength of leader identity relates to both your meaning of leader identity and the levels of leader identity. Your leader identity strength will vary based on how much your behaviors reflect your meaning of identity and the progression of your abilities from being driven by individuation or self-interest compared to relating with others or serving a collective entity. Part of your leader identity strength relies upon the ease with which you enact appropriate leader behaviors. The activities and assessments in this chapter are provided to help you visualize certain leader behaviors and to become more aware of those you enact. For example, the leader meter illustrates your gauge of your own leader identity strength and the behaviors you use that serve as the foundation for this measurement. Understanding how you develop and practice those leader behaviors by enacting claiming and granting processes will help you identify opportunities for further development.

While the behavioral theories discussed do not provide a definitive list of effective leader practices, the enactment of leader behaviors over time and in pursuit of different outcomes helps strengthen one's leader identity. The strength of your leader identity can change over time, growing with opportunities or weakening as one experiences obstacles or challenges, as noted with the J-Shaped Development Curve. Concerted efforts to develop your strength of leadership identity can be successful.

The Claiming and Granting activity allows you to practice cataloging leader and follower behaviors and to create clear examples to help with your own leader or follower emergence. This will assist you in recognizing and embracing opportunities in the moment. Being able to anticipate such moments will continue to strengthen your leader identity.

We can look to the behavioral studies of Lewin, Lippitt, and White, the researchers at Ohio State and the University of Michigan, and Blake and Mouton for general approaches that both require task- and people-orientations and have positive impacts on follower and organizational outcomes. The findings show that democratic leadership approaches often reap more positive outcomes than authoritarian or laissez-faire leadership and that a combination of task and people approaches are typically more effective. However, situational constraints do limit the effectiveness of certain behaviors, so leaders must be able to adapt when required.

The next section details Blake and Mouton's Managerial Grid™, which maps prototypical behaviors on two axes: concern for people and concern for results. Each manager "type" illustrates a particular focus, although the research findings using the grid are mixed. Activity 3 asks students to find examples of leaders using prototypical behaviors to illustrate these approaches.

The final concept in this chapter adds the dimension of change-oriented behaviors, where the leader's focus is creating new and innovative approaches for continuous improvement. Activity 4 allows you to rate your own usage of these behaviors compared to task versus relational approaches.

The next chapter will focus on how leaders can develop their skills to better adapt to changing conditions and continue to find ways to be effective. Learning about your own competencies will help you identify areas for continued development and the most impactful behaviors for effective leadership.

Learning Objectives

Determine the strength of your leader identity

Leader identity strength is the extent to which individuals view themselves as leaders. You can gauge your leader identity strength by filling out your leader meter and including the behaviors you enact that build up that strength. You can develop your leader identity strength by seeking out new leadership challenges and learning from your successes and failures. Leader identity strength may fluctuate over time as you lead in new and different situations. Too much or too little leader identity strength can limit your effectiveness in leadership situations.

Summarize claiming and granting behaviors

Claiming behaviors are verbal or nonverbal acts that individuals can use to assert a particular role. Granting behaviors recognize another party's actions to secure those roles. The ongoing process of claiming and granting roles involves interactions between leaders and followers where all involved internalize their roles at the individual level, recognize the others' roles through interpersonal processes, and then collectively endorse each other for those roles. These behaviors may be overt and verbal, such as saying, "I take on this role," or they may be nonverbal and symbolic, such as choosing a specific seat at the table.

Evaluate classical leader behavior studies

The classical leader behavior studies of Lewin, Lippett, and White (1939) compared outcomes for authoritarian, democratic, and laissez-faire leaders. The findings showed the most positive outcomes for the democratic groups, where the participants felt cohesive and preferred to work under this particular leader. The laissez-faire group was the least productive, and there were mixed results for the authoritarian group. The Ohio State and Michigan studies evaluated the effectiveness of task-focused versus people-focused behaviors. Overall, there was a preference for leaders who combined both behaviors.

Describe the Blake and Mouton Managerial Grid™

The leadership grid maps out five managerial prototypes across the dimensions of concern for results and concern for people. Each type of leader has a particular focus and enacts behaviors toward expected outcomes. Managers who show low levels of people- and results- focused behaviors are "impoverished," those focused mainly on results are "authority-compliance," those who are people-focused are "country-club managers," those with some level of both are "middle of the road," and those who excel on both dimensions are "team managers". While the managerial grid is quite popular, the findings remain mixed as certain situations may require one focus at the expense of the other.

Key Terms

Leader Identity Strength (Pg. 120)

Claiming (Pg. 122)

Granting (Pg. 122)

Authoritarian (Pg. 124)

Democratic (Pg. 124)

Laissez-Faire (Pg. 124)

Change-oriented leadership (Pg. 127)

Critical Thinking Questions

1. In your own words, describe leader identity strength. Give examples of times you have worked with someone who has a high leader identity strength. What are some examples of their behaviors? Give examples of times you have worked with someone who has a low leader identity strength. How could you help them develop?

2. Have you felt your leader identity strength fluctuate over time? What conditions caused your identity strength to build or weaken? How can you work with a follower experiencing the J-shaped development curve with their leader identity strength?

3. What leader and follower claiming and granting behaviors do you use? How do you communicate to others your preference for a particular role? How do you grant role-taking to others? In the workforce, how do you ensure that a broad array of individuals have the opportunity to embrace leadership roles?

4. While the findings of the classic behavioral studies are mixed, what do you feel are the most important discoveries from these lines of research? What themes can you adopt from these studies to assist your own leadership development?

References

Blake, R.R., & Mouton, J.S. (1981). "Management by Grid® principles or situationalism: Which?" *Group & Organization Management*, 6(4), 439–455.

Cai, D. A., Fink, E. L., & Walker, C. B. (2019). Robert R. Blake, With Recognition of Jane S. Mouton. *Negotiation and Conflict Management Research*.

DeRue, D. S. (2011). Adaptive leadership theory: Leading and following as a complex adaptive process. *Research in organizational behavior*, *31*, 125–150.

DeRue, D. S., & Ashford, S. J. (2010). Who will lead and who will follow? A social process of leadership identity construction in organizations. *Academy of management review*, *35*(4), 627–647.

Dragoni, Oh, I.-S., Vankatwyk, P., & Tesluk, P. E. (2011). Developing executive leaders: The relative contribution of cognitive ability, personality, and the accumulation of work experience in predicting strategic thinking competency. *Personnel psychology*, 64(4), 829–864. Https://doi.org/10.1111/j.1744-6570.2011.01229.x

Ekvall, G., & Arvonen, J. (1991). Change-centered leadership: An extension of the two-dimensional model. *Scandinavian Journal of Management*, 7(1), 17–26.

Hammond, M., Clapp-Smith, R., & Palanski, M. (2017). Beyond (just) the workplace: A theory of leader development across multiple domains. *Academy of Management Review*, 42(3), 481–498.

Kahn, R. L. (1956). The prediction of productivity. *Journal of Social Issues*, 12(2), 41–49.

Katz, D., Maccoby, N., & Morse, N. C. (1950). Productivity, supervision, and morale in an office situation. Part I. Institute for Social Research. University of Michigan. Ann Arbor: MI.

Kerr, S., Schriesheim, C. A., Murphy, C. J., & Stogdill, R. M. (1974). Toward a contingency theory of leadership based upon the consideration and initiating structure literature. *Organizational Behavior and Human Performance*, 12(1), 62–82.

Kniffin, Detert, J. R., & Leroy, H. L. (2020). On Leading and Managing: Synonyms or Separate (and Unequal)? *Academy of Management Discoveries*, 6(4), 544–571. https://doi.org/10.5465/amd.2018.0227

Kragt, D., & Day, D. V. (2020). Predicting leadership competency development and promotion among high-potential executives: The role of leader identity. *Frontiers in Psychology*, 1816.

Kragt, D., & Guenter, H. (2018). Why and when leadership training predicts effectiveness: The role of leader identity and leadership experience. *Leadership & Organization Development Journal*.

Lanaj, K., Gabriel, A. S., & Chawla, N. (2021). The self-sacrificial nature of leader identity: Understanding the costs and benefits at work and home. *Journal of Applied Psychology*, 106(3), 345.

Lanka, E., Topakas, A., & Patterson, M. (2020). Becoming a leader: Catalysts and barriers to leader identity construction. *European Journal of Work and Organizational Psychology*, 29(3), 377–390.

Lewin, K., Lippitt, R., & White, R. K. (1939). Patterns of aggressive behavior in experimentally created "social climates". *The Journal of Social Psychology*, 10(2), 269–299.

Likert, R. (1979). From production-and employee-centeredness to systems 1-4. *Journal of Management*, 5(2), 147–156.

Miscenko, D., Guenter, H., & Day, D. V. (2017). Am I a leader? Examining leader identity development over time. *The Leadership Quarterly*, 28(5), 605–620.

Morse, N. C., and Reimer, E. (1956). The experimental change of a major organizational variable. *Journal of Abnormal and Social Psychology,* 52(1), 120–129.

Scheidlinger, S. (1994). The Lewin, Lippitt and White study of leadership and "social climates" revisited. *International Journal of Group Psychotherapy, 44*(1), 123–127.

Skinner, S. (2020). An empirical investigation of leader identity formation and implications for executive coaching and leadership development. *Philosophy of Coaching: An International Journal, 5*(2), 18–39.

Yukl, G. (1999). An evaluative essay on current conceptions of effective leadership. *European Journal of Work and Organizational Psychology, 8*(1), 33–48.

Yukl, G., Gordon, A., & Taber, T. (2002). A hierarchical taxonomy of leadership behavior: Integrating a half century of behavior research. *Journal of Leadership & Organizational Studies, 9*(1), 15–32.

Zheng, W., & Muir, D. (2015). Embracing leadership: A multi-faceted model of leader identity development. *Leadership & Organization Development Journal.*

CHAPTER 8

Competency and Skills-Based Theories

CHAPTER OUTCOMES

1. Define competence and competence models
2. Evaluate management systems theory
3. Explain the skills-based model of leadership
4. Assess your leadership skills

Purpose of This Chapter

This chapter focuses on the competencies of effective leaders and the leadership skills model. We define competencies and discuss how individuals can acquire and hone capabilities as part of their development. We describe Management Systems Theory (Likert, 1961; 1967; 1979) and the Skills-Based Model of Leadership (Mumford et al., 2000). We end the chapter by describing practical methods you can use to develop specific leadership skills, such as influence tactics, political skills, and negotiation skills. You will also learn how to connect these skills with the strength of your leader identity.

What Are Competencies?

Competence is the ability to interact effectively with one's environment (White, 1959). Competencies include knowledge, skills, or abilities that allow an individual to perform appropriately within a specific context. Competencies prove to be adaptable and agile, which is particularly important given the increasingly complex business environment. In the Iceberg Model illustrated in Figure 1, knowledge and skills sit at the top of the iceberg. They are seen as easier to change and more dependent upon conditions. The competencies below the surface, such as self-image and traits, are more difficult to change and slower to adapt to the environment. We've discussed in previous chapters how self-awareness regarding your traits, motives, and self-image is imperative to understanding how you can enact effective leadership behaviors. This chapter highlights capabilities like knowledge and skills—both of which are extremely likely to benefit from focused developmental efforts.

A **competency model** is a descriptive approach that specifies the requisite capabilities an individual needs to perform effectively on assigned tasks. Examining leadership

COMPETENCE: The ability to interact effectively with one's environment. (White, 1959)

COMPETENCY MODEL: A descriptive tool to ascertain the interconnected skills, knowledge, personal characteristics, and behaviors needed to effectively perform a task. (Lucia & Lepsinger, 1999)

Chapter 8: Competency and Skills-Based Theories

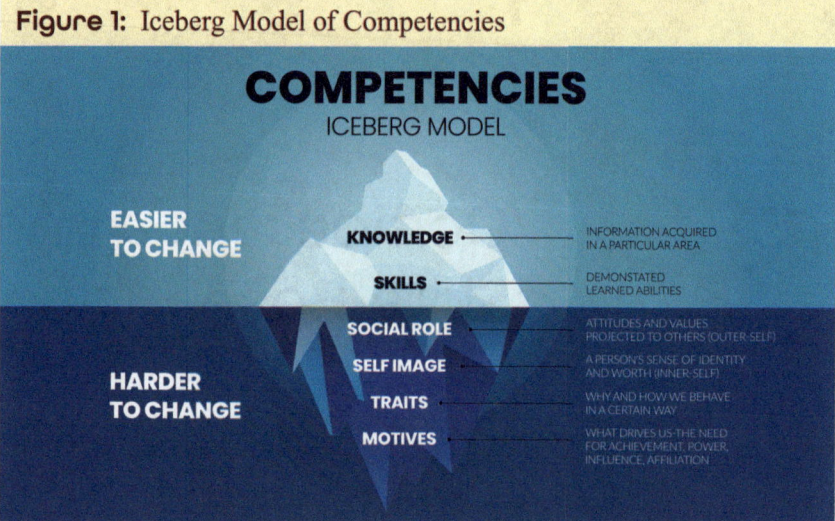

Figure 1: Iceberg Model of Competencies

from a competency model approach—regardless of the industry—uncovers certain knowledge, skills, and abilities necessary for successful performance.

Leadership competency models begin by establishing a clear understanding of the leadership performance requirements. Next, they define the knowledge and skills needed to deliver on those requirements. Leadership competencies are developable abilities that help leaders enact effective performance. To be successful, leaders should employ complex problem-solving skills, generate solutions, and possess the necessary social judgment to know when and how to use their competencies (Mumford et al., 2000). Experiences, education, and exposure to different people, processes, and organizations allow these capabilities to develop. Traits and personality factors can certainly impact the ease with which capabilities develop—however, the acquisition of such skills is open to anyone willing to deploy the skills when a leadership opportunity arises. We present these "competency models," exemplified by management systems theory (Likert, 1961; 1967) and the skills-based model of leadership (Mumford, Zaccaro, Harding, Jacobs & Fleishman, 2000).

Management Systems Theory

The interest in leadership skills grew out of the Michigan Leadership Studies, which we discussed in Chapter 7. Likert and colleagues (1961; 1967) began to explore beyond a production vs. employee orientation to examine the management approaches within different organizational systems and performance levels. In summarizing the results from a decade of studies across industries, Likert recognized that skill and outcome patterns aligned with different management approaches. These patterns were then labeled **Management Systems 1-4** (summarized in Table 1). Managers and leaders at the highest-performing organizations approached their work in a much more participative manner (System 4). On the other hand, organizations focused on earnings and productivity exhibited exploitive and authoritative skill deployment (System 1), resulting in decreased productivity and undesirable employee outcomes. This pattern held even in organizations that were initially high-performing but then experienced pressure for better financial results.

MANAGEMENT SYSTEMS THEORY: "An orderly, systematic relationship among all the different variables that are important in the management of human resources." (Likert, 1979)

Chapter 8: Competency and Skills-Based Theories

Table 1: Management Systems 1-4

System	Title	Description
1	Exploitive-Authoritative	• Mediocre productivity • Pure economic focus • Coercive power • Decision-making power concentrated at the highest levels • Distrust among employees • General dissatisfaction • Downward communication • High turnover
2	Benevolent-Authoritative	• Fair to good productivity • Economic and status focus • Balanced reward and coercive power • Policy decisions made at the top; other decision-making power exists at the appropriate level • Frequent conflict between employees • Moderate dissatisfaction to moderate satisfaction • Mostly downward communication • Moderately high turnover
3	Consultative	• Good productivity • Economic, status, and innovation focus • Predominant use of reward power • Broad policy decisions are made at the top; other decision-making occurs at lower and mid-levels • Some conflict among employees • Some dissatisfaction to moderately high satisfaction • Downward and upward communication • Moderate turnover
4	Participative	• Excellent productivity • Economic, status, innovation, and group focus • Reward and referent power • Little conflict—employees motivated collectively toward goals • Decision-making takes place throughout the firm at the appropriate level • Relatively high satisfaction • Downward, upward, and peer-to-peer communication • Low turnover

Source: Gretchen Vogelgesang Lester and Paul Lester

To illustrate the different management systems, imagine an organization producing an excellent product or service—so excellent that it draws attention from investors. A participative system of management in this organization drives productivity and innovation. However, as investors begin to examine the "fundamentals" of the firm, they might question how decisions are being made and resources are being used and then narrow

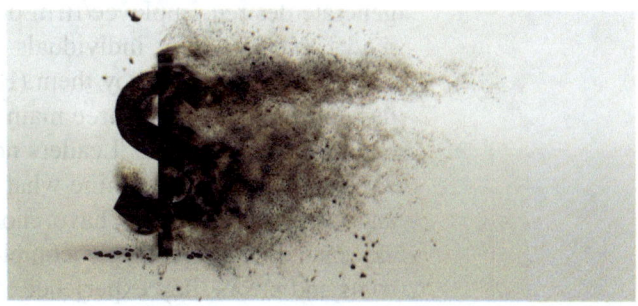
© Oliver Denker/Shutterstock.com

the focus to the firm's earnings and operating costs. This fixation on financials incentivizes the firm's leadership to explore cost-cutting measures. Through this process, the participative approach to management declines—decision-making is centralized, and staff is reduced to boost earnings. The cost-cutting measures and decision-making approaches hollow out the employee focus, stunt innovation, and ultimately lead to worse performance. This downward spiral compels leaders to become even more authoritative and punitive, generating even lower productivity. It's a cycle that can be summed up by paraphrasing a popular movie quote: The more management tightens its grip, the more the positive organizational returns slip through its fingers (Lucas, 1977).

While Likert's work in the 1960s and 1970s predicted this detrimental cycle, organizations continue to make the same mistakes. Recent evidence points to CEOs with MBAs as contributing to this negative environment (Miller & Xu, 2019). A recent working paper by Acemoglu, le Maire, and He (2022) surmises that the focus on maximizing shareholder value—coupled with lean management practices popularized in the late 1970s—promotes the view that investing in employees/human capital are superfluous costs. This approach is institutionalized in certain business schools, management consulting firms, and the evaluation of economic returns by investors and analysts. As MBAs move into executive positions in global organizations and stock prices continue to rise (with shareholders enjoying high returns), the turnover of high-performing employees increases, and overall wages decrease (Acemoglu et al., 2022).

Likert (1961; 1967) instead recommended that firms continue investing in their human capital and training their leaders to use System 4 participative approaches to boost productivity. Perhaps it is time to review these seminal studies and approaches to management. What if we broaden the current economic view of the firm to include a focus on employees and participation described by System 4 management? If some MBAs continue to focus on maximizing shareholder wealth, others can increase the focus on leadership skill acquisition to develop their employees and spur productivity.

Skills-Based Model of Leader Performance

The management systems approach presents a coordinated organizational structure to facilitate better communication, productivity, and performance. Inherent in the system is the ability of managers and leaders to adapt their skills to generate desired employee/firm outcomes. Furthering this idea, the skills-based model explores how individuals adopt new capabilities and determine when, where, and how to deploy them (House & Howell, 1992; Mumford, 1986). Skills development occurs in three main areas: problem-solving skills, social judgment skills, and social skills. Leaders not only define the problems facing the organization—they also determine what information is required to solve the problems and evaluate when they have enough information to make decisions. As leaders encounter increasingly complex problems, they gain wisdom through the trials and errors they experience. As they see different solutions succeed or fail, social judgment develops. Social skills are sharpened as they observe varying motivational tools that aid in solution implementation.

The types of skills and how quickly they develop depend on the experience level of the leader, traits, and motivation toward development. Novice leaders have expertise and social judgment challenges—they may not be able to define the problems facing the organization, and they may not know the abilities of their followers or the limits of their own knowledge. Contrastingly, expert leaders—with the benefit of experience and maturity—most likely have encountered similar problems in the past, have a deep knowledge of their followers' skill sets, and have self-awareness regarding their own limits. Thus, expert leaders adapt and quickly deploy the necessary skills to solve complex and unique problems (Mumford et al., 2000). Skill adoption can be accelerated due to traits such as intelligence (Mumford et al., 2000). Other characteristics (such as motivation to lead) can also assist in leadership skills acquisition. The skills you acquire can have a measurable impact on your leader identity strength.

Activity 1: Leadership Identity Strength—Identity Circles

For this activity, let's visualize your leader identity strength on a continuum from novice to expert. The image below is of nine stages of an eclipse. Picture your identity as the sun and your leader identity as the moon moving into that sun in front of the sun to create an eclipse. The letter "A" represents a novice leader, where the leader identity is completely separate from the individual identity, as the moon is not visible in that picture. The letter "I" represents an expert leader, where the leader identity is the individual's identity, and the moon completely eclipses the sun. Thinking through the capabilities discussed in management systems and the skills-based theory of leader development, choose the image that best represents the space/overlap between the leader identity and your self-identity.

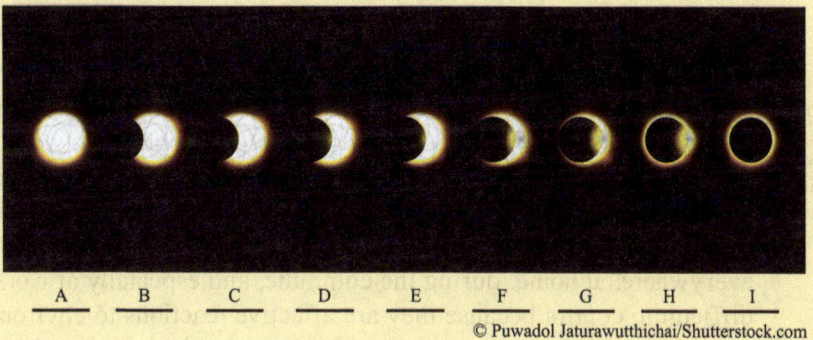

© Puwadol Jaturawutthichai/Shutterstock.com

Once you have chosen the letter that best represents the space/overlap between your self-identity and a leader identity, reflect on your selection:

- Write down why you selected this degree of overlap.
- Document the skills shared between the leader identity and your self-identity.
- Identify the skills you would like to adopt to move towards a stronger leader identity.

Activity 1: Learning Outcomes

Visualizing the overlap between your self-identity and your leader identity may also reflect your motivation to lead and your overall leader identity strength. It may show you areas for opportunity or growth or may indicate that your leader identity strength is quite strong (maybe even too strong). As noted in Chapter 7, those with little to no leader identity strength may not benefit from development opportunities, and those with too much may find they enact self-sacrificial behaviors or have work-life conflict.

Often, our leadership skills coalesce around two basic questions. First, in what ways are you able to make connections with people in the workplace? (This varies—for example, some may use humor while others rely on sincerity or affability.) Second, because the workplace can be stressful and emotions are likely to emerge at predictable or random times, are you able to "read the room" and adapt your approach based on your interpretation of the emotions? Below, we describe two competencies that help you do so.

Social Intelligence

SOCIAL INTELLIGENCE: The ability to perceive what is occurring between people (i.e., between leader and followers) and then adapting one's behavior to fit the needs of the group. (Zaccaro et al., 1991)

According to Steve Zaccaro and coauthors (1991), socially intelligent leaders have two important competencies: social perceptiveness and behavioral flexibility. They state that "[l]eaders are able to ascertain demands, requirements, and affordances in organizational problem scenarios and tailor their responses accordingly" (p. 317). In other words, socially intelligent leaders can perceive what is happening at the interpersonal level, then adapt their behaviors to fit the needs of the group *at that time*. The social intelligence concept was extended further to include a range of social traits, including sociability, communication style, empathy, sensitivity, and tact—all of which are backed by considerable research (Bass & Bass, 2008). Each of these helps leaders make connections with their followers, and as that connection grows, they are, in turn, better suited to interpret follower emotions and consequently adjust.

Emotional Intelligence

EMOTIONAL INTELLIGENCE: A set of skills hypothesized to contribute to the accurate appraisal and expression of emotion in oneself and in others, the effective regulation of emotion in self and others, and the use of feelings to motivate, plan, and achieve in one's life. (Salovey & Mayer, 1990)

As described throughout this text, our identity as leaders is shaped not only by what we think about ourselves but by how we *feel* about ourselves (in other words, the emotions engendered when leading). We often hear leaders say they wish people would "check their emotions at the door" before reporting to work. After all, emotions are messy—Both a quick-tempered boss or a sensitive coworker who tears up at the first sign of criticism create discomfort for others. But omitting emotions from the workplace is unrealistic, as they have no boundaries. You feel emotions everywhere: at home, during the commute, and especially at work. Emotions are difficult to control because they are affective reactions to environmental stimuli. They are "hot" reactions, meaning they occur quickly and without much thought

© Rei Imagine/Shutterstock.com

(as opposed to "cold" cognitions, such as when you think and deliberate carefully before making an important decision). Being able to control and direct emotions in the workplace is considered a *Holy Grail* for leaders because emotions channeled in a positive way can do a lot of good.

Building on some of the themes from social intelligence, Daniel Goleman is largely credited for ushering in the popularity of emotional intelligence. According to Goleman (2004), emotionally intelligent leaders show five key traits: self-awareness, self-regulation, motivation, empathy, and social skills.

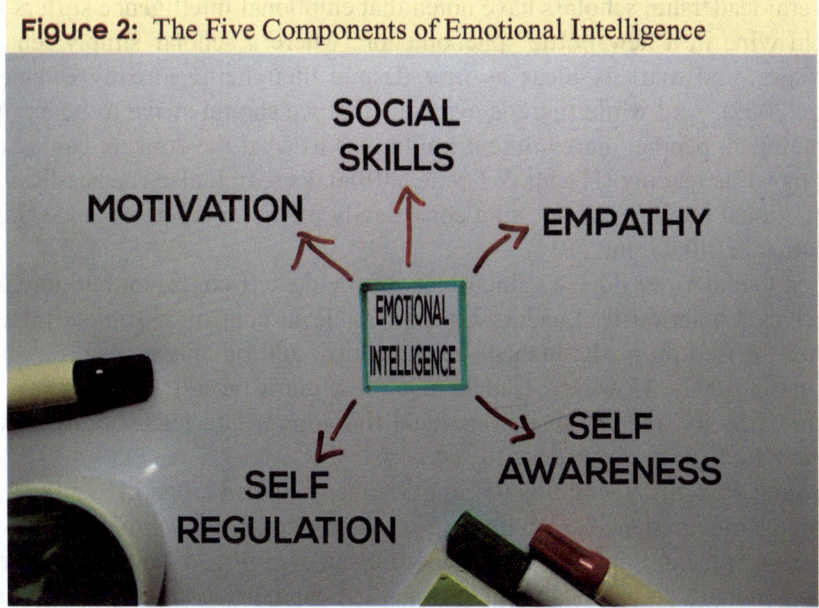

Figure 2: The Five Components of Emotional Intelligence

© bangoland/Shutterstock.com

Self-Awareness is the ability to recognize and understand your moods, emotions, and drives, as well as their effect on others. **Self-Regulation** is the ability to control or direct disruptive impulses and moods and the control to suspend judgment and to think before acting. **Motivation** is the passion to work for reasons that go beyond money or status and the propensity to pursue goals with energy and persistence. **Empathy** is the ability to understand the emotional makeup of other people and treat people according to their emotional reactions. **Social Skill** is proficiency in managing relationships and building networks, plus an ability to find common ground and build rapport.

There is little question that all of these are admirable qualities, and there is research showing that each helps leaders in a variety of ways (Harms & Credé, 2010a). However, a meta-analysis of 62 studies between emotional intelligence, transformational and transactional leader behaviors generated interesting findings. The hypothesis presumed emotionally intelligent leaders would enact more relational (transformational) leader behaviors than directive (transactional) leader behaviors. The initial results found a modest relationship between emotional intelligence and transformational leadership; however, the relationship practically disappeared when they accounted for who completed the survey. In other words, when you ask leaders if they are both emotionally intelligent and utilize transformational leadership behaviors (inspiring, motivating, and developing close relationships with followers), the scores are high. Conversely, when leaders reported their own emotional intelligence while followers *also* rated the leader behaviors, the scores were much lower. In a follow-up paper, the same authors (Harms & Credé, 2010b) added the Big Five personality factors into their study and found that when they did so, emotional intelligence assessments provided by leaders were not at all related to how followers rated their leaders' behavior. In other words, these researchers could not find a relationship between a leader's emotional intelligence and the type of behaviors they enact as leaders—at least through the eyes of followers.

Several leadership scholars have noted that emotional intelligence suffers from the "old wine in a new bottle" phenomenon, where a scholar simply renames, repackages, and markets ideas as new despite their being already established (Locke, 2005). And while there is evidence that we should strive to be emotionally intelligent people, there are real limitations to what the concept can actually do for us while leading (Harms & Credé, 2010a). Research also repeatedly shows that emotional intelligence does not consistently predict job performance (Joseph & Newman, 2010; Grant, 2014)

Taken together, we do see value in leaders being self-confident but not taking themselves too seriously. Leaders should be able to control disruptive impulses and stay focused on goals, manage relationships, and be able to read emotional reactions in others. However, leaders also must mesh these traits with what the situation calls for and be able to marshal the appropriate leadership behaviors necessary for their organizations to succeed.

Organizations that recognize the importance of leadership skill acquisition as an outcome of experience are deliberate about creating both technical and professional developmental assignments. According to *Training*, a trade magazine for HR professionals, companies spent between 25% and 30% of their entire training budget on leadership training over the last decade (Leimbach, 2021). However, deployment of resources throughout organizations is not always equitable or available to all employees. In Chapter 11, we present approaches for self-development of leadership capabilities. Skills develop as a function of proficiency, so individuals can target opportunities for leadership deployment. To acquire new skills, you must put yourself in the right position to gain experience, model the behaviors of others, and have the opportunity to practice the skills and learn from both success and failure. Recognizing the skills you plan to adopt is the first step toward strengthening your leader identity.

© garagestock/Shutterstock.com

Skill Development

It can take years—decades, even—to acquire the complex leadership skills required for expert leaders to effect positive performance. Some researchers suggest it can take at least ten years, and most likely more, to become proficient at deploying the appropriate skills at the optimal time. The types of skills required for effective leadership—such as communication and interpersonal skills, team skills, and problem-solving skills—require a "whole person learning" approach. This involves emotional, cognitive, and behavioral resources (Hoover, Giambatista, Sorenson, & Bommer, 2010). Another integral aspect to skill development is that it must be learner-driven to be effective (Cranton, 1994). One must be highly involved in their learning process, use goal-setting techniques, access support systems, and receive feedback throughout the skill development process.

Next, we will look at skills that consistently relate to positive leadership performance: decision-making skills, influence tactics, political skills, and negotiation skills. While we note that these skills contribute to leadership effectiveness, this is by no means an exhaustive list. New technologies, ways of working, and unique problems require unique skills. Understanding how leaders can acquire new skills to further their development is a valuable skill in itself.

Decision-Making

Those who claim leadership positions or are granted leadership authority are often decision-makers. Leaders decide the direction of the organization and must influence others to accept decisions and move forward. Likert (1971; 1967) posited that followers would buy into the decisions if they had a chance to participate in the process. The **Normative Decision-Making Model**, by Vroom and colleagues, focuses attention on the type of problem (Vroom & Yetton, 1973). Different types of problems require varying levels of participation, and higher participation often requires more time to come to a decision. The time available for the decision-making process and the opportunity for follower development—other factors included in this model—increase the complexity of this approach. Figure 2 highlights the five different actions leaders may take regarding the involvement of followers in the decision-making process. Autocratic (A1) actions can be taken in problem sets where the leader has the required information, and the team trusts the leader, and follower commitment is not necessary. The leader makes the decision quickly and without input from others. The graphic shows the leader communicating the decision to the team. Autocratic (A2) actions require the leader to gather more information from the team, but the final decision is still solely made by the leader. The graphic indicates the circular flow of information. Consultative (C1) actions include the leader meeting individually with followers to gather intelligence and opinions, but then the leader makes the final decision. The graphic indicates that while the leader consults individually, they still are responsible for the overall solution. Consultative (C2) actions include larger group discussions and brainstorming for solutions, but decision-making authority is still with the leader. The graphic suggests a conference call or webinar for interactive discussion. Finally, collaborative (G2) actions include large group dialogues where the leader facilitates the process toward a final decision.

Figure 3: Vroom-Yetton Decision Model

© Skyline Graphics/Shutterstock.com

NORMATIVE DECISION-MAKING MODEL: A model that specifies the process by which leaders come to solutions by structuring problems in a systematic way. (Vroom & Jago, 1988)

Each successive action set takes more time, drives different levels of commitment, and requires different knowledge bases. The leader must keep in mind which choices should drive the intended outcomes (Vroom, 2003). If a problem comes up that is fairly routine, does not require follower buy-in for the decision, and the leader has the knowledge to solve the issue, then A1 is the optimal action. But if a unique problem comes up that requires special knowledge and will take a major effort of time and engagement to solve, G2 is the correct approach—this way, the leader can uncover as much intelligence as possible and create enthusiasm for implementing the agreed-upon solution. This is a simplified description of normative decision-making. Advanced versions use computer programs with algorithms to help guide leaders through the decision-making process (such as https://www.decisionmakingforleaders.com/, which can be accessed for a fee). The strength of this approach is that it focuses on the problem as the unit of analysis and considers the advantages/drawbacks of enlisting participation through the decision-making process (Vroom, 2003). Yes, you can enroll in a training program specifically designed to use the normative approach. But this skill can also be learned through thoughtful reflection on your own previous problems and reflection on the requirements, steps taken, and outcomes that will better prepare you for future challenges.

Influence Tactics and Power

INFLUENCE TACTICS: Behaviors directed towards others that individuals use to gain compliance, resources, or affirmations from others in the workplace. (Smith et al., 2013)

As noted throughout this text, leadership is an influence process whereby a leader persuades followers to aid in the achievement of some goal. **Influence tactics** are an integral part of this persuasion process. Influence can be directed in multiple directions in an organization: upward appeals (aimed at supervisors and those higher in the chain of command), lateral appeals (aimed at peers), and downward appeals (aimed at those lower in rank). Leaders can wield these appeals in a variety of ways to create commitment, compliance, or resistance (Yukl, 1989). **Commitment** infers that influence tactics have aroused emotion towards completing the goal. **Compliance** results in task completion without enthusiasm. **Resistance** generates opposition. The difference in a leader's skill level can also determine the outcome. For example, an individual using ingratiation in a skilled manner may gain compliance through flattery because the target may not recognize the influence. Another individual may be obvious in their ingratiation, creating resistance. An effective or ineffective use of influence tactics will make the difference between success and failure.

Table 2 presents the most commonly employed influence tactics observed in organizations (Schriesheim & Hinkin, 1990; Falbe & Yukl, 2001; Kipnis, Schmidt, & Wilkinson, 1980; Smith et al., 2013). These tactics can be used to ensure follower commitment to organizational goals, arrange or avoid work, and pursue organizational advancement (among many other organizational goals). The tactics are typically combined, particularly by those capable of deploying them to achieve desired outcomes. There are also implications based on sex and minority status in the usage of these influence tactics, where some individuals may be more successful in using tactics such as assertiveness or sanctions, while others may be expected to use tools like collaboration or exchange to achieve commitment.

Table 2: Common Influence Tactics and Typical Outcomes

Tactic	Description	Power Base(s)	Example	Outcome(s)
Inspirational Appeals	Goal alignment with followers' beliefs creates enthusiasm for goals	Referent Legitimate	A manager assigns an employee to a Corporate Social Responsibility (CSR) project because of their interest in the topic.	Commitment
Consultation	Followers' advice is requested in pursuit of shared goals	Expert Legitimate	A manager seeks the assistance of a follower due to prior expertise.	Commitment

Chapter 8: Competency and Skills-Based Theories   145

Tactic	Description	Power Base(s)	Example	Outcome(s)
Rational Persuasion	Facts and reasonableness convince followers to assist in the pursuit of goals	Expert Information	A department manager explains the reasons behind a procedural change.	Commitment Compliance
Ingratiation	Aid is cajoled from followers through flattery	Reward Coercive	An employee fawns over their manager's credentials.	Compliance Resistance
Personal Appeals	Personal connections to powerful others pressure followers to help pursue goals	Legitimate Reward Coercive	A manager reminds subordinates that upper management is invested in the goal.	Compliance Resistance
Exchange Tactics	Transactional approaches enlist the followers in pursuing the goals	Legitimate Reward	An employee offers to cover one shift in exchange for another.	Commitment Compliance
Assertiveness/ Pressure Tactics	Rewards or coercion enlist the assistance of followers	Reward Coercive Legitimate	A project manager sets an aggressive due date for an assignment.	Compliance Resistance
Legitimating Tactics	Position of power requires followers to assist in pursuing the goals	Legitimate	A project manager reminds followers of what is in their employment contract.	Compliance Resistance
Coalition	Others' commitment to help pressures followers to assist in pursuing the goals	Reward Coercive Legitimate	A manager reminds the employees that everyone is counting on each team member to do their part.	Compliance Resistance
Intimidation/ Sanctions	Threats or authority used to force followers to assist	Coercive	A manager reminds employees that their jobs are in danger if they do not complete the work.	Compliance Resistance
Self-Promotion	Advocating for oneself by highlighting achievements to peers and managers	Expert Coercive	An employee reminding a manager of their excellence on a project.	Commitment Compliance Resistance
Supplication	Feigning incompetence to enlist the help of others to complete a task	Referent	To avoid a task, an employee tells coworkers that the new software package is impossible to learn.	Compliance Resistance
Apprising	Explaining how working together will assist the follower	Referent Coercive Reward	A manager tells an employee that this particular project will look good on their resume.	Commitment Compliance
Exemplification	Sacrifices personal well-being to arouse guilt in others so they will contribute	Referent	An employee works over the weekend; team members then stay late to match commitment.	Commitment Compliance Resistance
Collaboration	Offering assistance in exchange for aid	Referent Reward Coercive	A manager jumps in to help others during busy times.	Commitment Compliance

Source: Gretchen Vogelgesang Lester and Paul Lester

Figure 4: French and Raven's Organizational Power Bases

© Kheng Guan Toh/Shutterstock.com

POLITICAL SKILL: The ability to effectively understand others at work, and to use such knowledge to influence others to act in ways that enhance one's personal and/or organizational objectives. (Ferris et al., 2005)

Organizational dynamics instill influence automatically based on position, but even leaders without formal role authority can use influence tactics to build momentum toward goals. French and Raven (1959) defined organizational power as it relates to five different sources (depicted in Figure 3). **Reward power** arises from an individual's ability to bestow compensation and incentives. **Coercive power** is the capability to threaten others with negative outcomes. **Legitimate power** accompanies a specific position in an organization. (These first three powers exist within the organization and rely upon roles and responsibilities, not necessarily leadership ability.) **Expert power** arises from one's knowledge or wisdom in a specific area. **Referent power** exists when followers trust and like the leader, increasing their willingness to act. (Expert and referent power are seen as personal qualities that can exist regardless of one's position or role in an organization.)

There is one more power: **information power**. This distinct attribute manifests because of one's personal network and their access to intelligence that is not readily available to others (Raven, 1965). The expected result from the use of power and influence is a major determinant of how the leader chooses to exercise these skills (Kipnis, et al., 1980). Context is also important. Some types of influence and power are effective in person; others may be more applicable in a virtual setting. We recommend practicing the influence tactics that typically result in commitment or compliance—taking into account the desired outcomes, context of the situation, and the type(s) of power available to the influencer.

Political Skill

Political skill describes how leaders perceive others and wield their influence to achieve organizational effectiveness (Treadway et al., 2002). Leaders who possess political skills figure out what needs to be done and then execute a plan to do it. Political skill is not a trait or cognitive ability—it can be developed through formal and informal leadership experiences (Treadway et al., 2004). Leaders who possess higher levels of political skill portray a sense of ease and confidence. They focus on others and organizations, are accountable, and typically are high in conscientiousness. There are four main factors that comprise political skill: Social Astuteness—being able to observe and identify with others; Interpersonal Influence—being flexible and enacting behaviors appropriate for changing conditions; Networking Ability—creating and then using diverse networks of colleagues; and Apparent Sincerity—appearing or being perceived as open, candid, and forthright.

Activity 2: Political Skill Inventory

Instructions: Using the following 7-point scale, please assign a number to each item that best describes how much you agree with each statement about yourself.

1 = strongly disagree   2 = disagree   3 = slightly disagree   4 = neutral   5 = slightly agree   6 = agree   7 = strongly agree

1. I spend a lot of time and effort at work networking with others. (NA)
2. I am able to make most people feel comfortable and at ease around me. (II)
3. I am able to communicate easily and effectively with others. (II)
4. It is easy for me to develop good rapport with most people. (II)
5. I understand people very well. (SA)
6. I am good at building relationships with influential people at work. (NA)
7. I am particularly good at sensing the motivations and hidden agendas of others. (SA)
8. When communicating with others, I try to be genuine in what I say and do. (AS)
9. I have developed a large network of colleagues and associates at work whom I can call on for support when I really need to get things done. (NA)
10. I know a lot of important people at work and am well-connected. (NA)
11. I spend a lot of time at work developing connections with others. (NA)
12. I am good at getting people to like me. (II)
13. It is important that people believe I am sincere in what I say and do. (AS)
14. I try to show a genuine interest in others. (AS)
15. I am good at using my connections and network to make things happen at work. (NA)
16. I have good intuition or savvy about how to present myself to others. (SA)
17. I always seem to instinctively know the right things to say or do to influence others. (SA)
18. I pay close attention to people's facial expressions. (SA)

Scoring: This scale has four subscales: SA = social astuteness, II = interpersonal influence, NA = networking ability, and AS = apparent sincerity. Add up the scores for the subscale items. High scores are as follows: SA between 25-35; II between 20-28; NA between 30-42; and AS between 15-21.

Gerald R. Ferris, Darren C. Treadway, Robert W. Kolodinsky, Wayne A. Hochwarter, et al., *Journal of Management*, vol. 31, no. 4, pp. 126-152, copyright © 2005 by SAGE Publications. Reprinted by Permission of SAGE Publications.

Activity 2: Learning Outcomes

The political skill inventory captures some aspects of social intelligence, influence tactics, sociability, and even impression management. These skills are all adaptive to study and practice, so if your scores a lower in one or more areas, you may highlight this as an area for development. As noted above, those who demonstrate political skills are often more effective due to how others perceive their abilities.

Evidence suggests that leader political skill positively impacts team and organizational effectiveness (Ahearn et al., 2004) and enhances the reputation of the leader (Ammeter et al., 2002). It also specifically affects individual, team, and organization outcomes through the perception of positive organizational support (Treadway et al., 2004). It appears that a key component of followers' perceptions of a leader's political skill is the belief that the organization provides resources and assistance to further task completion. Leaders help create this belief with their political skills and through interactions with their followers.

There is evidence that political skills can be developed. And they are popular skills *to* develop, as evidenced by the continued popularity of one of the best-selling self-help books of all time, *How to Win Friends and Influence People* by Dale Carnegie (over 30 million copies sold!). Corporate training programs that provide executive coaching, feedback, and role-playing scenarios are useful. But beyond that, individuals can focus on developing their political skills and enhancing their self-awareness by completing personality inventories described in Chapter 4 (Big 5, Hexaco, Core Self Evaluations). They can also seek out 360-degree feedback or developmental feedback sessions regularly with a manager, watch a video of themselves to analyze their political skill, and practice in leadership opportunities outside of the workplace (Ferris et al., 2002). Networking with mentors—both inside and outside of your workplace—can also offer opportunities to learn from individuals who have astute political skills. After all, we learn from modeling others' behaviors. **Mentoring** is "a relationship between a more experienced individual and a less experienced individual that has consistent, regular contact over a period of time and is intended to promote mutual growth, learning, and development within the career context." (Astrove & Kraimer, 2022). Research shows that the most productive mentoring relationships develop naturally (Underhill, 2005; Johnson & Andersen, 2010). Thus, protégés who observe leaders with political skills should seek a mentoring relationship in order to adopt this skill set through vicarious learning processes.

MENTORING: A relationship between a more experienced individual and a less experienced individual that has consistent, regular contact over a period of time and is intended to promote mutual growth, learning, and development within the career context. (Asgrove & Kraimer, page 486)

Negotiation and Conflict-Management Skills

The final skill set we'll cover is imperative to leader performance—the ability to negotiate effectively. There are entire courses dedicated to teaching negotiation skills, and what we cover here barely scratches the surface. However, like problem-solving skills, one's approach to negotiation will vary depending on the problem. General skills such as self-awareness, your preferred approach to negotiation and conflict management, creativity, and the use of reflection to learn from past negotiations are important tools in honing your negotiation effectiveness (Foster & Farquharson, 2011). As with all the skills covered in this chapter, the development of these competencies is maximized during experiential learning episodes where the learner can reflect on their skill sets. Observing others and receiving real-time feedback adds even greater benefit to the learner.

There are multiple aspects of negotiation skills. The first is focused on the actual negotiator as a person. Effective negotiators set high goals, have self-awareness and self-control, show respect for others, and have integrity.

Figure 5: Qualities of Effective Negotiators

Source: Gretchen Vogelgesang Lester and Paul Lester

This means that the other parties feel they can develop trust with the person and can reasonably predict their actions and responses.

These negotiators also have analytical and technical skills in addition to their people skills. Effective negotiators understand the environment, the fine details of the potential deal, and how to read others in the room. Negotiating is a combination of social and emotional intelligence, interpersonal influence tactics, decision-making expertise, and political skill.

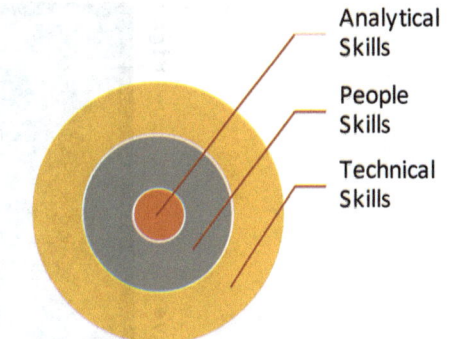

Figure 6: Skills of Effective Negotiators

- Analytical Skills
- People Skills
- Technical Skills

Source: Gretchen Vogelgesang Lester and Paul Lester

Beyond the skills that can be studied and practiced by individuals, there is also the process by which negotiation occurs. Those that prepare for a negotiation activity often see stronger results. Thus, the **planning** and **assessment** phases are integral for success. The **BATNA**, or Best Alternative To Negotiated Agreement is another set of options, which may include the point at which you walk away. You spend time **examining** the other side, using the social or people skills necessary to negotiate effectively. You can then **choose how to communicate** by defining the conditions of the negotiation, how different requests will be handled, and how long the negotiation will continue. As the discussion continues, you will need to **make decisions** regarding your different requirements, potentially prioritizing some needs over others. During the debates, you should **match styles**, which means that you reflect the same tone and approach as your partner. Through this, you can **establish rapport** and potentially build trust as you near an agreement. Finally, even if you come to a decision acceptable to all parties, you should **continue to seek information** in case new material is introduced.

While differing from conflict management skills, negotiation skills are similar to a commonly used approach to managing conflict. **Conflict** is "the process which begins when one party perceives that another has frustrated, or is about to frustrate, some concern." (Thomas, 1992, pg. 265). The approaches to managing conflict detailed in this section grew out of Blake and Mouton's (1964) behavioral approach, discussed in detail in Chapter 7. While negotiation does not always

CONFLICT: The process which begins when one party perceives that another has frustrated, or is about to frustrate, some concern. (Thomas, 1992)

Figure 7: The Negotiation Process

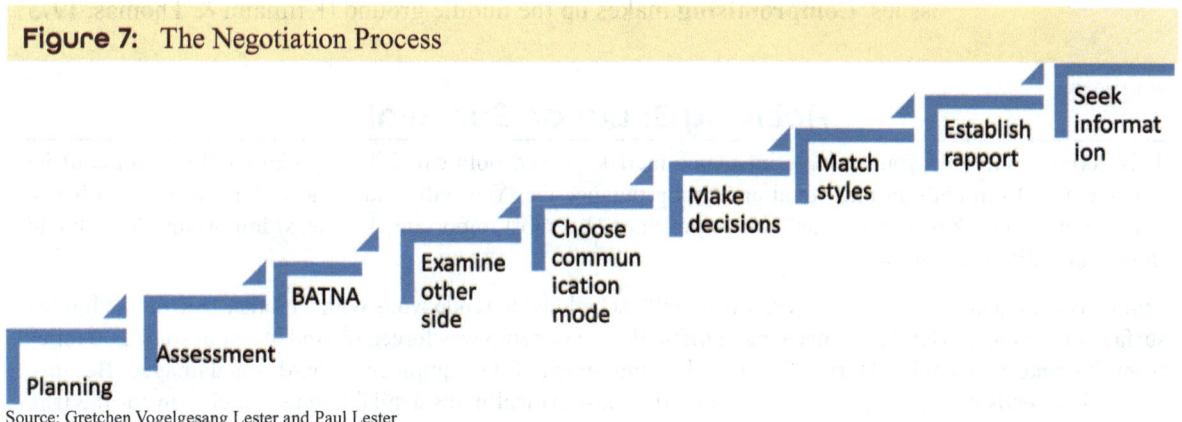

Source: Gretchen Vogelgesang Lester and Paul Lester

Figure 8: Approaches to Conflict

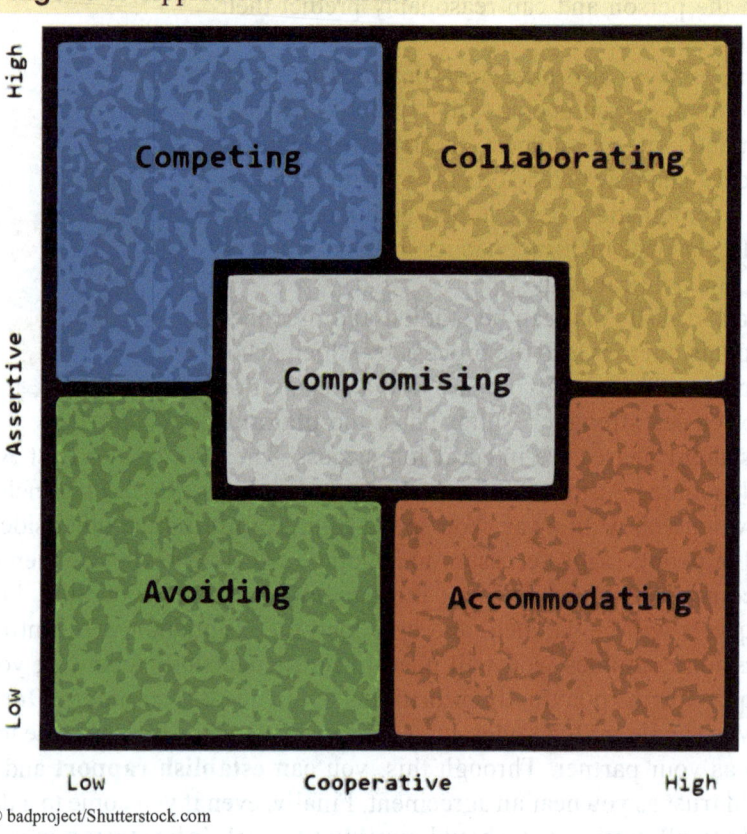

© badproject/Shutterstock.com

entail the frustration of concerns, the classification approach presented in Figure 8 is a helpful way to describe how people often approach conflict. The vertical axis ranges from low assertiveness to high, while the horizontal axis ranges from low cooperation to high. Starting at the low-low quadrant, **avoiding** denotes withdrawal or the failure to engage. **Competing** is a highly assertive approach that conveys a win-lose mentality and low cooperation. **Accommodating** is an action where one party seeks to appease the other party—a lose-win. **Collaborating** involves the willingness to creatively problem-solve to find solutions and confront issues. **Compromising** makes up the middle ground (Kilmann & Thomas, 1975).

Activity 3: Lunar Survival

This activity will help you evaluate influence tactics, power, political skill, negotiating skill, and conflict management from both an individual and group perspective. You will read a short story, evaluate a list of items, and then rank them based on their importance (1 = most important; 15 = least important). You should time your individual ranking.

Story: You are a member of a space crew originally scheduled to rendezvous with a mother ship on the lighted surface of the moon. But due to mechanical difficulties, your ship was forced to land at a spot some 200 miles from the rendezvous point. During the crash landing, much of the equipment aboard was damaged. Because survival depends on reaching the mother ship, the most critical items available must be chosen for the trip. In the graph below are the 15 items left undamaged after landing.

Chapter 8: Competency and Skills-Based Theories 151

Task 1: Rank items in terms of their importance in allowing your crew to reach the rendezvous point. Time your individual ranking.

Items:	Task 1: Individual Ranking	Task 2: Team Ranking	3 Expert Ranking	4 Individual Score (Difference between Individual and Expert)	5 Team Score (Difference between Team and Expert)
Box of matches					
Food concentrate					
50 feet of nylon rope					
Parachute silk					
Portable heating unit					
Two .45 caliber pistols					
1 case of dehydrated milk					
2 100-pound tanks of oxygen					
Stellar map (of the moon's constellation)					
Life raft					
Magnetic compass					
5 gallons of water					
Signal flares					
First aid kit containing injection needles					
Solar-powered FM receiver transmitter					

Task 2: In a team of 4-5 individuals, re-rank the items. Time your group ranking. Note why you made your team decisions.

Scoring: Your instructor will share the expert rankings with you (write them down in column 3 in the table). Calculate the difference in scores—first between your individual score and the expert and then between your group score and the expert. The difference scores (columns 4/5) are the absolute difference (there are no negative values). The lower your difference score, the closer you are to the expert rankings.

Jay Hall, W. H. Watson, *Human Relations*, vol. 24, no. 3, pp. 299-317, copyright © 1970 by SAGE Publications. Reprinted by Permission of SAGE Publications.

Activity 3: Learning Outcomes

After you compare your individual difference score with the group difference score, determine which is lower. If your individual score was lower, you might question why the group influenced you to change your scores. What types of power were on display? If the group score was lower, again, think about why you re-evaluated your initial rankings. This activity can provide insight into how power dynamics work, even in a setting where true experience is unlikely.

The activity can also spur may realization of your conflict management preferences, leading you to agree, even if you disagreed, or gaining insight into effective influence processes used to convince your groupmates to change their answers.

The competencies set out in this chapter transpire at the surface of the iceberg model (pictured in Figure 1). The knowledge and skills related to decision-making, influence tactics, power, political skill, and negotiation are learned abilities that can positively impact a leader's effectiveness. The inventories and assessments throughout this chapter are designed to help you improve your self-awareness regarding your current proficiency in deploying these competencies as part of your leader identity. The more skilled you are at enacting leadership competencies, the more likely your self-identity and leader identity will overlap. If you feel deficient in your leadership skills, you may find there is a greater distance between your self- and leader identity.

Activity 4: Leader Identity Strength—Identity Circles

Revisit Activity 1 from earlier in the chapter. Based on the activities and content presented in the chapter, choose an image that illustrates the space/overlap between a leader identity and your self-identity. If you have opted for a different choice than earlier, write down why you have made this change. Visualized like an eclipse, the more you adopt new leadership skills, the more aligned your identity (the moon) becomes with your leader identity (the sun).

© kersonyanovicha/Shutterstock.com

Activity 4: Learning Outcomes

As you begin to ascertain your competencies, you may recognize that you already have adopted some skill sets that will help you become a successful leader. If so, you may choose a different stage of the eclipse. On the other hand, you may realize that there are numerous competencies you have not mastered, and your eclipse stage may put more space between the sun and the moon. As we have discussed over the past two chapters, your identity strength will wax and wane as you accept new challenges, adopt new skills, and recognize areas for development.

In Review

Chapter 8 presents the competencies and skills that effective leaders and managers must develop in order to perform beyond expectations. While each of us has a unique set of inherent traits that are less changeable, the competencies presented here are easy to adopt and hone with focused effort.

When we describe competencies, we mean the knowledge, skills, and abilities that leaders and managers can develop to be more effective across multiple tasks. The generation of competency models that describe the skills required to complete tasks can help leaders and managers identify areas for development and create motivation toward those goals. Two theories describe specific competencies required for firm performance: the Management Systems Theory and the Skills-based Model of Leadership.

While there is a range of skills that can help leaders be effective, Management Systems Theory presents a consistent pattern (System 4) where participative behaviors allow for high-performing organizations to excel as compared to more exploitive approaches. The organizations that fostered participation had excellent productivity, higher economic status, little conflict and collective progress towards organizational goals, high job satisfaction, and low turnover. Unfortunately, while the evidence strongly suggests this approach, many organizations and particularly those focused on the financials, feel a focus on participation is less efficient and increases costs to the organization. Those who adhere to the theory of maximizing shareholder value, including MBAs, choose instead to enact System 1 behaviors like a purely economic focus, and instead damage the employer-employee relationship and see turnover of their highest performing employees. The evidence is clear that this approach is harmful, yet leaders must continually convince their stakeholders that the effort and investment in employees as followers with a stake in the organization is worth the time and money. Leaders and managers must become skilled advocates for their employees to maximize their performance potential.

The skills-based model described additional competencies such as problem-solving skills, social judgment skills, and social skills. As leaders gain experience and mature, they become more adept at deploying these skills. Social judgment and social skills may be easier for those with specific personality traits such as extraversion, but again, these are learned behaviors. Social intelligence stems from creating strong interpersonal bonds that allow leaders to adapt as required by the followers' needs. Emotional intelligence incorporates self- and other-awareness along with self-regulation to channel emotions appropriately, given the contest. While the research on emotional intelligence does not find a strong relationship with job performance, many would agree that leaders being able to moderate their emotions and use them appropriately based on the situation helps stabilize the organizational culture.

Skill development is a long-term investment, with some research finding that it may take up to ten years to gain proficiency in a certain area. While many organizations spend quite a bit of money on training programs, they don't typically envision such a long time horizon. Again, some skills develop faster based on individual characteristics and traits, so organizations should be strategic about how they deploy such opportunities. In addition, individuals should constantly be scanning all domains for leadership skill development opportunities to more quickly accrue the experience necessary for skill adoption.

The last part of the chapter identifies specific skills that are integral to leader and manager success. Decision-making skills, influence tactics and power, political skill, conflict management approaches, and negotiation skills are all important components to managing and leading people. Decision-making applications can vary based on the type of challenge, the time allotted, and the importance for follower buy-in. The Vroom-Yetton model describes one approach that can help a leader categorize these factors to enact a particular approach, but each individual may have to find their own unique approach based on the situational needs in the moment.

Table 2 presents a list of influence tactics that can be enacted based on the resulting outcomes of commitment, compliance, or resistance. It also details the direction in which the influence can be directed—to peers, to those who report to you, or those to whom you report. Power dynamics can also be used to a leader's advantage—those who wield reward, coercive, legitimate, expert, referent, and information power judiciously will see positive returns, while those who are more directive in their power may fuel resistance and negative outcomes. The activities in this chapter, including Lunar Survival and the Political Skill Inventory, are meant to help you identify how you wield and react to different types of influence tactics, political behaviors, the use of power, and negotiation skills. It also may help you recognize your preferred response to conflict management as you work with others to make decisions.

The next chapter articulates the integration of leader identity, along with discussions regarding the full-range leadership model and transformational leadership. Your identity strength can also impact how you integrate or splinter your identity across domains. As you strengthen certain skill sets, it may be easier for you to create connections across domains to more fully master the competency. For those skills that are still developing, you may contain them to a specific domain while you practice that specific competency.

Learning Objectives

Define competence and competence models

Competence is the ability to interact effectively with one's environment. Thus, they are tools you use to complete and manage tasks. Competence is adaptable and trainable through focused developmental efforts and includes knowledge, skills, and abilities. A *competency model* describes the required competencies for a specific job or task. They are the knowledge, skills, and abilities necessary for completing a goal in an effective manner. They include performance, skill, and resource requirements. Typical leadership competencies include decision-making skills, solution generation, and social judgment.

Evaluate management systems theory

Management systems theory expands upon the task orientation/people orientation approach of the earliest leadership studies to describe a management pattern found in high-performing organizations. Management systems 1-4 outline particular management structures related to variable performance outcomes. System 1, an exploitive-authoritative approach, highlights a strong focus on economic outcomes, the use of coercive power, and high employee turnover. System 4, a participative approach, specifies high productivity, innovation, the use of reward and referent power, and low turnover. While numerous organizations were evaluated based on these characteristics, the research shows that in the ensuing decades since this theory's publication, very few organizations adhere to System 4 guidelines. Thus, while the theory touts high performance related to participative management approaches, the prevailing approach by many organizational leaders is an economic focus on shareholder value, which has been shown to disadvantage many employees while rewarding shareholders.

Explain the skills-based model of leadership

The skills-based model depicts the adoption of new capabilities and the decision-making process for when to deploy those skills. The three main capabilities are problem-solving skills, social judgment skills, and social skills. As leaders encounter more complexity, they learn from their mistakes and increase their social judgment. Novice leaders are challenged in all three areas, but as they develop, they become more skilled at understanding how to define problems, they increase their self-awareness, and they recognize their followers' skill sets. Social intelligence, or the accurate perception of follower and group requirements, can help leaders create strong connections with their followers, motivating them toward positive outcomes. Emotional intelligence includes the ability to read others' emotions and regulate one's own emotions, which is quite important as leaders work to overcome challenges. It is important to note that while we might think emotional intelligence contributes to a leader's performance, meta-analytic studies have not found a consistent link between the two.

Assess your leadership skills

The second half of this chapter highlights the skills most highly related to leadership effectiveness. The normative decision-making model is one approach to decision-making that requires the leader to ascertain the type of problem, the follower requirements, and the time constraints for a specific problem. Learning to analyze these components can increase positive decision-making outcomes. Table 2 presents the most common influence tactics, the power base from which they arise, and the typical outcomes of each tactic. The political skill inventory can give you insight into the types of political machinations you currently use in the workplace and highlight areas for potential growth. Finally, the section on negotiation and conflict-management skills offers a brief overview of the personal and procedural approaches that can increase your chances for negotiation success. Activity 3 allows you to work independently and then with others to examine a particular problem. The most important learning outcomes, though, are how you worked with a group, how you used the skills presented in the chapter and your reflections on areas for development.

Key Terms

Competence (Pg. 135)

Competency Model (Pg. 135)

Management Systems Theory (Pg. 136)

Social Intelligence (Pg. 140)

Emotional Intelligence (Pg. 140)

Normative Decision-Making Model (Pg. 143)

Influence Tactics (Pg. 144)

Political Skill (Pg. 146)

Mentoring (Pg. 148)

Conflict (Pg. 149)

Critical Thinking Questions

1. What competencies have you currently mastered? Which ones are areas for development? How can you practice these competencies to become adept at deploying them across domains?

2. Although the chapter covers a range of competencies, what other knowledge, skills, and abilities influence the leadership process?

3. Using management systems theory, categorize your current workplace based on its organizational culture and approach to work. If it is not system 4, what do you think you could do to increase the participative nature of the work to increase productivity?

4. When you completed the Lunar Survival activity, what did you learn about yourself? What influence tactics were used by group members? What conflict management approaches occurred? How did the group members use power to reach a decision?

References

Acemoglu, D., He, A., & le Maire, D. (2022). *Eclipse of rent-sharing: the effects of managers' business education on wages and the labor share in the US and Denmark* (No. w29874). National Bureau of Economic Research.

Ackerman, P. L. (1990). A correlational analysis of skill specificity: Learning, abilities, and individual differences. *Journal of Experimental Psychology: Learning, Memory, and Cognition, 16*(5), 883.

Astrove, S. L., & Kraimer, M. L. (2022). What and how do mentors learn? The role of relationship quality and mentoring self-efficacy in mentor learning. *Personnel Psychology, 75*(2), 485–513.

Cranton, P. (1994). Self-directed and transformative instructional development. *The Journal of Higher Education, 65*(6), 726–744.

Ferris, G. R., Treadway, D. C., Kolodinsky, R. W., Hochwarter, W. A., Kacmar, C. J., Douglas, C., & Frink, D. D. (2005). Development and validation of the political skill inventory. *Journal of Management,* 31(1), 126–152. https://doi.org/10.1177/0149206304271386

Foster, T. N., & Farquharson, E. R. (2011). Assessment procedures for skills-based MBA courses adapted from the US Army Reserve Officer Training Corps Leadership

Development Program. *Negotiation Journal*, *27*(3), 367–386.

Hoover, J. D., Giambatista, R. C., Sorenson, R. L., & Bommer, W. H. (2010). Assessing the effectiveness of whole person learning pedagogy in skill acquisition. *Academy of Management Learning & Education*, *9*(2), 192–203.

House, R. J., & Howell, J. M. (1992). Personality and charismatic leadership. *The Leadership Quarterly*, *3*(2), 81–108.

Johnson, W. B., & Andersen, G. R. (2010). Formal mentoring in the US military: Research evidence, lingering questions, and recommendations. *Naval War College Review*, *63*(2), 113–126.

Kolodinsky, R. W., Treadway, D. C., & Ferris, G. R. (2007). Political skill and influence effectiveness: Testing portions of an expanded Ferris and Judge (1991) model. *Human Relations*, *60*(12), 1747–1777.

Leimbach, M. (2021, May 18). 2021 Leadership Development Survey: The times they are a changing…*Training*, May 2021, 24–33.

Likert, R. (1961). *New patterns of management*. McGraw-Hill: New York.

Likert, R. (1967). *The human organization: Its management and values*. McGraw-Hill: New York.

Likert, R. (1979). From production-and employee-centeredness to systems 1-4. *Journal of Management*, *5*(2), 147–156.

Lucas, G. (Director). (1977). *Star Wars*. [Film]. Lucasfilm.

Lucia, A. D., & Lepsinger, R. (1999). Competency models: Pinpointing critical success factors in organizations. *San Francisco: Jossey-Bass/Pfeffer*.

Miller, D., & Xu, X. (2019). MBA CEOs, short-term management and performance. *Journal of Business Ethics*, *154*(2), 285–300.

Mumford, M. D. (1986). Leadership in the organizational context: A conceptual approach and its applications 1. *Journal of Applied Social Psychology*, *16*(6), 508–531.

Mumford, M. D., Marks, M. A., Connelly, M. S., Zaccaro, S. J., & Reiter-Palmon, R. (2000). Development of leadership skills: Experience and timing. *The Leadership Quarterly*, *11*(1), 87–114.

Mumford, M. D., Zaccaro, S. J., Connelly, M. S., & Marks, M. A. (2000). Leadership skills: Conclusions and future directions. *The Leadership Quarterly*, *11*(1), 155–170.

Mumford, M. D., Zaccaro, S. J., Harding, F. D., Jacobs, T. O., & Fleishman, E. A. (2000). Leadership skills for a changing world: Solving complex social problems. *The Leadership Quarterly*, *11*(1), 11–3

Salovey, P., & Mayer, J. D. (1990). Emotional intelligence. *Imagination, Cognition and Personality*, *9*(3), 185–211.

Smith, Watkins, M. B., Burke, M. J., Christian, M. S., Smith, C. E., Hall, A., & Simms, S. (2013). Gendered influence: A gender role perspective on the use and effectiveness of influence tactics. *Journal of Management*, *39*(5), 1156–1183. https://doi.org/10.1177/0149206313478183

Thomas, K. W. (1992). Conflict and conflict management: Reflections and update. *Journal of Organizational Behavior*, 265–274.

Treadway, D. C., Hochwarter, W. A., Ferris, G. R., Kacmar, C. J., Douglas, C., Ammeter, A. P., & Buckley, M. R. (2004). Leader political skill and employee reactions. *The Leadership Quarterly*, *15*(4), 493–513.

Underhill, C. M. (2006). The effectiveness of mentoring programs in corporate settings: A meta-analytical review of the literature. *Journal of Vocational Behavior*, *68*(2), 292–307.

Vroom, V. H. (2003). Educating managers for decision making and leadership. *Management Decision*.

Vroom, V. H., & Jago, A. G. (1988). *The new leadership: Managing participation in organizations*. Prentice-Hall, Inc.

White, R. W. (1959). Motivation reconsidered: the concept of competence. *Psychological Review*, *66*(5), 297.

CHAPTER 9
Integration of Leadership Identity

CHAPTER OUTCOMES

1. Define and explain the eight components of the Full Range Leadership Model (FRLM)
2. Identify behaviors you have witnessed that align with the 4 I's of transformational leadership
3. Explore and understand the ways in which transformational leadership and other components of the FRLM can be applied ethically and unethically
4. Understand how you might accelerate the development of your Full Range Leadership behaviors

Purpose of This Chapter

In this chapter, we start with integration of leader identity, then we expose you to the theory behind transformational leadership and the practical application of a Full Range system of leadership with eight distinct components (with the transformational approach on one end of a continuum). This system we describe has some of the strongest evidence of leadership effectiveness that we cover in this book, and we discuss the range of outcomes you can expect to see with each component. We also present some best practices and use cases for each component, plus some developmental techniques that have shown to be effective. Finally, we conclude the chapter with a practical exercise in which you rate a leader from your past on a range of leader behaviors and then reflect on your experiences with this leader.

What is Leader Identity Integration?

Before we begin this chapter, we must slow down and recognize that Part 4 of this textbook focuses on integrating your leader identity. Integrate our leader identity into what, you ask? As we have hinted throughout (or at times, said directly), our goal for you is to integrate your leader identity with other *already present* aspects of your identity—those parts of yourself you know well. To do so, start with a practical exercise called "**Domain Circles**", which illustrates exactly what we mean by leader identity integration. The practical exercise has four steps, and you will need a few clean sheets of paper and approximately 30 minutes to complete the work. Integration of leader identity helps you move from the being of leadership to the doing of leadership — it connects your meaning, level, and strength of leader identity to the actions you take to lead in all domains of your life.

Activity 1: Domain Circles

Step 1: Let's Draw. On a clean sheet of paper, please draw a circle to represents each of your life's domains. Most people have at least three circles—work, community, and friends/family—but you can and probably will have more. Before you begin, think about how big or small you should make each circle compared to the others. The size of each circle represents the domain's importance in your life relative to the other domains. Go ahead and draw and label your domain circles. The results will probably look something like Figure 1, seen below.

Domain Circles

Figure 1: Your Identity   **Figure 2:** Variations of Leader Identity Integration

Source: Gretchen Vogelgesang Lester and Paul Lester

© Art Kovalenco/Shutterstock.com

Step 2: Reflect. Now that you have drawn and labeled your domain circles, reflect for a few minutes on how your leader identity cuts across the boundaries of each domain circle. In other words, write down the ways in which you are influencing others in each domain, and also capture how your leading others might transcend boundaries across multiple domain circles.

Step 3: Now draw what you *really* want. In the first two steps, we asked you to think about and draw your *current* life's domains and leader identity. In this final step, we want you to redraw the domain circles and their overlap as you'd like them to be in the future. **Integration** of leader identity across domains can be a matter of preference or, due to necessity, a matter of domain characteristics. If you aspire to have a highly integrated leader identity, yet the job calls for segmentation (i.e., separation from other aspects of your life), then you might feel stress or be motivated to seek out other work that allows you to be integrated. For example, we know that leaders tend to develop faster and more completely if the other domains of their life are integrated. However, some fields are more segmented than others (e.g., police work, financial management, certain legal work, military service, etc.).

Step 4: Meaning-making. You may discuss your results in class, but we also recommend you set aside your domain circles for a week or two and revisit them after you have had longer to reflect on them. Think through the differences in how the circles look as they are today vs. how you want them to look in the future. What do you need to do in the coming weeks, months, and years to move closer to your desired end state of leadership identity integration? Who might help you think these steps through? Here's a hint: Your loved ones and your mentors know you best—start by having a conversation with them.

Introduction

When we ask our students to describe the kind of leader they want to become—to offer more detail than simply cataloging a chain of single-word adjectives—what we hear most often is this: They want to be a leader who can adroitly communicate an inspired vision oriented towards the future, and they want to do it so well that people intuitively know it is the right thing to do. This ideal leader can say and do just the right things to motivate others to perform beyond expectations. "Is that a brick wall in front of us? No problem, we'll scale it, dig under it, go around it—or if all else fails, we'll blast right through it because that's exactly what our leader needs us to do." This leader challenges followers to use their own capabilities to solve problems. The leader acknowledges the fact that *each follower* has special talents and encourages them to grow and develop as people and emerging leaders. Lastly, there's no question in anyone's mind that this leader is an ethical exemplar for all to emulate, and that followers willingly do so because in the end they want to be like this leader.

The ideal leader our students usually describe is what we commonly refer to as a **transformational leader**, and since the early 1980s, arguably no other theory of leadership has been as dominant as transformational leadership. Thousands of research studies, papers, and books have been written about transformational leadership, and a quick Google Scholar search returns over 750,000 hits. In terms of its scholarly study, transformational leadership emerged from three related fields: sociology, political science, and psychology. First, sociologist James Downton's *Rebel Leadership* (1973) described how leaders leverage charisma, inspiration, and transactions with followers to drive deep commitment towards organizational goals. And Downton's work underscores how these leverage points can be used for tremendous good or unspeakable evil. Second, political scientist James MacGregor Burns' *Leadership* (1978) chronicled how President Franklin Delano Roosevelt transformed the United States by employing a range of techniques to lead the country out of the Great Depression and through the darkest days of World War II. The world today would likely look very different were it not for FDR's leadership. Third, in the early 1980s, psychologist Bernard Bass and a group of scholars at State University of New York-Binghamton (including Bruce Avolio and Francis Yammarino) set out to theorize on, create and evaluate measures for, and then assess the validity of transformational leadership. These researchers are most credited with giving the leadership field the framework we cover throughout this chapter.

> **TRANSFORMATIONAL LEADERSHIP:** A highly consequential form of leadership that influences people or groups to look past their immediate needs or motivations and instead work towards achieving highly challenging goals and performing beyond typical expectations. (Bass, 1985)

© Chan2545/Shutterstock.com

The Full Range Leadership Model

One conclusion that the early scholars of transformational leadership made was that context looms large and shapes both leader and follower motivation and behavior—so, certain leader behaviors are likely to be more effective in some situations than others (Avolio, 1999). For example, there is little question that FDR's leadership during the Great Depression and World War II was highly consequential. But would it resonate with people as much had the country's economy not faltered and Germany not invaded much of Europe? Or for a smaller-scale example, think where you have worked in the past. Do you need your manager to give you an inspirational speech or convey a strategic vision every day you come to work? The answer to both questions is probably "no"—you realize that there is a time and a place for different leadership techniques. An important sign of a leader's growth is being able to read a situation and understand what approach is most appropriate.

FULL RANGE LEADERSHIP: A broad conceptualization of leadership that accounts for an array of leadership and non-leadership behaviors that are common in organizations. The model includes both transformational and transactional leadership, along with laissez-faire behaviors. (Bass & Avolio, 1997)

Research shows that in many circumstances, employees need little more than to understand the task ahead of them, grasp the purpose of the work, and feel supported by their leaders (Sims et al., 2009). Yet there are times when the organizational context becomes quite serious (e.g., a crisis). In these situations, leaders must know how to tap into the emotions and motivations of their followers and direct that energy towards completing difficult tasks that are important to the group (Bass, 1985). The cynic may cry, "That sounds manipulative!" Yes, that's exactly the point. Leadership is an influence process, and being able to manipulate the emotions, motivations, and behaviors of followers when it matters the most is what effective leaders do—particularly when stakes are highest. Keep that in mind.

Much of the remainder of the chapter is dedicated to the **Full Range Leadership Model** (Bass & Avolio, 1997), which incorporates transformational leadership and includes other approaches to leadership that tend to be more common (you will likely recognize them from your own work experiences). Unlike other leadership texts that tend to start with transformational leadership, we have worked from the opposite direction by first describing laissez-faire leadership (i.e., the absence of leadership), covering the three forms of transactional leadership (passive and active management by exception, plus contingent reward), then transitioning into the "4 I's" of transformational leadership.

LAISSEZ-FAIRE LEADERSHIP: The general absence of leadership, commonly characterized by leaders offering little input, avoiding use of influence to shape outcomes. (Bass & Avolio, 1997)

Laissez-Faire Leadership. If you ever took a class on government, you likely recall that laissez-faire means to avoid interfering and let things take their natural course. The absence or avoidance of leadership is all too common in many organizations and—in extreme cases—it can be a sign of a rotting organizational culture. Organizations employ leaders to avoid things taking their natural course, which can be an eventual decline towards disorder and dysfunction.

However, our own experience suggests that laissez-faire leadership within organizations tends to be specific to domains within the workplace, where leaders either intentionally choose to not interfere or—because leaders are often stretched too thin—simply lack the time/

© canbedone/Shutterstock.com

energy to focus on it. As you might expect, there are many costs and few benefits to laissez-faire leadership. For example, when senior leaders avoid taking an active role in promoting diversity, equity, and inclusion efforts and instead espouse a "meritocratic" approach to hiring and promotion, they often regret their laissez-faire approach when complaints of gender and racial bias emerge (Seijits & Milani, 2021).

Though they are often conflated, laissez-faire leadership is *not* the same as empowering leadership. Empowering leadership is a decentralized influence process that pulls followers into the decision-making process—the leader is involved, albeit in a somewhat muted way compared to other active forms of leadership (Wong & Geissner, 2018). As one paper touting laissez-faire leadership suggests, "[a] hands-off approach by a leader can allow employees to feel respected and autonomous, suggesting that there are beneficial effects of low or non-involvement on the part of leaders" (Yang, 2015, p. 1247). But there is little evidence that the *absence* of leadership actually accomplishes this.

When is laissez-faire leadership appropriate? The answer is *rarely*, especially considering the research suggesting that laissez-faire leadership can be destructive (Skogstad et al., 2007). Perhaps what makes laissez-faire leadership so dangerous within organizations is that while the leader may be present, he or she abdicates responsibility for decision-making and avoids taking an active role in organizational success. This leads to a toxic mix of follower stagnation, the search of ineffective "work arounds" that intentionally circumvent the weak leader, or both (Bass & Avolio, 1990).

Management by Exception—Passive. Management by exception is about correcting follower mistakes. While all leaders will take on this role periodically, the passive form is particularly insidious because of its timing. Leaders employing the passive form of management by exception withhold their involvement until the context is so severe that recovery is doubtful (Antonakis et al., 2003). Or, within the leader-follower dynamic, they may wait to correct followers' performance errors until well past the time these followers can take corrective action (Avolio, 1999). For example, imagine you take on a new role at work. While you know you struggle at times in this role, you generally feel as though you are on the right track because your leader never offers criticism or coaching. But when you sit down with your leader for your annual appraisal, you receive a poor evaluation and are told that you will revert to your old job. Because you received the feedback so late in the evaluation period, there is no way for you to improve. Imagine what you could have done with that information six months ago?

Clearly the passive form of management by exception is ineffective. It should rarely be used intentionally by leaders. We often see passive management by exception when leaders are spread thin, stressed, or are themselves poorly led by senior management. We also know that passive management by exception is detrimental to followers in a variety of ways, including follower resilience (Harland et al., 2005), motivation, group or organizational performance, and followers' satisfaction with their leader (Judge & Piccolo, 2004). Thus, passive management by exception should be avoided, and there are several ways to do so. First, you must manage your own workload to ensure you have enough bandwidth to regularly communicate with members of your team. You must understand the challenges they are facing, which keeps you from having to "swoop in" at the last minute to

MANAGEMENT BY EXCEPTION–PASSIVE: An influence process whereby leaders tend to only become involved in a context or try to influence behaviors after followers have made serious mistakes. (Avolio, 1999)

try to save the day. Second, setting and adhering to regular informal and formal counseling sessions ensures that you are giving the proper feedback to followers. This way, they can continue to improve their performance, and if done properly, you (the leader) can hold people accountable for their performance in the fairest way possible.

Management by Exception—Active. The active form of management by exception is primarily focused on making "on the spot" corrections of follower mistakes as they perform their jobs. If you have ever had a leader looking over your shoulder and providing immediate feedback on your errors, then you know exactly how this feels. As Avolio (1999, p. 49-50) notes, this "form of corrective transaction tends to be more ineffective, particularly when used in excess … the leader arranges to actively monitor deviations from standards, mistakes, and errors in the follower's assignments and to take corrective action as necessary."

While it may not feel great to receive this form of feedback—and there is evidence that excessive active management by exception can degrade performance (Wang et al., 2011)—we diverge from the research by pointing out that it can be highly useful in certain contexts, especially job training. Indeed, requiring immediate corrective action by followers when learning their job can prevent a continuum of future harm. For example, actively correcting errors by a junior accountant may save your company money and prevent perceptions of unethical conduct; correcting errors by a nursing student may prevent infections and death in future patients; immediately correcting use of force errors in police recruits may prevent future civil rights violations; and actively correcting pilot trainee errors may one day be

> **MANAGEMENT BY EXCEPTION—ACTIVE:** An influence process whereby leaders tend to vigilantly participate in performance monitoring and quickly make corrections from performance deviations before the situation deteriorates. (Avolio, 1999)

the difference between hundreds of passengers enjoying their vacation or a major catastrophe. Thus, we submit that active management by exception is a valid leader behavior, but only in specific contexts.

Contingent Reward. At its most basic level, contingent reward is a quid pro quo between leaders and followers—leaders set expectations or goals and, pursuant to followers meeting them, followers in turn receive a reward for performance. A simple contingent reward is receiving pay for coming to work and doing your job, but there are others. As we have highlighted a few times in this textbook, salespeople commonly expect to receive some sort of commission or annual bonus if they hit the sales quotas established by their leaders. The foundational concept on which contingent reward is built is **Expectancy Theory of Motivation** (Vroom, 1964), which holds that employees will exert effort into their work if they believe they will receive an award for success.

There are other forms of contingent rewards that you should closely track when leading others. For example, in exchange for performing work, most jobs allow employees to earn vacation days annually or accrued across pay periods. However, earning those vacation days is only half of the contingent reward. Employees expect to be allowed to take those vacations days as they wish if they give enough notice in accordance with company policy. So, if a leader enters into a tacit or explicit contingent reward transaction with followers, the costs of leaders failing to follow through can be high—*leaders who fail to deliver lose credibility and trust* (Yammarino et al., 1998). Thus, transactional leadership—and explicitly contingent rewards—serves as the foundation on which transformational leadership can be built (Bass et al., 2003). As we turn to the transformational components of the Full Range Leadership Model, consider the following: Leaders who deliver on contingent rewards when followers perform establish a bond of trust between leaders and followers. If you—the leader—need followers to try harder in their jobs and perform beyond expectations, why would they bother doing so if they do not trust you?

Transformational Leadership

Transformational leadership is a significant component of the Full Range Leadership Model. As touched on previously, it consists of individualized consideration, intellectual stimulation, inspirational motivation, and idealized influence, all of which are described in greater detail below. And, as we chronicle later in this section, there are specific *behaviors* that are associated with transformational leadership, which you can adopt as you develop as a leader.

Individualized Consideration. Because every person within an organization has a unique array of talents, transformational leaders use individualized consideration to recognize, respect, and leverage those capabilities for the betterment of the organization. Beyond tapping into individual capabilities, transformational leaders also recognize that employees have unique needs and goals that must be met if the leader hopes to retain employees within the company. Whereas active management by exception is squarely focused on correcting followers' errors or work behavior, individualized consideration is often operationalized (i.e., how it actually occurs) within organizations by leaders serving as coaches, mentors, teachers, and counselors (Avolio, 1999).

Individualized consideration can be thought of as encompassing two distinct "buckets" of leader behaviors—specifically being developmental and supportive

CONTINGENT REWARD: A transactional form of leadership whereby leaders exchange a reward for performance or compliance by a follower. (Avolio, 1999)

EXPECTANCY THEORY OF MOTIVATION: A theory of work motivation that combines expectancy (belief that a stated goal can actually be attained), instrumentality (belief that a reward will be given for performance), and valence (the value an individual places on a reward). (Vroom, 1964)

(Rafferty & Griffin, 2006; Bass, 1985). Developmental behaviors occur when leaders serve as career counselors and mentors, assist in social networking, and recommend followers for professional education and training. In other words, the individually considerate leader is not only the "boss," but also the facilitator of future success for the follower; they help followers see the path towards attaining personal goals. Supportive behaviors occur when leaders show concern and account for follower needs and goals in organizational decisions. This is not to say that follower needs surpass those of the organization, but rather the impact on employees is part of the decision calculus. Broadly, individualized consideration should be common practice for leaders for a variety of reasons—it reinforces trust, provides followers with a sense of psychological safety, and proves that leaders care about them.

Intellectual Stimulation. Shrewd leaders recognize that they are hardly the oracle of all knowledge and that sometimes they are too deep in the weeds to create innovative solutions on their own. When you consider all the roles that a manager fills daily—planner, organizer, coordinator, scheduler, communicator, and resources administrator—it's no surprise that little time remains for ideation and innovative problem solving. Transformational leaders instead actively look outward towards those on their teams to solicit input for problem solving. Put simply: Your employees are *smart,* they want to put that intelligence to good use, so *let them.*

Leaders operationalize intellectual stimulation among employees by transparently challenging the assumptions under which the team operates (Avolio, 1999). While "the way we've always done it" may sometimes be acceptable, that refrain should be questioned periodically as situations change. Doing so presents transformational leaders with an opportunity to give employees the tacit permission they seek to be creative, which then creates a greater sense of follower buy-in because intellectual stimulation makes them part of the solution. A great example of this is military leaders, who provide followers with both the task (i.e., the what/mission) and purpose (i.e., the why). However, they tend not to explicitly state *how* the work must be completed, though it is implied that the work must be completed ethically and within a given standard. Nevertheless, limiting leader guidance to task and purpose gives followers an opportunity to engage their own intellect to find novel solutions to problems that they face. Meanwhile, leaders remain available to help remove obstacles and offer other forms of support *when needed.*

Inspirational Motivation. Returning to the origins of transformational leadership, Burns (1978) exhaustively examined the language and rhetorical devices used by FDR during the Great Depression and throughout his presidency during World War II. What emerged was an image of a transformational leader optimistically framing future organizational goals and presenting them as difficult yet attainable. Thus, when scholars frame transformational leadership as being about performance beyond expectations (Bass, 1985; Avolio, 1999), the lever leaders most often use to get that kind of performance is inspirational motivation. Inspirational motivation has four operational components: Leaders must view the future optimistically and talk about it as such, frame their vision in a compelling way that clearly articulates the necessity of reaching that vision, express excitement about the work ahead and convey that to team members, and convey confidence in the group's ability to reach goals through an unwavering conviction (Bass & Avolio, 1997).

What becomes clear when inspiring people in these ways is the nested nature of transformational leadership. Keep in mind that motivation is derived individually; what motivates you, Employee A, and Employee B will likely vary. To inspire followers, it is not enough to just transmit an inspirational message. Transformational leaders must know what would motivate their followers based on their needs (individualized consideration) and in turn speak to the pathways in which they will rely on followers to play a major role in the development and execution of the vision (intellectual stimulation). Recognizing the nested nature of transformational leadership then allows leaders to convey the *right kind* of resonant, inspirational message to followers.

Idealized Influence. As we discussed in Chapter 5, there is much to learn in life by watching others. The same must be said for the leader-follower dynamic. Followers look to leaders to serve as role models—being a role model is the essence of idealized influence—and it is well established that transformational leaders expend significant effort developing followers into leaders (Avolio, 1999). Transformational leaders exert idealized influence by openly talking about their most important personal values and by actively working towards living those values ethically. They self-sacrifice for the good of the group. They frame the vision in terms of "we-ness" rather than focus on their personal goals. They reinforce the notion that the goals and work ahead have a strong purpose. And they instill a sense of pride in being a part of the organization.

Given that we place such emphasis on identity in this textbook, it is worth noting that idealized influence is the component of the Full Range Leadership Model—and *specifically* transformational leadership—that most closely aligns with your identity because it calls for you to *be* a role model for others to emulate. As we will cover in Chapter 10, being this kind of role model is in some ways built on experience and authenticity. Stated differently, one challenge facing novice leaders is the gulf between lacking credibility and wanting to be taken seriously when enacting idealized influence behaviors. In such cases, we recommend consistency in behaviors—consistently talking about and acting in alignment with your important values and willingly sacrificing for the good of the group. Over time, people in your team will take notice, and you will develop credibility and **idiosyncratic credit** (Hollander, 1992) that can be drawn upon when you pitch challenging visions and/or ask for the subsequent extra effort needed to meet stretch goals.

Summary: A Healthy Dose of Reality. As you have undoubtedly discovered, this book covers a wide variety of conceptualizations of leadership and the Full Range Leadership Model is one approach. As an approach to leading, the FRLM is attractive to students and practitioners for three important reasons. First, unlike many descriptive models of leadership, it is behaviorally prescriptive. So, if you are in a context calling for close supervision and immediate corrective action of followers who fail to perform in a specified way, the model offers a series of behaviors that are likely to be successful (e.g., management by exception-active). Need to inspire people to work harder than they ever have so the company can reach an important milestone? There is a set of behaviors within the model that allow you to do that (e.g., inspirational motivation). This range of behaviors meshes well with the real world and therefore is not pollyannish; the approach accounts for needing to be directive, transactional, or transformational depending on what the leader faces at a given moment in time.

Second, as we cover in greater detail shortly, there is a significant amount of empirical research supporting the benefits of the FRLM. This matters because the components of the model were not thought up by a self-anointed leadership guru trying to sell books in the airport giftshop, but rather it is based on evidence from rigorous

IDIOSYNCRATIC CREDIT:
The latitude a leader has to bring about change as a function of followers' perception of that leader's competence and signs of loyalty that engender trust. (Hollander, 1992, p. 49)

studies that tested the components many times. While far from perfect, the model holds up to scientific scrutiny better than many others.

Third, we view the model as approachably aspirational. While it may appear as though becoming a transformational leader is a daunting task accomplished by only a rarified few, novice leaders can in fact adopt these behaviors and, with practice, hone them and integrate them into their identity. Reading a situation and then knowing when or how to employ contingent reward vs. intellectual stimulation may not be intuitive for some. But gaining and then reflecting upon experiences sets the conditions for future growth as a Full Range leader.

The Case *Against* the Full Range Leadership Model

Despite our view that the Full Range Leadership Model has many advantages, it also has a few shortcomings, and there are several scholars who have leveled withering criticism against the model. For example, van Knippenberg and Sitkin (2013, p. 2) stated "charismatic-transformational leadership research enjoys the reputation of explaining particularly effective leadership—indeed, implicitly or explicitly, the *most* effective form of leadership ... [b]ut have we really reached the state where we can sign off on this conclusion and file it as fact?" Some criticisms of the model fall outside the scope of this textbook, but others are worth exploring a bit. After all, understanding the model's shortfalls can help you make a more informed decision regarding how to apply transformational leader behaviors.

The 4 I's. One of the more noteworthy concerns about the Full Range Model of Leadership focuses on the 4 I's of transformational leadership—individualized consideration, intellectual stimulation, inspirational motivation, and idealized influence. Several scholars have noted that the research does not consistently show that these dimensions are separate. They state that too much overlap exists across the 4I's, suggesting that transformational leadership is instead just a grab bag of positive leader behaviors (van Knippenberg & Sitkin, 2013; Alvesson & Karreman, 2016). This could matter to leaders, as without dimensional distinction, leaders face difficulties in discerning which set of transformational leader behaviors they should employ. For example, if idealized influence and inspirational motivation are not distinct, then the leader is left to guess which set of behaviors to enact.

Transformational Leadership is Too "Leader-Centric." There is little question that the Full Range Leadership Model focuses on specific behaviors that leaders should enact to varying degrees based on the context. The point is for these behaviors to get followers to perform exceptionally well, and it can be argued that influencing others to perform this way is the whole point of the FRLM. Critics of the model, however, point out that followers are underrepresented. This is a valid point. They tend to fixate on the "specified" behaviors espoused in the model (i.e., spending time teaching and coaching or talking optimistically about the future) while glossing over the "implied" context on which transformational leadership is built (i.e., establishing quality relationships with followers via social exchange)

(Gerstner & Day, 1997). But because the model is prescriptive—it suggests specific behaviors to be performed by leaders—it is by necessity lopsided towards the leader; after all, the model is about how leaders *influence others*. These points aside, that the Full Range Model is somewhat underspecified and could account for more of the follower's role underscores a point: You should take the follower's organizational role quite seriously as you continue your leadership development journey.

The Cult of Transformational Leadership. An additional problem facing transformational leadership is that the academic literature largely *defines* effective or successful leadership as transformational leadership. As we discussed in Chapter 2, studies of Romance of Leadership (Meindl et al., 1985) found that individuals tend to attribute individual and organizational outcomes to the behavior of leaders, thus discounting the influence of environmental factors or the impact that outstanding followers have on the organization. This heroic view of leadership has arguably been exacerbated within the study of transformational leadership due to the **tautologic** nature of defining the model (that is: based on the espoused behaviors associated with the model rather than defining its actual dimensional properties). As Alvesson and Karreman (2016, p. 141) wrote, "[a] person that is said to be into work that 'Empowers and develops potential,' and is an 'Inspirational networker and promoter' must per definition be better than one that dis-powers, does not develop (but hinders) potential, and is uninspiring. Someone offering intellectual stimulation or inspirational motivation in a managerial/leadership position is surely better than someone that does not. Someone assessed to have 'extraordinary' qualities will probably not be assessed as having poor results."

TAUTOLOGY: A statement that must be true in all circumstances based on the logic used to form it. In this case, transformational leadership is tautologically defined by what it does (behaviors) rather than what it is. (APA, 2022)

They have a valid point—one that highlights something all emerging leaders must come to grips with as they take on greater responsibilities. Specifically, there may be a divergence between how you and your boss measure your performance. For example, you may be tremendously transformational—your followers are inspired and motivated to do great things, you are developing them into leaders, they have completely bought into the vision—but despite this, you receive a poor evaluation because you failed to meet objective performance metrics set by your manager. In other words, you did everything "right" and were a beloved leader, but a highly transactional peer down the hall got the promotion because they focused on pay rewards for increased performance. Rapid "on the spot" corrections ensured higher team productivity.

Finally, critics of transformational leadership express concern that it lacks a moral core, that charisma and other components of the model can be used for highly unethical and immoral ends (Price, 2003). Indeed, some of the worst human atrocities—the genocide during the Holocaust, the Tutsis in Rwanda, the Killing Fields of Cambodia—were perpetrated by leaders who employed aspects of transformational leadership. Yet, proponents of transformational leadership point towards the correct use of idealized influence as an ethical guardrail. Bass and Steidlmeier (1999) label those who employ transformational leadership for evil ends as "pseudo-transformational leaders." Despite the relabeling, logic nevertheless dictates that effective influence tactics from a determined transformational leader can do both tremendous good *and* bad depending on the true motivations and power of the leader, as discussed in chapter 6.

© Lemonsoup14/Shutterstock.com

The Case *for* the Full Range Leadership Model

There are several ways to justify the use of nearly any approach to leadership, and the Full Range Leadership Model is no exception. But our preference is to turn towards the empirical evidence showing its benefits. As we repeatedly state in this chapter, the Full Range Leadership Model, and transformational leadership more specifically, has been extensively researched in a wide variety of settings—in labs, universities, for-profit organizations, non-profit organizations, the military, national, state, and local governments, and in international contexts (Lowe & Gardner, 2000)—and the common research questions focus on three broad areas. First, who are transformational leaders? Second, under what conditions are the various components of the Full Range Leadership Model most effective? Third, what are the primary outcomes of the Full Range Leadership Model, particularly of transformational leadership? We highlight some of the results from published meta-analyses.

Who are Transformational Leaders? A meta-analysis of 26 independent studies examined the link between the Big Five personality factors (covered in Chapter 4) and both transformational and transactional leadership. In short, this meta-analysis attempted to determine if transformational and transactional leadership behaviors were rooted in personality dispositions, such as extraversion. Although the researchers found a positive link between extraversion, idealized influence, and inspirational motivation (combined within the study as "charisma"), the overall link between personality/transformational (the 4 I's) and transactional leader behaviors (contingent rewards and both active/passive forms of management by exception) was consistently weak (Bono & Judge, 2004). This is good news in terms of leader development because it suggests that one does not need a particular personality type to employ the Full Range Leadership Model.

Researchers also performed a meta-analysis of 45 empirical studies of transformational leadership that examined transformational leadership and gender. Here, the researchers wanted to know if followers viewed men and women differently along the various components of the Full Range Leadership Model. The results clearly showed that, compared to women, men were seen by followers as being more laissez-faire and more likely to use both passive and active forms of management by exception. Conversely, women tended to be viewed by followers as slightly more charismatic and were significantly more likely to use individualized consideration. Likewise, followers who worked for women who were viewed as transformational leaders gave significantly more effort in their work, were more satisfied with their work, and evaluated their leaders as more effective compared to male leaders (Eagly et al., 2003). This research is particularly important because it challenges the stereotypical view that followers view men as "dynamic" leaders, and it shows that the charisma of women leaders is noticed and valued by followers.

Full Range vs. Context. Is the Full Range Leadership Model effective in all situations? This is a challenging question to answer—there are hundreds of studies that have tested the model in nearly every conceivable context—but the answer is generally yes (Bass, 1997), at least in the West. There are two corollaries already mentioned that are worth restating. First, in terms of effectiveness and performance, research repeatedly shows that regardless of organizational setting, followers respond better to transformational leadership behaviors than they do to transactional and laissez-faire behaviors. For example, a meta-analysis found that transformational leadership outperformed transactional leadership in both public and private organizational contexts (Dumdum et al., 2013). Second, transformational leadership augments transactional leader behaviors. In other words, transactional behaviors set the foundation for transformational leader behaviors to be effective. This augmentation effect has been seen in many studies going back more than 35 years (Waldman & Avolio, 1986). A third corollary proposed by Bass (1997), that transformational leadership is effective across all national cultures, has recently been challenged in a meta-analysis using data from 215 samples across 34 countries. These researchers found that transformational leadership was generally more effective when leader behaviors were in line with cultural values and practices, but much less so when followers perceived a misalignment between leader behavior and cultural norms (Crede et al., 2019).

Transformational Leadership & Outcomes. The available research has examined a variety of outcomes, but here we focus on follower job satisfaction, **organizational citizenship behavior (OCBs)**, **psychological capital**, and organizational and follower work performance. Regarding transformational leadership's influence on follower job satisfaction and performance effectiveness, a meta-analysis found that the statistical effect of transformational leadership on job satisfaction and performance effectiveness was approximately twice that of transactional leadership (Dumdum et al., 2013). Another meta-analysis examined the differential effects of the Full Range Leadership Model on follower performance and found that transformational leadership had stronger effects on team and organizational performance than did transactional leadership (Wang et al., 2011). Other researchers found that transformational leadership and follower OCBs were linked (Crede et al., 2019), thereby suggesting that transformational leaders influence followers to go above and beyond their job requirements to help the organization (i.e., performance beyond expectations). Additionally, other scholars found that, when compared to other leadership styles, working for a transformational leader was the strongest antecedent of psychological capital in followers (PsyCap) (Loghman et al., 2022). Taken together, the scientific picture of the Full Range Leadership Model that has come into focus over several decades of research suggests the following: The model—and transformational leadership in particular—is a highly consequential form of leadership that impacts important organizational outcomes.

ORGANIZATIONAL CITIZENSHIP BEHAVIORS: Discretionary behaviors of employees that are not part of their job and generally are not rewarded but go above and beyond job requirements for the overall good of the organization. (Organ, 1988)

PSYCHOLOGICAL CAPITAL (PSYCAP): A constellation of psychological strengths comprised of Hope, Efficacy, Resilience, and Optimism that has repeatedly been shown to be highly influential in follower performance, job satisfaction, retention, and other areas. (Luthans et al., 2007)

Activity 2: Practical Exercise: Assessing Transformational & Transactional Leadership

The gold standard for measuring Full Range Leadership is the Multifactor Leadership Questionnaire (MLQ), written by Bernard Bass & Bruce Avolio (1997) and published by Mindgarden (https://www.mindgarden.com/16-multifactor-leadership-questionnaire). Because it's copyrighted, we cannot reprint the MLQ in this text. However, other scholars have developed effective measures of transformational and transactional leadership, and we selected the Transformational Leadership Inventory (TLI) (Podsakoff et al., 1990) to use in this practical exercise.

Instructions. Below you will see a questionnaire with 28 items. Using this questionnaire, rate your current leader or the one you most recently worked for on a range of transformational and transactional behaviors, with frequency occurring on a 7-point scale (1 = Strongly Disagree; 7 = Strongly Agree). Please read each statement and place an X in the box you most closely associate with your leader's behavior.

	My leader...	Strongly Disagree 1	Disagree 2	Somewhat Disagree 3	Neutral 4	Somewhat Agree 5	Agree 6	Strongly Agree 7
1	Has a clear understanding of where we are going							
2	Paints an interesting picture of the future for our group							
3	Is always seeking new opportunities for the organization							
4	Inspired others with his/her plans for the future							
5	Is able to get others committed to his/her dream							
6	Leads by "doing" rather than simply by "telling"							
7	Provides a good model for me to follow							
8	Leads by example							
9	Fosters collaboration among work groups							
10	Encourages employees to be "team players"							
11	Gets the group to work together for the same goal							
12	Develops a team attitude and spirit among employees							
13	Shows us that he/she expects a lot from us							
14	Insists on only the best performance							
15	Will not settle for second best							
16	Acts without considering my feeling (R)							
17	Shows respect for my personal feelings							
18	Behaves in a manner thoughtful of my personal needs							
19	Treats me without considering my personal feeling (R)							
20	Challenges me to think about old problems in new ways							
21	Asks questions that prompt me to think							
22	Has stimulated me to rethink the way I do things							
23	Has ideas that have challenged me to reexamine some of the basic assumptions about my work							
24	Always gives me positive feedback when I perform well							
25	Gives me special recognition when my work is very good							
26	Commends me when I do a better than average job							
27	Personally compliments me when I do outstanding work							
28	Frequently does not acknowledge my good performance (R)							
	(R) denotes a reverse-scored item, so 1=7, 2=6, etc							

Scale Crosswalk

- Items 1-5: Articulating a vision (i.e., inspirational motivation)
- Items 6-8: Role modeling (i.e., idealized influence)
- Items 9-12: Establishing goals
- Items 13-15: Setting performance expectations
- Items 16-19: Individualized consideration
- Items 20-23: Intellectual stimulation
- Items 24-28: Transactional leadership (i.e., contingent reward)

Activity 2: Learning Outcomes

This scale will give you insight into the types of transformational or transactional behaviors your leader uses. You can also reflect on the behaviors that seem to most motivate your own performance. Use the discussion questions to guide your thinking.

Discussion Questions

- Thinking back to your experiences with your leader, can you identify the specific instances that weighed more heavily in how you responded to the questionnaire?
- If you cannot recall specific instances, what general sense or feeling about the leader nudged you towards responding in the way you did?
- Items 1-8 and 16-23 are associated with transformational leadership. What was it about your leader that made him/her more or less transformational?
- We discussed in the chapter that transformational leadership was additive to transactional leadership, meaning that transactional leadership serves as a foundation from which transformational leadership can be built. What did your leader do particularly well on the transactional side of leadership? See items 24-28?
- Lastly, we know that transformational leaders tend to excel at developing other leaders. What were the most impactful things you learned from your time working for your leader?

In Review

We largely concur with other noted scholars in the leadership field who point out that *transformational leadership* is the most consequential approach to leadership. After all, time and again the evidence shows that when transformational leadership is effectively applied in contexts where it is needed, the resulting effect is individual, team, and organizational performance beyond expectations. Transformational leadership taps into follower psyche by leveraging four behavioral patterns: *inspirational motivation* (being charismatic), *idealized influence* (serving as a role model), *intellectual stimulation* (promoting inclusive problem solving), and *individualized consideration* (being developmental and supportive).

However, we balance our enthusiasm for transformational leadership with the fact that some transformational components are rarely needed because most contexts call for a simple transaction between the leader and follower. In other words, leaders need not make emotional appeals or lean too heavily on charisma for simple tasks; doing so is overkill. Thus, the *Full Range Leadership Model* provides an array of behaviors from which leaders may choose to employ in the right circumstances. As described in the chapter, most leaders spend the majority of their time influencing others transactionally via contingent reward, which is important because it helps establish trust and sets the conditions for followers being open to the leader's future use of transformational approaches.

The Full Range Leadership Model also offers excellent descriptions of approaches to leadership we usually ought to avoid. For example, laissez-faire leadership—the absence of leadership—has been shown to be destructive to organizations because followers look to leaders for guidance and structure. Likewise, both Management by Exception-Passive and Active are often problematic because the leader engages in the influence process once mistakes are made. There are, however, times when the active form of Management by Exception makes sense, particularly when providing task training and coaching.

The Full Range Leadership Model is appealing to practitioners for three reasons. First, the model is prescriptive, meaning that if one wants to lead inclusively and identify novel solutions (intellectual stimulation), then he or she should ask followers questions that prompts them to rethink the way they work. Second, the model has amassed volumes of empirical research supporting efficacy. So, the science says the model works. Third, the transformational components of the model are what we tear *approachably aspirational*, meaning that emerging and early-career leaders can practice these behaviors and see improvements over time. While many of us may blanch at the thought of charismatically giving an inspirational talk within the workplace, this is indeed a skill that can be honed via practice.

Learning Objectives

Define and explain the eight components of the Full Range Leadership Model.

The Full Range Leadership Model consists of eight components, including laissez-faire leadership, or the absence of leadership; management by exception-passive and -active, where the leader typically intervenes only after errors have occurred; contingent reward, commonly referred to as transactional leadership; and the transformational components of leadership, which include idealized influence, inspirational motivation, intellectual stimulation, and individualized consideration. The Full Range Leadership Model should be viewed as a continuum, so the challenge for leaders is to understand when each component of the model is appropriate, which is commonly based on the context and the followers being influenced.

Identify behaviors you have witnessed that align with the 4 I's of transformational leadership.

While each of us have unique experiences, the research suggests that aspects of transformational leadership are universally applicable across contexts and cultures. There are, of course, nuances to the universality as some organizations and cultures eschew charisma in leaders, for example. That aside, most of us can likely recall a teacher, coach, boss, or mentor who made a strong connection with us, made us feel that our opinions and strengths were relevant to the organization, and had an approach to leadership that made us want to emulate them. These people serve as our mental model of transformational leadership.

Explore and understand the ways in which transformational leadership and other components of the Full Range Leadership Model can be applied ethically and unethically.

As this book takes an identity approach towards leading others, the key to understanding the ethical use of transformational leadership may be tied back to many of the concepts covered elsewhere in the book, such as character and identity integration across multiple contexts. Indeed, transformational leadership has been a factor in some of the most important successes throughout history. For example, much of the theory was modeled after the leadership behaviors of President Franklin Delano Roosevelt during the height of the Great Depression and World War II. However, while one need not be the leader of a nation to apply transformational leadership, at the same time leaders with ill intent have used aspects of transformational leadership towards unethical ends. Thus, the ethical-unethical transformational leadership question largely comes down to the leader's identity.

Understand how you might accelerate the development of your Full Range Leadership behaviors.

The call for practice and repetition has been called for several times in this chapter. Developing efficient and effective behaviors requires practice and reflection, so accelerating the development of Full Range Leadership behaviors is no different. Admittedly, some of the behaviors called for in the model may initially seem daunting and may not mesh well with how you see yourself as a leader. We advocate for practice because even those leaders who may not be the most charismatic or may not easily make connections with others can grow in these areas by *practicing the behaviors* over time, then reflecting on how they might improve in the future.

Key Terms

Transformational Leadership (Pg. 161)

Full Range Leadership (Pg. 162)

Laissez-Faire Leadership (Pg. 162)

Management by Exception-Passive (Pg. 163)

Management by Exception-Active (Pg. 164)

Contingent Reward (Pg. 165)

Expectancy Theory of Motivation (Pg. 165)

Idiosyncratic Credit (Pg. 167)

Tautology (Pg. 169)

Organizational Citizenship Behavior (Pg. 171)

Psychological Capital (Pg. 171)

Critical Thinking Questions

1. Can you recall a time when a leader inspired you? How did that make you feel? What specifically did the leader do that you found inspirational?
2. Can you describe the eight components of the Full Range Leadership Model? How would you describe contexts where each component should be applied?
3. Thinking back over your life so far, can you identify times when you witnessed aspects of the Full Range Leadership Model? What were the outcomes?

4. In your mind, what constitutes the ethical use of transformational leadership? Do you have personal examples where you witnessed (or read about) the unethical use of transformational leadership?
5. Why is important that the Full Range Leadership Model has so much scientific support behind it?

References

Alvesson, M., & Kärreman, D. (2016). Intellectual failure and ideological success in organization studies: The case of transformational leadership. *Journal of Management Inquiry*, 25(2), 139–152.

American Psychological Association (2022). Definition of tautology. Retrieved June 20, 2022, from https://dictionary.apa.org/

Antonakis, J., Avolio, B. J., & Sivasubramaniam, N. (2003). Context and leadership: An examination of the nine-factor full-range leadership theory using the Multifactor Leadership Questionnaire. *The Leadership Quarterly*, 14(3), 261–295.

Avolio, B. J. (1999). *Full leadership development: Building the vital forces in organizations*. Sage.

Bass, B. M. (1997). Does the transactional-transformational leadership paradigm transcend organizational and national boundaries? *American Psychologist*, 52(2), 130–139.

Bass, B. M. (1985). *Leadership and performance beyond expectations*. Collier Macmillan.

Bass, B. M., & Avolio, B. J. (1997). *Full range leadership development: Manual for the Multifactor Leadership Questionnaire*. Mind Garden.

Bass, B.M., & Avolio, B.J. (1990). Developing transformational leadership: 1992 and beyond. *Journal of European Industrial Training*, 14(5), 21–27.

Bass, B. M., Avolio, B. J., Jung, D. I., & Berson, Y. (2003). Predicting unit performance by assessing transformational and transactional leadership. *Journal of Applied Psychology*, 88(2), 207–218.

Bono, J. E., & Judge, T. A. (2004). Personality and Transformational and Transactional Leadership: A Meta-Analysis. *Journal of Applied Psychology*, 89(5), 901–910.

Bass, B. M., & Steidlmeier, P. (1999). Ethics, character, and authentic transformational leadership behavior. *The Leadership Quarterly*, 10(2), 181–217.

Burns, J. M. (1978). *Leadership*. Harper & Row.

Crede, M., Jong, J., & Harms, P. (2019). The generalizability of transformational leadership across cultures: A meta-analysis. *Journal of Managerial Psychology*, 34(3), 139–155.

Downton, J. V. (1973). *Rebel leadership: Commitment and charisma in the revolutionary process*. Free Press.

Dumdum, U. R., Lowe, K. B., & Avolio, B. J. (2013). A meta-analysis of transformational and transactional leadership correlates of effectiveness and satisfaction: An update and extension. In *Transformational and charismatic leadership: The road ahead 10th anniversary edition*. Emerald Group Publishing Limited.

Eagly, A. H., Johannesen-Schmidt, M. C., & van Engen, M. L. (2003). Transformational, transactional, and laissez-faire leadership styles: A meta-analysis comparing women and men. *Psychological Bulletin*, *129*(4), 569–591.

Gerstner, C. R., & Day, D. V. (1997). Meta-Analytic Review of Leader-Member Exchange Theory: Correlates and Construct Issues. *Journal of Applied Psychology*, *82*(6), 827–844.

Harland, L., Harrison, W., Jones, J. R., & Reiter-Palmon, R. (2005). Leadership behaviors and subordinate resilience. *Journal of Leadership & Organizational Studies*, *11*(2), 2–14.

Hollander, E. P. (1992). Leadership, followership, self, and others. *The Leadership Quarterly*, *3*(1), 43–54.

Judge, T. A., & Piccolo, R. F. (2004). Transformational and transactional leadership: a meta-analytic test of their relative validity. *The Journal of Applied Psychology*, *89*(5), 755–768.

Loghman, S., Quinn, M., Dawkins, S., Woods, M., Om Sharma, S., & Scott, J. (2022). The Comprehensive Meta-Analyses of the Nomological Network of Psychological Capital (PsyCap). *Journal of Leadership & Organizational Studies*, 15480518221107998.

Lowe, K. B., & Gardner, W. L. (2000). Ten years of the leadership quarterly: Contributions and challenges for the future. *The Leadership Quarterly*, *11*(4), 459–514.

Luthans, F., Youssef, C. M., & Avolio, B. J. (2007). *Psychological capital: Developing the human competitive edge* (Vol. 198). Oxford University Press.

Meindl, J. R., Ehrlich, S. B., & Dukerich, J. M. (1985). The romance of leadership. *Administrative Science Quarterly*, *30*(1), 78–102.

Organ, D. W. (1988). *Organizational citizenship behavior: The good soldier syndrome*. Lexington books.

Podsakoff, P. M., MacKenzie, S. B., Moorman, R. H., & Fetter, R. (1990). Transformational leader behaviors and their effects on followers' trust in leader, satisfaction, and organizational citizenship behaviors. *The Leadership Quarterly*, *1*(2), 107–142.

Price, T. L. (2003). The ethics of authentic transformational leadership. *The Leadership Quarterly*, *14*(1), 67–81.

Seijts, G. H., & Milani, K. Y. (2021). The application of leader character to building cultures of equity, diversity, and inclusion. *Business Horizons*. https://doi.org/10.1016/j.bushor.2021.07.007.

Sims Jr, H. P., Faraj, S., & Yun, S. (2009). When should a leader be directive or empowering? How to develop your own situational theory of leadership. *Business Horizons*, *52*(2), 149–158.

Skogstad, A., Einarsen, S., Torsheim, T., Aasland, M. S., & Hetland, H. (2007). The destructiveness of laissez-faire leadership behavior. *Journal of Occupational Health Psychology*, *12*(1), 80–92.

Van Knippenberg, D., & Sitkin, S. B. (2013). A critical assessment of charismatic—transformational leadership research: Back to the drawing board? *Academy of Management Annals*, *7*(1), 1–60.

Vroom, V. H. (1964). *Work and motivation*. Wiley.

Wang, G., Oh, I. S., Courtright, S. H., & Colbert, A. E. (2011). Transformational leadership and performance across criteria and levels: A meta-analytic review of 25 years of research. *Group & Organization Management*, *36*(2), 223–270.

Wong, S. I., & Giessner, S. R. (2018). The thin line between empowering and laissez-faire leadership: An expectancy-match perspective. *Journal of Management*, *44*(2), 757–783.

Yammarino, F. J., Spangler, W. D., & Dubinsky, A. J. (1998). Transformational and contingent reward leadership: Individual, dyad, and group levels of analysis. *The Leadership Quarterly*, *9*(1), 27–54.

Yang, I. (2015). Positive effects of laissez-faire leadership: Conceptual exploration. *The Journal of Management Development*, *34*(10), 1246–1261.

CHAPTER 10
Authenticity and Ethicality in Identity

CHAPTER OUTCOMES

1. Define and explain the components of impression management
2. Describe what it means to be an ethical leader based on the two-pillar ethical leadership model
3. Explain the ways in which the four components of justice have impacted your work life
4. Understand how you might accelerate your authentic leader development using the four components of authentic leadership theory

Purpose of This Chapter

In this chapter, we describe three leadership approaches that will likely weigh heavily on shaping your leader identity. They are as much about influencing others as they are about leveraging how others perceive and form opinions about you. These approaches include impression management, ethical leadership, and authentic leadership. As this chapter unfolds, you will learn that while all three approaches are highly applicable when leading, they also require different degrees of leader identity activation and integration.

Introduction

Many people go through a stage of social development in their teens and early 20s where they convince themselves—and perhaps even say aloud—that they do not care what others say or believe about them. Similarly, we respect the once-starving artist who does not compromise her craft to please the masses. Politicians who buck the trend of taking the safe stance on controversial topics often get an approval bump because there is something invigorating about watching someone take a risk by saying aloud what many of us are already thinking. Rebellious entrepreneurs enjoy cultivating this same persona, as people who break the rules and fight the status quo are interesting and brave. Indeed, most of us want to become the kind of leader who succeeds because we stay true to who we are. After all, history—at least the version that Hollywood likes to tell—is full of defiant idealists who faced long odds yet somehow "made it" while staying true to their beliefs.

Or did they? If you are drawn to these types of stories and people, you have likely noticed the paradox that eventually emerges. On the one hand, in addition to our penchant to root for the underdog, we are also drawn in by what we perceive to be genuine beliefs and behavior. Lacking pretense, these leaders seem *real* and *authentic*, and we respect authenticity because it suggests other virtues like integrity (Avolio et al., 2004). And if we define trust as our willingness to be vulnerable to someone else (Mayer et al., 1995), then logic suggests we gravitate towards those we believe to be exactly who they say they are—they are authentic and therefore worthy of our trust.

On the other hand, we must also keep in mind that the stories we hear about rebellious leaders who never compromised their values are rarely completely true, especially if they are the ones telling the stories (Pfeffer, 2010). Instead, they are *a version* of the truth the leaders want to be told. Starving artists eventually get fed by selling their art to *someone* who decides to underwrite the work. Entrepreneurs bring their ideas to fruition by convincing investors to provide seed funding. Politicians win elections to office because *you* vote for them. The compelling story that all three want to be told is that they did not compromise, but instead, *you* came around to their way of thinking. They were right all along; it just took you a little longer to figure it out and trust them. But the truth likely rests somewhere in the middle—they probably softened somewhat and used certain influence tactics that appealed to you, and you probably saw in them enough of what you needed to satisfy your needs. One could argue that this phenomenon has the characteristics of a compromise, but from the leader's end of things, we refer to this as impression management.

IMPRESSION MANAGEMENT: The active measures taken via social interaction designed to shape the perceptions of others about another person or event. (Goffman, 1959)

Impression Management

There is a long history of theory and research on impression management within the leadership field. **Impression management** is defined as the active measures taken via social interaction designed to shape the perceptions of others about another person or event (Goffman, 1959). Think of the daily work we put into trying to shape how others see us. For example, because we want to be seen by prospective employers as professionals, we make the effort to dress up for job interviews. When we go to parties, we may carefully choose what we say to make new friends and avoid offending others. At work, when an employee does something that enrages us, we usually do not say the first thing that comes to mind. Instead, we stifle our "inside voice," slowly count to five, and respond in a way that avoids a referral by the human resources office to attend anger management classes. Impression management is an adaptive measure we use every day. It helps us get ahead, maintain relationships with others, and

© fizkes/Shutterstock.com

makes our lives easier. Impression management is also a bedrock concept within leadership (Peck & Hogue, 2018)—however, it tends to be discounted because it has an inauthentic connotation. Stated differently, because impression management calls for a leader's active participation in projecting a desirable image, others make **attributions** about this projected image (some will say your efforts show the "real you," while others will call it fake). There are several frameworks for how leaders use impression management—below, we describe the dominant view plus some additional considerations.

ATTRIBUTION:
An inference regarding the cause of a person's behavior or an interpersonal event. (APA, 2022)

Dramaturgical Approach

The dramaturgical approach (Gardner & Avolio, 1998) frames impression management in the common lexicon of the theater. It harkens to the lines from Shakespeare's (1623, p. 83) *As You Like It*, where Jaques says, "All the world's a stage, and all the men and women merely players; They have their exits and their entrances; And one man in his time plays many parts." Here, leaders are actors performing roles on sets (i.e., the workplace). They use physical acts and rhetoric to convey a message while the audience for the play (i.e., followers) derives meaning from what is happening.

As Gardner and Avolio state (1998, p. 33), "… how people express themselves to, and in conjunction with, others to create meaning and influence is the central focus of dramaturgy." So, if the leaders (actors) are convincing and use rhetoric properly, then the followers (audience) walk away from the play with a uniform meaning of what the play was about and the message the leader/actor conveyed (i.e., the leader successfully managed impressions). But if the leader/actor is less successful, then followers/audience members will walk away with different interpretations of the play's meaning and will likely make different attributions about the leader's intent or personal character. This latter result is commonly experienced in organizations. For instance, people who depart from the same meeting may have very different interpretations and recollections of what their leader said (Sosik et al., 2002).

FRAMING:
A quality of communication that causes others to accept one meaning over another. (Fairhurst & Sarr, 1996, p. xi)

SCRIPTING:
The development of a set of directions that define the scene, identify actors and outline expected behavior. (Benford & Hunt, 1992, p. 38)

In practice, the dramaturgical approach to leading with impression management has four distinct stages: framing, scripting, staging, and performing (Gardner & Avolio, 1998). **Framing** is a concept-shaping effort whereby leaders use rhetoric to define the terms, orientation, and limits of a discussion or concept. For example, the CEO of a mid-sized custom cabinetry manufacturer may state that her company's vision is "to become the #1 purveyor of custom cabinetry in California." But she could change the frame dramatically by adjusting the ending to "… on the West Coast." This would then reorient followers to expansion beyond the previous frame, which is limited to a single geographical location. **Scripting** extends framing beyond shaping a concept and instead shapes the scene, describes expected behaviors and specifies roles. Using our same CEO example, she scripts by stating that "Tom Parker has been with our company for seven years, but prior to joining us, he worked in sales in both Oregon

© Fer Gregory/Shutterstock.com

STAGING:
Appropriating, managing, and directing materials, audiences and performing regions. (Benford & Hunt, 1992, p. 43)

PERFORMING:
The actual enactment of scripted behaviors and relationships. (Gardner & Avolio, 1998, p. 44)

TYPOLOGY:
An analysis of a particular category of phenomena (e.g., individuals, things) into classes based on common characteristics. (APA, 2022)

PRO-SELF BEHAVIORS:
Actions that are specifically geared to result in a desirable outcome for the leader, such as using self-promotion and ingratiation tactics. (Peck & Hogue, 2018)

PRO-SOCIAL BEHAVIORS:
Actions that are specifically geared to result in a desirable outcome for the leader and others, such as promoting teamwork, exemplifying group norms or standards, and personal sacrificing. (Peck & Hogue, 2018)

and Washington. He will lead our expansion effort in Oregon and stand up a manufacturing shop in Portland." **Staging** is related to how leaders set the conditions for organizational success and thus convey to followers the leaders' commitment to the endeavor. Here, our CEO might state, "As you know, we've built up a hefty company cash reserve, so I'm allocating 50% of that reserve towards the expansion into Oregon, which will cover our procurement of a facility, employee salary for the next two years, and allow us to bring on a marketing firm to promote our growth in that region." Finally, **performing** is the actual motion or acting out of the play the leader describes. There are reinforcing behaviors that the leader can exhibit to ensure the performance "sticks," such as periodic communication with followers to remind them of the goals and the progress made. The dramaturgical approach is a useful and elegant way to frame a leader's use of impression management, and it effectively shows the follower's part in the process.

There are five main strategies associated with impression management (Gardner & Cleavenger, 1998). **Ingratiation** is an approach individuals use to make themselves more likable, often by complimenting others or doing favors for others. **Self-promotion** strategies are activities that individuals can do to highlight their competence, such as displaying their educational credentials, publicizing awards, or participating in social media activities. **Exemplification** behaviors create the perception the leader is worthy of being followed, such as self-sacrificial behaviors like working 80-hour weeks or sleeping at the office. These behaviors can also display adhering to organizational values or living by one's principles. **Intimidation** uses coercive power or threats to demand compliance. Finally, **supplication** behaviors signal helplessness to persuade another to do the work. An example might be an employee who refuses to learn a new software package and then asks others to complete the work for them. Research on these differing approaches finds exemplification and ingratiation are both highly correlated with transformational leadership, perceptions of effective performance, and follower satisfaction (Gardner & Cleavenger, 1998). Conversely, intimidation and self-promotion were negatively associated with transformational leadership, perceptions of effective performance, and follower satisfaction (Gardner & Cleavenger, 1998).

Additional Considerations. You may recall that in Chapter 8, we described a range of influence tactics and the bases of power from which those tactics emerge. Leaders employ these tactics to shape follower commitment and ultimately help the organization reach important goals (for a review, please turn back to Table 2 in Chapter 8, p. 144). These same tactics can be used by the leader to help manage follower impressions of the leader or a host of follower perceptions related to the leader's goals. But as you might imagine, a common criticism of impression management is that leaders can misuse influence tactics towards unethical and/or immoral ends. Questions of referent inevitably also come up when discussing impression management. In other words: Is the leader using impression management to promote goals that benefit the organization, or is he using impression management to promote himself? A recent theory offered by Peck and Hogue (2018) addresses these concerns by outlining a **typological** model of impression management (parts of which we describe below).

Regarding the referent—is impression management used to promote the leader or the good of the organization?—this dichotomy is framed in terms of **pro-self** vs. **pro-social** leader behaviors. It is worth noting that, at first glance, these terms are **valance-neutral** until we understand the leader's intent. You can think of pro-self behaviors as occurring along a continuum. At one end are truly egoistic pro-self behaviors intended to enhance narcissistic tendencies, which result in an outcome that only benefits the leader (i.e., boasting or over-claiming credit), while at the other end are altruistic pro-self behaviors intended to help the leader make connections with followers (i.e., telling self-deprecating stories). Your followers are perceptive and will quickly identify where your pro-self behaviors land on the continuum. And—despite your best efforts to authentically communicate your true intent—followers who are distrustful of leaders in general (or of you specifically) may view your pro-social behaviors as self-serving. We address this problem set more later in this chapter when we cover the components of ethical leadership and authentic leadership theories.

In a similar vein, the moral and ethical intent behind a leader's use of impression management matters greatly. Returning to the components of transformational leadership theory from Chapter 9, you may recall that a leader's charm is often framed as a combination of idealized influence (e.g., role modeling) and inspirational motivation (e.g., use of optimistic and uplifting language, conveying a future vision), which together can influence followers to perform beyond expectations (Bass & Avolio, 1997). But as you lead by managing impressions, you must also carefully assess the moral and ethical ends you desire. For example, as we discussed in Chapter 6, researchers have shown that charismatic leaders can use impression management toward *socialized* or *personalized* ends (Howell, 1988; Howell & Avolio, 1993; Sosik et al., 2002). Specifically, socialized charisma is used to shape ethical collective action in a pro-social way, whereas personalized charisma is used towards unethically manipulating others in a pro-self way (Sosik et al., 2002).

Summary: Impression Management. Regardless of how you feel about impression management, it is both necessary and useful in the leadership domain. As the dramaturgical approach to impression management suggests, there are specific components leaders should focus on as they shape the perceptions of others—framing, scripting, staging, and performing are essential to effective impression management. But you must also balance impression management in two ways. First, leaders should understand that followers are quick studies who will rapidly assess if your impression management attempts fall into either an egoistic pro-self or altruistic pro-social category. Second, when impression management is coordinated with effective influence techniques, the result is a powerful tool that can do tremendous good or be misused towards unethical and immoral ends.

Ethical Leadership

Just as leadership is learned behavior, so is leading ethically. **Ethics** is defined as how we judge behavior to be right or wrong. **Morality**, on the other hand, is related to the standards we individually or collectively set for what is considered to be right or wrong. While there is evidence that our ability to judge morality is at least somewhat heritable, that research is only now emerging and likely will not mature for many years (Zakherin & Bates, 2022; Smith & Hatemi, 2020). Instead, we learn the most by watching and interacting with other people (as you will read more about in Chapter 11). And as humans have debated ethics and morality for thousands

VALENCE-NEUTRAL: Seen as neither positive nor negative until more information can be gathered. (APA, 2022)

ETHICS: The framework we use to judge behavior to be right or wrong. (APA, 2022)

MORALITY: The standards we individually or collectively set for what is considered right or wrong. An example of moral standards set within an organization includes a Code of Conduct that governs acceptable behavior. (APA, 2022)

of years, the literature is correspondingly extensive and consistently suggests that our ethics and morality are derived from a variety of sources—family members, neighbors, clergy, schools, and work organizations, to name just a few. Given our focus on leading others, evidence from empirical research suggests that followers respond in kind to the ethical behavior of leaders (Kalshoven et al., 2016).

ETHICAL LEADERSHIP: The demonstration of normatively appropriate conduct through personal actions and interpersonal relationships, and the promotion of such conduct to followers through two-way communication, reinforcement, and decision-making." (Brown et al., 2005, p. 120)

Ethical leadership is defined as "the demonstration of normatively appropriate conduct through personal actions and interpersonal relationships, and the promotion of such conduct to followers through two-way communication, reinforcement, and decision-making" (Brown et al., 2005, p. 120). This definition is important because it conveys three key behaviors by ethical leaders. First, ethical leaders are those who *demonstrate* behaviors that are considered ethically normal within an organization. So, for leaders to be ethical, they must be seen by others as doing what the organization accepts as being "right," meaning they model proper behavior for followers. Second, ethical leaders actively *promote* ethical conduct to followers by communicating their expectations of ethical follower behavior. It is not enough for leaders to simply role model the behavior—they must also actively foster ethical behavior in others by verbalizing expectations. Third, ethical leaders *reinforce* organizational ethical standards not only via their personal behavior but also through their decisions. These decisions can range from how the leader goes about fairly implementing promotion, reward, and punishment systems to—more importantly—how the leader specifically rewards ethical and punishes unethical behavior (Treviño et al., 2000). For example, imagine you are a mid-level executive at an airline. How would you judge a senior leader who seemingly is the company's ethical standard bearer and does everything "above board," yet hands over a huge bonus to an employee known for taking shortcuts that save the company money while simultaneously placing customers and employees at risk? Ethical standards within organizations are established for many reasons and must be upheld—otherwise, there is no value in establishing them.

While there are clearly a set of behaviors related to ethical leadership, the practice is deeply rooted in our identity. As emerging leaders, you almost certainly know what the "right" thing to do is in most situations—you do not necessarily need an ethics course to learn this. But acting as an ethical leader can be challenging for some as there are many forces that may be working against you (e.g., peer pressure, toxic leadership, morally bankrupt organizational practices). In other words, a common paradox facing emerging leaders is a "knowing-doing gap." While that phrase was popularized by organizational scholars who work outside of the ethics field (Pfeffer & Sutton, 2000), it is highly relevant here. In short, it is not enough for you to *know* what must be done to lead ethically—if this were the case, then unethical behaviors within organizations would rarely occur—but rather a case of consistently and courageously *acting* ethically so you (the leader) can develop an identity and reputation for *being* an ethical leader. Ethical leadership scholars developed a two-pillar model of ethical leadership, where a leader must be both a *moral person* and a *moral manager* (Treviño et al., 2000). This is described in greater detail below

Moral Person. As discussed in Chapter 4, you have multiple *selves* based on the varying roles you fulfill throughout your life. And since life is complex at times, most of us juggle multiple selves at any one time (e.g., spouse, parent, shift leader, etc.). However, keep in mind that one developmental goal we should seek in terms of leader development is greater integration of characteristics across our various selves. Stated another way, we do not want to be entirely different people at work vs. at home, and there should be some immutable features common to all selves. This is especially germane to ethical leaders because, as outlined by Treviño and coauthors (2000), in the eyes of our followers, we must first be a moral person before we can effectively be a moral leader.

Being a moral person is comprised of several features, including having certain traits that include integrity (overall completeness of character), honesty (being candid and factual), and trustworthiness (being consistent and dependable). Moral people also consistently exhibit moral behaviors such as showing concern for others, making the right ethical choices, being open to feedback from followers, and having and communicating a personal moral code. Importantly, the personal moral code extends to situations in both professional *and* personal life. Lastly, moral people make decisions in a particular way—decisions that specifically are consistent with their values, are typically objectively fair, and show concern for the organization and the larger community. Moral people also adhere to rules they set for making ethical decisions.

Admittedly, these characteristics seem highly aspirational. Few of us can live up to each facet in every context. The aspirational nature of the "moral person" pillar is designed the way it is because, according to Treviño and her research team (2000), the goal is to develop a reputation bestowed upon you by others as being both a moral person and a moral manager. So, while puritanical perfection is not required, you do need to be seen by others as being a moral person.

Moral Manager. If being a moral person is foundational to ethical leadership, then being a moral manager is the natural extension of ethical leadership behavior within the workplace. According to Treviño and coauthors (2000), this second pillar of moral leadership has three features. First, as touched on in the introduction to this theory, ethical leaders model proper behavior via visible action. Followers must hear *and* see leaders acting ethically. Ethical leader role modeling, in turn, sets the conditions for that behavior to be emulated by followers, a social learning phenomenon supported by empirical research (Badrinarayanan et al., 2019). Second, ethical leaders actively promote ethical behavior by communicating to followers the importance of acting with ethical and moral intent, and they show their sincerity by discussing their personal values and describing how they enact those values at work. Now, when discussing their personal values, leaders should carefully balance their desire for sincerity and connectedness with concern for being perceived as overbearing or self-righteous. And because our values stem from our personal experiences with family and religion and from our political views of society, you should be mindful that some followers may feel as though you are pushing a particular agenda. Instead, we recommend you frame your values—such as integrity, courage, humility, and accountability (Seijts et al., 2015)—in terms of how you use them to help your organization.

DISTRIBUTIVE JUSTICE:
The perceived fairness of how rewards and punishments are allocated. (Alexander & Ruderman, 1987)

PROCEDURAL JUSTICE:
The perceived fairness of the decision-making process related to how outcomes are distributed. (Colquitt, 2001)

INTERPERSONAL JUSTICE:
The perception that people are treated properly, with dignity, professionalism, and respect. (Colquitt, 2001)

INFORMATIONAL JUSTICE:
The perception that people receive enough explanation (i.e., candid, reasonable, etc) regarding why and how an organizational system was used. (Colquitt, 2001)

Third, ethical leaders create ethical systems within the organization. At its most basic level, employees want to be treated fairly: they want fair pay, accountability processes, and promotion opportunities. For example, some researchers call for leaders to ensure that rewards and discipline systems within companies are ethical (Treviño et al., 2000)—and while this is certainly warranted, ethical systems transcend far beyond rewards and discipline. In fact, the research on organizational justice describes four considerations for leaders creating or operating ethical systems. Organizational systems must be constructed with **distributive justice** in mind, helping to ensure that both tangible and intangible assets (e.g., pay and praise) are applied fairly (Alexander & Ruderman, 1987). Distributive justice is an area where many organizations fall woefully short. Surveys conducted by the Society for Human Resource Management and other organizations suggest that women make approximately 82 cents for every $1 made by men (even lower for women of color) (Miller, 2022). Further, ethical leaders must consider **procedural justice** when creating organizational systems. Doing so ensures that the processes governing decisions related to functions (hiring, promotion, financial compensation decisions, disciplinary systems, etc.) actually work as designed, which helps employees trust those systems (Konovsky, 2000). Research on procedural justice shows that there are important secondary effects, including greater job satisfaction (Lambert et al., 2020), organizational commitment, knowledge sharing, and organizational performance for companies who are seen as having procedural justice (Imamoglu et al., 2019).

Additionally, ethical leaders must consider if their systems account for **interpersonal justice**, which is related to the respect shown to employees when they are impacted by organizational systems. For example, workplace terminations are unfortunate facts of organizational life, but how an organization terminates people says a lot about the degree to which its leaders respect employees. When someone is terminated, is it handled quietly and professionally, or is the affected employee publicly humiliated? Since other employees are closely watching your behavior, your reputation as a leader is affected greatly by how you handle these situations. Ethical leaders must also account for how their systems address **informational justice**, which is related to the sufficiency of information provided that explains why or how a particular system was used to make decisions. Referring to our previous example, followers who have been terminated are looking to leaders to explain why it is happening and help them make meaning of the situation. And those who are not terminated are also looking to leaders to help them understand why an employee was terminated and what they can do to ensure it does not happen to them. Leaders should consider sharing what they can within legal and ethical limits. Here, informational justice can have a significant impact on followers. Their perceptions of the quality and sufficiency of the information they receive can impact a range of outcomes, including their intent to stay with a company during turbulent times (Kim, 2009).

Summary: Ethical Leadership. The twin-column moral person/moral manager is an outstanding way to frame how we should lead ethically. Like the other views of leadership we have covered thus far, most of the research on ethical leadership suggests that improving ethical decision-making and moral development occurs over a lifetime and is reinforced via experience and reflection (Kohlberg, 1971; Rest et al., 1999). While leaders at every level should set high personal expectations for themselves and hold themselves accountable to lead ethically, you should also manage your own expectations and recognize that you will likely fall short at times. Perhaps you will lose your temper at an inopportune time, make a rash decision that impacts an employee, or fail to stand up to a boss who is being a bully. But overall, are you being both a moral person and a moral manager *most* of the time? Are you doing your best to get the difficult ethical decisions—the ones that affect your followers and your organization—right? Lastly, what are you doing to *show* others that you are leading ethically? And how are you communicating your expectations for them to behave accordingly?

Activity 1: The Ethical Leadership Scale

Ethical leadership can be measured in a variety of ways, but perhaps one of the better measurement tools is the Ethical Leadership Scale (ELS), developed by scholars in the Penn State University System and published in 2005 (Brown et al., 2005). The ELS forms the basis for the following practical exercise.

- First, think of your most recent leader—the one you have in a job now or the last one you had—and then complete the 10-item scale below.

	My leader...	Highly Unlikely	Unlikely	Somewhat Unlikely	Neutral	Somewhat Likely	Likely	Highly Likely
1	Conducts his/her personal life in an ethical manner							
2	Defines success not just by results but also the way that they are obtained							
3	Listens to what employees have to say							
4	Disciplines employees who violate ethical standards							
5	Makes fair and balanced desisions							
6	Can be trusted							
7	Discusses business ethics or values with employees							
8	Sets an example of how to do things the right way in terms of ethics							
9	Has the best interests of employees in mind							
10	When making desisions, asks "what is the right thing to do?"							

- Next, look at how you endorsed each question. Did you indicate that your leader was highly unlikely, unlikely, or somewhat unlikely to behave in those ways? If so, can you recall the specific instances that came to mind as you responded to each question? Lastly, what would you have done differently?
- What about the items you endorsed positively? How did your leader's ethical behavior shape your view of leading others? Does anything come to mind?
- Reflect on these questions and come to class prepared to discuss.

Activity 1: Learning Outcomes

Gauging someone's perceived ethical actions can help you diagnose your organizational culture. If you find your leader is not working in your best interests or allows unethical behaviors to continue, you may want to seek out a more ethical leader. You can also evaluate your own score on these items to see if you are acting in accordance with your own ethical beliefs or if you are allowing the organization to create boundaries for you.

Authentic Leadership

AUTHENTICITY:
As it relates to people, being true to oneself across a range of thoughts, emotions, and behaviors. (Gardner et al., 2005)

As described in the introduction, **authenticity** carries considerable allure when we think about leadership. Perhaps Gardner and colleagues (2005, p. 344) said it best when they wrote, "With today's pressures to promote style over substance, dress for success, embrace flavor-of-the-month fads and fashions, and compromise one's values to satisfy Wall Street's unquenchable thirst for quarterly profits, the challenge of knowing, showing, and remaining true to one's real self at work has never been greater." The emergence of **authentic leadership theory** in the early 2000s came during a turbulent intersection of Western history. Around then, the first dot-com bubble burst occurred, and people began to understand that much of the internet and those who promoted it lacked substance; companies like Enron, WorldCom, and Tyco were run by ethically bankrupt hacks, and when those companies collapsed, jobs and retirement savings for thousands of people vaporized; and American leaders willfully misled the world by convincing the UN that invading Iraq under the guise of eradicating weapons of mass destruction was a good idea (there of course were no WMDs). In turbulent times, people look for authenticity—they want to place their trust in something real, and they search for that same quality in their leaders.

© Faizal Ramli/Shutterstock.com

AUTHENTIC LEADERSHIP THEORY:
An approach to leadership that calls upon individuals to develop and rely on four qualities—self-awareness, balanced processing, internalized moral perspective, and relational transparency (defined below)—to influence others. (Avolio & Gardner, 2005)

The leadership field struggled to keep up with the rapidly changing world around it (as is the case with many scholarly domains). Some scholars argued (and continue to argue) that our yearning for authenticity was overly nostalgic and too "feel good" to be a utility to organizations, much less have any significant bearing on performance (Alvesson & Einola, 2019). But while established approaches and theories of leadership—such as transformational and transactional leadership, ethical leadership, and others—overlapped significantly in some ways, they ultimately failed to fully account for what it meant to be an authentic leader. What emerged was an influence process that relied on applying deep knowledge about oneself to help guide leaders to self-regulate their behaviors in ethical ways (Gardner et al., 2005). The tethering of self-awareness to self-regulation is an important feature of leading authentically, as having a deeper sense of the self helps you moderate negative behaviors (i.e., keeping yourself from being an "authentic jerk"). As described below, the theory has four tenets: leaders must be self-aware and use such knowledge throughout the leadership process; they must employ balanced processing in decision-making; they must have and follow an internalized moral perspective; and they must foster honest, transparent personal relations with followers.

SELF-AWARENESS:
Having a deep understanding of one's strengths, weaknesses, emotions, drives or motivations, and preferences. (Gardner et al., 2005)

Self-awareness. Most views of leadership suggest that for leaders to effectively influence others, they should know themselves well. Authentic leadership is no different. But the more germane question is: What *about* yourself should you know? In Chapter 3, we discussed how authentic leaders understand the different aspects of their self-concept, including their strengths, weaknesses, values, motivations, emotions, and goals (Gardner et al., 2005). Self-aware leaders have an appreciation for how these factors might impact other people (either intentionally or unintentionally).

Importantly, there is a difference between *being* self-aware and *gaining* self-awareness. Gaining self-awareness can come from a variety of sources—senior leaders, peers, followers, and family members—but what you learn about yourself must be integrated into your self-concept via reflection and perspective-taking. As Gardner and colleagues (2005, p. 347) wrote, "authentic leaders build understanding and a sense of self that provides a firm anchor for their decisions and actions, and we would argue a more authentic self. They continually ask themselves, 'Who am I?'" According to authentic leadership theory, gaining a deeper sense of self-awareness allows authentic leaders to self-regulate their behaviors via the other three components of the theory: balanced processing, internalized moral perspective, and relational transparency.

Balanced Processing. Authentic leaders are those "inclined and able to consider multiple sides of an issue and multiple perspectives as they assess information in a relatively balanced manner" (Avolio & Gardner, 2005). Being receptive to and seeking out input from multiple stakeholders—especially followers—allows you to keep cognitive biases in check, in turn helping you make a more informed decision. There are also added benefits to balanced processing beyond making good decisions, namely that it shows that you are humble and willing to seek out advice, which in turn will likely ingratiate you with followers and potentially strengthen the quality of your relationship.

BALANCED PROCESSING: Actively pursuing input from multiple points of view and carefully considering new information before making a decision. (Avolio & Gardner, 2005)

Internalized Moral Perspective. Authentic leaders have a clear sense of their values, morality, and ethics, which by extension, helps them regulate their behavior and consistently act within their beliefs (May et al., 2003). One way to think about this is as such: Authentic leaders do not hesitate to refer to their moral compass, and more often than not, they will *defer* to it. Because they follow their personalized code of ethics, they may go against peer pressure or organizational norms to speak out when they believe the organization is heading in the wrong direction, especially when facing moral peril (Gardner et al., 2005).

INTERNALIZED MORAL PERSPECTIVE: Acting within a well-understood and accessible moral and ethical framework that is based upon personal values. (Gardner et al., 2005)

Relational Transparency. At the root of relational transparency is communication, which researchers have defined as "perceptions that a leader listens, follows up, makes recommendations, and takes action exhibiting open communication" (Vogelgesang et al., 2013, p. 406). Here, leaders openly express their true thoughts—their true selves—and ask others to do the same, which in turn allows leaders to receive input that assists with balanced processing. Can you lead too transparently, suggesting that you self-disclose too much information with employees? Or are you so transparent in your relationships with those outside your company that you place your organization at a competitive disadvantage? Yes—but fostering relational transparency does not mean you should abandon discretion. Instead, a reasonable degree of transparency in communication and relationship-building efforts by leaders helps do away with perceptions of being "fake." Followers and other stakeholders get the sense that they are seeing more than the just leader—they are seeing the authentic person behind the leadership mask (Avolio et al., 2004).

© Stockbakery/Shutterstock.com

RELATIONAL TRANSPARENCY: Honest, open, two-way communication between leaders and followers. (Vogelgesang et al., 2013)

Authentic Leadership & Outcomes: Authentic leadership theory has approximately two decades' worth of research behind it, and the results are admittedly mixed. On the one hand, meta-analytic research across 100 samples that included over 25,000 participants showed a strong positive correlation between authentic leadership and organizational performance, follower trust in the leader, follower job satisfaction, ratings of leader effectiveness, and follower organizational commitment. The study also found a modest negative relationship between authentic leadership and follower **counterproductive work behaviors (CWBs)**, follower stress, and follower intentions to resign from the organization (Banks et al., 2016). Based on these findings, authentic leadership appears to work exactly as theorized and designed—the influence process leads to many desirable results while staving off a range of negative outcomes.

On the other hand, because of the ubiquity of leadership approaches like transformational and ethical leadership, scholars have rightly questioned the relative value of adding *yet another* multi-dimensional theory into the mix of already well-understood leadership approaches (Alvesson & Einola, 2019). In other words, scholars questioned if authentic leadership theory provided added benefit over/above those other leadership approaches. This question matters for many reasons, but it is especially important because the answer can shed light on the areas at which leaders could focus their developmental efforts. In two meta-analyses (Banks et al., 2016 and Hoch et al., 2018), researchers found that authentic leadership was measurably additive to transformational leadership (i.e., combining the approaches was better than employing one or the other), but adding authentic leadership behaviors led to arguably modest gains (see Gardner et al., 2021 for a more in-depth discussion).

These latter results point to two takeaways you should consider as you work towards becoming an authentic leader. First, while the research may suggest that the effects of authentic leadership are somewhat limited compared to transformational leadership, remember that the theory is continuing to evolve, and new research results are being reported regularly. What we frame as being authentic leadership today may be decidedly different in the future. Second, the theory's tenets would seem to be beneficial to most leaders. Stated differently, we see little downside to leaders knowing their strengths and how to use them, seeking input from others so they can make more informed decisions, having a sense of ethics and operating within a moral code, and working to establish relationships built upon transparency rather than false pretense.

COUNTERPRODUCTIVE WORK BEHAVIORS (CWBs): Volitional acts that harm or are intended to harm organizations or people in organizations. (Spector & Fox, 2005, p. 151)

Activity 2: Carlos the Inspired Case Study

Introduction. We wrap up this chapter with an in-depth case study that pulls together many of the foundational concepts in this book. Here, we introduce you to Carlos, a CEO of a mid-sized marketing company who faces a range of obstacles that will challenge his leader identity and call upon his multiple approaches to leadership. At the close of the case, we offer several discussion and reflection questions for your consideration.

Carlos the Inspired: Making Sense of Leadership Challenges

Carlos awoke feeling ready and energized about the upcoming day's events. He had spent the last two months crafting a vision for his team, which today he would unveil. Not only did he feel confident that the vision would inspire his company, but he also had been practicing how to deliver the message with a leadership coach. This would be his ultimate display of charismatic leadership, and he was full of anticipation to experience its positive effects.

Visioning

First, Carlos had undertaken a process to devise his vision, which involved taking his company's pulse. Where did his company stand today? As CEO of Carloco, Carlos believed he had a solid grasp on the current reality. But income statements from the last few years indicated that sales were leveling off. They hadn't yet dropped, but there hadn't been any growth in the last three years. Carlos worried that sales could decrease in the next few years if a change wasn't implemented.

The market had experienced some challenges, and his company was initially slow to recognize the consequences. First, technology had changed the purchasing habits of Carloco's customer base. Second, certain global trends had affected the customer's bottom line, shrinking budgets. (For example, the price of oil had placed additional costs on clients, and erratic exchange rates made certain markets volatile and risky.) Finally, Carloco's own cost structure had been influenced by these global trends—and despite flat sales, costs had risen.

To address these major challenges, Carlos identified a three-pronged approach. He believed he knew exactly what was needed in Carloco's future. For the first challenge (technology changing purchasing habits), he assumed that face-to-face time had become less important to Carloco's customer base and that much of the sales process could be faster and more customer-friendly if it moved to web-based technologies. This would mean embracing the new technologies that had recently changed the landscape of the market, something Carloco initially was slow to recognize. Regarding the second challenge, Carloco was not in a place to reduce its prices. But given the strain on clients' budgets,

© Ground Picture/Shutterstock.com

Carlos knew that Carloco also couldn't *raise prices* to make up for its own cost structure. What Carloco needed was to make a stronger value proposition to clients. This way, they would feel as though they were getting more from Carloco at the same competitive prices. If the value proposition was stronger, the client base would grow. Acquiring new clients, Carlos believed, was the path to sales growth (rather than selling existing clients more services). As for the third challenge—Carloco needed to revamp how it did things to bring its costs under control. Carlos believed that introducing new technologies would help, but he also understood that the entire company had to change the way it thought about managing its costs. This meant challenging every detail, from small expenses like paper use to larger ticket ones such as choice of hotels and company cars.

The resulting vision Carlos came up with was: *"To innovate in everything we do."*

Carlos believed his vision was sufficiently inclusive—that it would be meaningful for everyone in the company. He believed it would inspire a new way of thinking. This change was to be radical: a few process changes would not be sufficient for Carloco to address the three main challenges. Rather, Carloco's entire way of thinking needed to change.

Practicing Charisma and Presenting the Vision

While preparing for the unveiling of his vision, Carlos realized that the content of the vision was inspiring, but his delivery was not. So, he took time to practice certain charismatic leadership tactics (Antonakis et al., 2012) and developed a meaningful presentation to explain his vision. Working with a leadership coach, he identified three behavioral tactics that would help communicate his vision in a compelling way. First, the coach explained that three-part lists are a nice way to distill a message into clear takeaway points. Since the vision involved a three-pronged approach, this step was easy. Next, Carlos wanted to portray confidence in the vision and make sure he did not dwell on the lackluster results of the last few years. Therefore, he carefully wrote and edited a speech that used language reflecting confidence. He also knew that metaphors are a powerful tool that charismatic leaders use, so he inserted a couple to help reflect his confidence. Finally, his coach helped him see that his tone and body language would also convey messages, and it was crucial that they showed confidence and emphasized the most important points. After practicing hand gestures, facial expressions, and pauses in front of a mirror, Carlos was confident in his tone and body language.

To deliver his message, Carlos had his staff organize a company-wide event that involved an opening address, small team meetings, and a closing reception. During his motivational address, he could feel the energy in the room, and he sensed that his employees were ready for a change. Spurred by the atmosphere and the tactics he'd practiced, Carlos thrived during the moment of delivery. During the meetings throughout the day and at the reception, employees approached Carlos and expressed their excitement about the new vision. Many thanked him for having the courage to make changes, while others conveyed their motivation to make the vision a reality.

In the following days, an exhilarating energy filled the company. The chatter at the water cooler revealed excitement for the future. There was a shared sense that together the employees would revitalize Carloco under Carlos' vision.

A Different Change Initiative

Feeling thrilled about how well his vision was received, Carlos opened a bottle of champagne over the weekend to celebrate with his wife, Anna. He recounted the event and the days following, reflecting on how it made him feel. Anna listened, encouraging his musings and affirming his effectiveness as a leader. Overall, Carlos felt convinced of his own leadership ability to take his company in this new direction. He told Anna that change required an inspiring and optimistic leader and that he had risen to the challenge.

That night, they received a phone call from their youngest daughter, Jacklyn, who was in her first year at university. She had just failed an assignment and was noticeably upset. As a top student through secondary school and an achievement-oriented child, her hard work usually paid off. She had been accepted to and now attended her top choice program at her top choice university. But the transition had been more difficult than she'd anticipated. The workload was more strenuous than in secondary school and required more independence and discipline. Carlos and Anna, being keenly aware of the challenges of first-year university, were as supportive as possible from afar.

Jacklyn explained that she had already met with the instructor, who suggested that she could still achieve passing marks in the class if she performed extraordinarily well on the next essay. But Jacklyn felt deflated by her failure. She did not believe she had the competence to improve her marks.

Carlos leaned on his charisma to give Jacklyn a pep talk. He reminded her of all her past successes and her ability to overcome challenges. He explained that this sort of learning experience was typical at university. He expressed his confidence in Jacklyn's ability to change her studying habits to meet the higher standards of the university, and he boosted Jacklyn's belief that she could achieve high marks on the next essay.

His remarks worked. The following week, Jacklyn called them to enthusiastically explain that she had indeed received a high mark on her essay *and* her instructor had provided glowing feedback that further boosted her confidence. Carlos quickly realized that the same charismatic tactics he had used to present his vision to his company had also worked with his daughter.

At the Soccer Club

After their children left home to attend university, both Carlos and Anna became active in community organizations. They took on leadership roles in organizations that had been influential in their lives and that of their children. Anna started volunteering for the United Way, joining the fundraising team and eventually becoming the coordinator for the local chapter. Her duties involved managing dues/fundraising schedules and deciding on the organizations that would receive donations. Carlos, an avid soccer enthusiast, missed coaching his kids' team in the local club, so he stayed involved. He joined the Board of Directors of the club, helping to manage finances, club memberships, and club facilities.

© matimix/Shutterstock.com

Unfortunately, the club's finances were in trouble. The board assessed the situation and discovered that membership was dropping while, at the same time, the facility's maintenance costs were rising. For Carlos, the corollary to Carloco was uncanny. He knew the club needed a strategic change and expressed his belief at a board meeting. The rest of the board agreed, and the general manager of the club, Patti, committed to presenting a vision and strategy to the board at the next monthly meeting.

That meeting was scheduled for soon, but Carlos wasn't confident that Patti would have much to report. Whenever he saw Patti at the club, she wasn't in her office. She never appeared to be working hard or drafting a strategy. Instead, she was out on the field or in the clubhouse, socializing with members. Carlos' most recent conversation with Patti contributed further to his concerns: she asked Carlos a series of questions about the club's present status and the future of the club. Carlos couldn't believe it—Patti was asking him to do her job!

When the day of the board meeting arrived, Carlos thought he'd be underwhelmed. He expected Patti to explain that she still didn't know what to do about the club. But he was completely shocked by what he had witnessed! Patti delivered a compelling vision that included elements Carlos himself had offered (which he was credited for). He looked around the room and saw heads nodding enthusiastically in agreement.

What appeared to Carlos as Patti goofing around, socializing, and generally avoiding facing her difficult task was actually a highly effective method of crafting a vision for the club. Patti had been gathering data and understanding the viewpoints of the many different constituents the club served. As it reflected all the voices of the club, it turned out to be a vision that everyone could get behind. Nothing about the vision needed to be sold to the constituents because they were *already* behind it.

Explaining this event to Anna later that evening, Carlos suggested that in a community organization such as the soccer club, perhaps Patti's style of leadership was more fitting. Maybe leadership in such a case needs to be more democratic—or at least participative—because the constituents pay dues rather than *being paid* by the organization. But from his experiences at Carloco, Carlos was convinced that such leadership would never work in the business world. There, a business style like his was necessary.

Implementation of the Change Strategies

A few months after the successful delivery of Carlos' vision, the reality of the change initiative took root. The positive energy had subsided, and employees started feeling the discomfort of the change. Carlos had expected—he knew that people would resist change—but these obstacles seemed larger than he'd anticipated. First, he didn't expect people to lose enthusiasm so quickly. The new web-based technology did not make the sales process easier. Rather, it seemed to become a burden both for sales staff and customers. The sales staff complained about being overworked and stressed, as much of their day was now spent deflecting angry customers who were frustrated by the new system. They also felt too much of their time was spent teaching the new technology to existing clients rather than selling to new clients. Frustrated with declining sales, John, the sales director, gave Carlos an earful. He explained that the problem with the new system was that it put a wedge between the salespeople and their clients. The salespeople had lost any direct involvement in the client relationship, John said.

"This company was built on strong client relationships," he continued. "Now the web-based technology has eroded that relationship. Our clients are complaining, and our salespeople are complaining. What we really needed was technology to help our sales staff free up their time so they could have more face-to-face time with clients—not *less*. This new technology was exactly the opposite of what we needed. Our clients want to see our salespeople in person. They see value in the personal touch we used to give. Now, they just see us the same as any other dehumanized service."

Carlos almost choked as he heard John's words. John was right, and what he said made complete sense. Carloco had always prided itself on the personalized touch. Since that had been taken away, sales were declining. Later that day, the marketing director, Jean, had similar complaints about how poorly the new value proposition was being received.

"I wish you had talked to me before moving ahead with this strategy. By the time you delivered it, it was too late to give you feedback. Worse, you never asked for feedback. You hired me to be your marketing person. How can I do that when you so recklessly change our entire value proposition? How much time did you spend with the clients before you decided that everything should move online? The sales department and the marketing department could have told you what we needed to improve sales. We've been trying to tell you for months before your vision unveils. You just refused to listen."

By this point, Carlos was seething. How dare John and Jean mouth off to him like this. Where had they been when he was figuring out the vision? And that's when Jean's words echoed in his head … he had refused to listen.

Carlos arrived home that night in a sullen mood. He didn't want to talk about it or have his bad mood spill into their home life, but Anna needed to know why he was so cranky. So, he recounted both conversations for her. She asked him what he would have done differently, and all he could say was "listen." But he realized he didn't know how to listen. Worse, he didn't know how to fix the damage his charisma had created. He had many questions but no answers.

By the weekend, he still felt awful. He had no idea what to do. He wanted to sit in a dark room and avoid everyone, but there was a celebration at the football club he had to attend as a member of the board. The change initiative at the club had been a huge success: membership dues were up, facility costs had come under control, and the members of the club were energized and excited about all the changes. The membership decided to host a thank you for Patti. The speeches at the celebration heralded Patti for doing such a good job of asking for feedback and listening to the many constituents. At that point, it dawned on Carlos even more how wrong he'd been about Patti's leadership style. Those times he'd thought Patti was too busy socializing to work, he realized that she was actually doing the hardest part of her job. And while he'd thought the way Patti crafted a vision could only work in a community organization, he realized he should've adopted her approach at Fresco.

Feeling even worse after realizing that his top-down approach to leading wasn't working, Anna consoled him. She asked him if he truly believed that charismatic leadership was the wrong type of leadership for his company. She then told him about how she'd been managing things at United Way and what that meant for her role at work. It was her job to inspire her teams, especially when things looked bad. "That's when I use my charisma," Anna said. "But when the team misses a fundraising goal, I listen to them about what they think could have been done better. Then I use their feedback to plan future events." Anna found that this approach also fits at work. She knows when to inspire them with a pep talk and when to be quiet and listen.

So—what should Carlos do now?

Discussion Questions

- Early in the case, when Carlos prepared and ultimately unveiled his new strategy, what leadership processes did he employ?
    - What aspects of transformational leadership do you see?
    - What aspects of authentic leadership do you see?
- The case then shifted to Carlos influencing his family members. What leadership approaches and influence tactics did he use when talking with his daughter?
- Why was Patti's leadership approach effective in her context? And why do you think Carlos initially resisted her approach?
- Near the end of the case, Carlos receives candid feedback from employees regarding the effectiveness of the strategy he formed. Think back to Chapter 1—specifically the discussion on sensemaking (noticing, interpreting, and enacting).
    - What questions should Carlos be asking himself to make sense of his current predicament?
    - If you were Carlos, what other perspectives would you seek out to help frame your next steps?
    - Based on the questions you formed and the perspectives you sought out, what would you do next if you were Carlos?

In Review

Chapter 10 covers a range of material that largely focuses on embedding what many scholars would consider to be higher-order leadership concepts—ethics, justice, and authenticity—within one's leader identity. These are not merely aspirational qualities we want in leaders, but indeed they serve as cornerstones of effective leadership within organizations.

Although novice leaders may want to be judged purely on objective measures because they may view this as the fairest assessment of performance, life as an organizational leader is more nuanced than "the bottom line", and how others perceive the leader matters greatly. Indeed, how we are perceived by others is of critical importance to our current and future success as leaders, so working towards managing the impressions of others is worth the effort. In the *dramaturgical* view of impression management, leaders play roles where they use rhetoric and actions to convey coherent and uniform messages via *framing, scripting, staging,* and *performing*. Each impression management technique serves a unique function that, when integrated with the others, can express a *pro-social* or *pro-self* narrative about what must be done (i.e., the mission) or who the leader is (i.e., personal values).

We next pivot to the nexus between the leader's identity and the practice *of ethical leadership*. We describe that while *knowing* what leader behaviors are ethical is necessary, knowing alone is not sufficient for one to be an ethical leader. Rather, one must both know what is ethical *and* take actions that are consistent with this knowledge. As Linda Treviño and other research scholars have noted, an ethical leader is one who is both a moral person and a moral manager. In other words, an ethical leader is a person who has defined their own understanding of what constitutes ethical behavior and acts in concordance with those beliefs within the workplace. Thus, at least in terms of behavior, there is little "daylight" between how one acts outside and inside the organization. Moral people enact their moral behaviors by showing concern for others, discussing their moral code with others, standing up for what they believe in, and making the right ethical choice even when it places them at a disadvantage. By extension, moral managers are those who role model ethical behaviors in the workplace, communicate to followers the importance of acting with ethical and moral intent within the organization, and create ethical systems to support the organization and followers.

Additionally, ethical leaders are those who support *justice* within the organization. Specifically, they advocate for distributive, procedural, interpersonal, and informational justice in the organization. This, of course, can take the form of creating and resourcing a just promotion and pay system that ensures that employees are treated fairly. Likewise, part of creating and sustaining this form of just promotion and pay system also necessitates a reasonable degree of transparency such that those who are affected by the system are provided with information on how it works.

The chapter closes with an examination of what it means to be an authentic leader. The Authentic Leadership Theory calls for leaders to have heightened self-awareness, engage in balanced processing, have an internalized moral perspective, and promote relational transparency with followers. Similar to transformational leadership described in Chapter 9, authentic leadership is more than just impression management, as there is a range of behaviors that are indexed to each component of authentic leadership. For example, authentic leaders actively seek out information from others (e.g., 360 feedback) that helps them become more self-aware, which in turn can assist them in regulating future behavior. Likewise, authentic leaders know themselves well enough to understand that they have biases that can be countered by seeking out input from followers and peers in problem-solving scenarios. As with the other approaches to leading covered in this book, authentic leadership takes time to develop. Yet, practicing authentic leadership behaviors—especially striving for greater self-awareness—can accelerate its development.

Chapter 10: Authenticity and Ethicality in Identity

Learning Objectives

Define and explain the components of impression management

Impression management is the active measures we take to shape how we are seen by others around us. While it tends to be viewed negatively—instead, much of the leadership literature espouses leaders to be their "authentic selves"—impression management is nevertheless pervasive and very useful. One conceptual frame used to describe how impression management influences leadership is the *dramaturgical approach*, where leaders and followers are viewed through the lens of actors in a theater; leaders and followers assume roles as if they are in a play. There are four stages within the dramaturgical approach, including *framing*, or the leader's use of rhetoric and other communication modalities to shape a joint understanding of terms within a conversation; *scripting*, or the leader's assigning of roles and responsibilities; *staging*, or the leader's effort to posture the organization for success, such as allocating resources; and finally *performing*, or the acting out of the work necessary to complete required tasks.

Describe what it means to be an ethical leader based on the two-pillar ethical leadership model

Recall that ethics is how we judge which behavior is right or wrong, whereas morality is linked to the standards or norms we set for ourselves—individually or collectively—for what is considered right or wrong. According to Linda Treviño and other noted leadership scholars, being an ethical leader has two broad components: being both a moral person *and* a moral manager. Moral people tend to have certain character traits, such as integrity, honesty, and trustworthiness, that are exhibited through their behaviors in their personal lives. With the firm foundation of being a moral person in place, one may serve as a moral manager by role modeling values and character qualities.

Explain the ways in which the four components of justice have impacted your work life

Although your personal experiences with justice likely differ from those of your peers, the ethical application of justice plays out in organizations every day, though it rarely makes the news. Rather, the misapplication of justice within organizations garners the most attention, and unfortunately, it occurs all too often. The four components of justice include *distributive* (allocation of rewards and punishment), *procedural* (perceived fairness of decisions and policies), *interpersonal* (perception of being treated with dignity and respect), and *informational* (receiving enough information about organizational systems). Every organizational member wants to be treated fairly, and thus, we look to our leaders to serve as the arbiters of justice.

Understand how you might accelerate your authentic leader development using the four components of authentic leadership theory

We tend to place a premium on authenticity in our leaders in part because our society and organizations afford leaders a great deal of power and influence over our lives. Authentic leadership is comprised of four components: *self-awareness* (understanding one's strengths, weaknesses, motivations, and emotions), *balanced processing* (seeking out input from stakeholders before making a decision), *internalized moral perspective* (understanding and applying one's values), and *relational transparency* (fostering open and honest conversations with others). To accelerate one's development of authentic leadership, we suggest that a focus on self-awareness is particularly helpful because gaining knowledge of the self, in turn, reinforces the growth of the remaining three components. Knowing yourself better will likely reduce your anxiety about seeking out input from others, will help you more clearly define your personal code of ethics, and will help you ease your way into establishing relationships with followers based on honest, transparent dialogue.

Key Terms

Impression Management (Pg. 180)
Attribution (Pg. 181)
Framing (Pg. 181)
Scripting (Pg. 181)
Staging (Pg. 182)
Performing (Pg. 182)
Typology (Pg. 182)
Pro-Self Behaviors (Pg. 182)
Pro-Social Behaviors (Pg. 182)
Valence-Neutral (Pg. 183)
Ethics (Pg. 183)
Morality (Pg. 183)
Ethical Leadership (Pg. 184)

Distributive Justice (Pg. 186)
Procedural Justice (Pg. 186)
Interpersonal Justice (Pg. 186)
Informational Justice (Pg. 186)
Authenticity (Pg. 188)
Authentic Leadership Theory (Pg. 188)
Self-Awareness (Pg. 188)
Balanced Processing (Pg. 189)
Internalized Moral Perspective (Pg. 189)
Relational Transparency (Pg. 189)
Counterproductive Work Behaviors (Pg. 190)

Critical Thinking Questions

1. What are the benefits and pitfalls of a leader's use of impression management?
2. Why might it be challenging for some leaders to be both a moral person *and* a moral manager?
3. Can you recall seeing each of the four components of justice in action? How did it make you feel? If you witnessed leaders fail to act in a just way, can you describe that context and the emotions you felt?
4. The Authentic Leadership Theory advocates for relational transparency between leaders and followers. As a leader, what personal limits have you put in place in terms of transparency? In other words, where do you draw the line?
5. The Authentic Leadership Theory also advocates for increasing your self-awareness and using the knowledge gained through self-awareness to lead others. How have you sought out feedback from others to gain greater self-awareness? Did you feel anxiety when seeking out such feedback?

References

Alexander, S., & Ruderman, M. (1987). The role of procedural and distributive justice in organizational behavior. *Social Justice Research*, *1*(2), 177–198.

Alvesson, M., & Einola, K. (2019). Warning for excessive positivity: Authentic leadership and other traps in leadership studies. *The Leadership Quarterly*, *30*(4), 383–395.

American Psychological Association. (n.d.). Definition of attribution, typology, valence-neutral, ethics, morality. In APA dictionary of psychology. https://dictionary.apa.org/

Antonakis, J., Fenley, M., & Liechti, S. (2012). Learning charisma. Transform yourself into the person others want to follow. *Harvard Business Review*, *90*(6), 127–30.

Avolio, B. J., & Gardner, W. L. (2005). Authentic leadership development: Getting to the root of positive forms of leadership. *The Leadership Quarterly*, *16*(3), 315–338.

Avolio, B. J., Gardner, W. L., Walumbwa, F. O., Luthans, F., & May, D. R. (2004). Unlocking the mask: A look at the process by which authentic leaders impact follower attitudes and behaviors. *The Leadership Quarterly*, *15*(6), 801–823.

Badrinarayanan, V., Ramachandran, I., & Madhavaram, S. (2019). Mirroring the boss: Ethical leadership, emulation intentions, and salesperson performance. *Journal of Business Ethics*, *159*(3), 897–912.

Banks, G. C., McCauley, K. D., Gardner, W. L., & Guler, C. E. (2016). A meta-analytic review of authentic and transformational leadership: A test for redundancy. *The Leadership Quarterly*, *27*(4), 634–652.

Bass, B. M., & Avolio, B. J. (1997). *Full range leadership development: Manual for the Multifactor Leadership Questionnaire*. Mind Garden.

Benford, R. D., & Hunt, S. A. (1992). Dramaturgy and social movements: The social construction and communication of power. *Sociological Inquiry*, *62*(1), 36–55.

Brown, M. E., Treviño, L. K., & Harrison, D. A. (2005). Ethical leadership: A social learning perspective for construct development and testing. *Organizational Behavior and Human Decision Processes*, *97*(2), 117–134.

Gardner, W. L., & Cleavenger, D. (1998). The impression management strategies associated with transformational leadership at the world-class level: A psychohistorical assessment. *Management Communication Quarterly*, *12*(1), 3–41.

Colquitt, J. A. (2001). On the dimensionality of organizational justice: A construct validation of a measure. *Journal of Applied Psychology*, *86*(3), 386–400.

Fairhurst, G., & Sarr, R. (1996). *The art of framing*. Jossey-Bass.

Gardner, W. L., & Avolio, B. J. (1998). The charismatic relationship: A dramaturgical perspective. *Academy of Management Review*, *23*(1), 32–58.

Gardner, W. L., Avolio, B. J., Luthans, F., May, D. R., & Walumbwa, F. (2005). "Can you see the real me?" A self-based model of authentic leader and follower development. *The Leadership Quarterly*, *16*(3), 343–372.

Gardner, W. L., Karam, E. P., Alvesson, M., & Einola, K. (2021). Authentic leadership theory: The case for and against. *The Leadership Quarterly, 32*(6), 101–495.

Goffman, E. (1959). *The presentation of self in everyday life.* Anchor.

Hoch, J. E., Bommer, W. H., Dulebohn, J. H., & Wu, D. (2018). Do ethical, authentic, and servant leadership explain variance above and beyond transformational leadership? A meta-analysis. *Journal of Management, 44*(2), 501–529.

Howell, J. M. (1988). The two faces of charisma: socialized and personalized leadership in organizations. In J. A. Conger & R. N. Kanungo (Eds.), *Charismatic leadership: The elusive factor in organizational effectiveness* (pp. 213–236). Jossey-Bass.

Howell, J. M., & Avolio, B. J. (1993). Transformational leadership, transactional leadership, locus of control, and support for innovation: Key predictors of consolidated-business-unit performance. *Journal of Applied Psychology, 78*(6), 891.

Imamoglu, S. Z., Ince, H., Turkcan, H., & Atakay, B. (2019). The effect of organizational justice and organizational commitment on knowledge sharing and firm performance. *Procedia Computer Science, 158*, 899–906.

Kalshoven, K., van Dijk, H., & Boon, C. (2016). Why and when does ethical leadership evoke unethical follower behaviour? *Journal of Managerial Psychology, 31*, 500–515.

Kim, H. S. (2009). Examining the role of informational justice in the wake of downsizing from an organizational relationship management perspective. *Journal of Business Ethics, 88*(2), 297–312.

Kohlberg, L. (1971). Stages of moral development. *Moral Education, 1*(51), 23–92.

Konovsky, M. A. (2000). Understanding procedural justice and its impact on business organizations. *Journal of Management, 26*(3), 489–511.

Lambert, E. G., Keena, L. D., Leone, M., May, D., & Haynes, S. H. (2020). The effects of distributive and procedural justice on job satisfaction and organizational commitment of correctional staff. *The Social Science Journal, 57*(4), 405–416.

May, D. R., Chan, A. Y., Hodges, T. D., & Avolio, B. J. (2003). Developing the moral component of authentic leadership. *Organizational Dynamics, 32*(3), 247–247.

Mayer, R. C., Davis, J. H., & Schoorman, F. D. (1995). An integrative model of organizational trust. *Academy of Management Review, 20*(3), 709–734.

Miller, S. (2022). Gender pay gap slowed during the pandemic. *Society for Human Resource Management.* https://www.shrm.org/resourcesandtools/hr-topics/compensation/pages/gender-pay-gap-improvement-slowed-during-the-pandemic.aspx#:~:text=Going%20into%202022%2C%20women%20earn,Gap%20Report%2C%20released%20March%2015.

Peck, J. A., & Hogue, M. (2018). Acting with the best of intentions… or not: A typology and model of impression management in leadership. *The Leadership Quarterly, 29*(1), 123–134.

Pfeffer, J. (2010). *Power: Why some people have it – and others don't.* Harper Collins.

Pfeffer, J., & Sutton, R. I. (2000). *The knowing-doing gap: How smart companies turn knowledge into action.* Harvard Business Press.

Rest, J. R., Thoma, S. J., & Bebeau, M. J. (1999). *Postconventional moral thinking: A neo-Kohlbergian approach*. Psychology Press.

Seijts, G., Gandz, J., Crossan, M., & Reno, M. (2015). Character matters: Character dimensions' impact on leader performance and outcomes. *Organizational Dynamics, 44*(1), 65–74.

Smith, K., & Hatemi, P. K. (2020). Are moral intuitions heritable? *Human Nature, 31*(4), 406–420.

Sosik, J. J., Avolio, B. J., & Jung, D. I. (2002). Beneath the mask: Examining the relationship of self-presentation attributes and impression management to charismatic leadership. *The Leadership Quarterly, 13*(3), 217–242.

Spector, P. E., & Fox, S. (2005). The stressor-emotion model of counterproductive work behavior. In *Counterproductive work behavior: Investigations of actors and targets.* (pp. 151–174). American Psychological Association.

Treviño, L. K., Hartman, L. P., & Brown, M. (2000). Moral person and moral manager: How executives develop a reputation for ethical leadership. *California Management Review, 42*(4), 128–142.

Vogelgesang, G. R., Leroy, H., & Avolio, B. J. (2013). The mediating effects of leader integrity with transparency in communication and work engagement/performance. *The Leadership Quarterly, 24*(3), 405–413.

Zakharin, M., & Bates, T. C. (2022). Testing heritability of moral foundations: Common pathway models support strong heritability for the five moral foundations. *European Journal of Personality*, 08902070221103957.

CHAPTER 11

Launching Your Identity Development

CHAPTER OUTCOMES

1. Describe Social Learning Theory
2. Explain Social Cognitive Theory
3. Design mentorship and transformative learning opportunities
4. Discuss positive outcomes of effective leadership
5. Create your personal leadership timeline

Purpose of This Chapter

The purpose of this chapter is to help you identify and initiate your leader identity development. We begin by describing human learning through the lens of Bandura's social learning and social cognitive theories. Next, we discuss approaches to transformative learning and using mentorship relationships as development opportunities. Goal-setting theory is presented as a method for action planning. We end with a comprehensive activity, which tracks your identity development from your earliest leadership memories to your retirement and describes the quantum approach to identity invention. By the end of this chapter, you will have a solid understanding of how your past behaviors can inform your present and future leader identities. You will also learn how to acquire the skills needed to manifest potential leader identities on your path to success.

What are Bandura's Social Learning and Social Cognitive Theories?

A thoughtful approach to developing your organizational behavior and leadership skills requires understanding how humans learn, acquire, adopt, and deploy new behaviors. Initial explorations of learning focused on direct experiences—where natural consequences of behaviors elicit subsequent behaviors. Think of a person who touches a hot pan—the resulting burn leads to their avoidance of hot pans.

On the other hand, trying a new food might result in a positive experience, leading a person to continue seeking different flavor profiles. Expectations of anticipated outcomes (either positive or negative) reinforce behaviors (Bandura, 1971). While this is clearly a method by which humans learn, it is also time intensive. Allowing natural consequences to drive adult learning would be quite inefficient for an organization—imagine waiting until a project manager fails and loses a client before the lesson is learned. Effective leaders and those motivated to lead often use more productive approaches to learning.

Social Learning Theory (SLT) is a framework created by Albert Bandura and colleagues to explain human learning processes. Bandura and Walters (1963) observed learning activities and the purely physiological responses evident with direct experience. The original focus of this approach centered on **observational learning** (learning by imitating others). This approach emphasizes the cognitive processes that underlie how children and adults observe activities in their social context and then enact or suppress behaviors (Bandura & Walters, 1963). Prior to deriving these theories, demonstration was not well understood as an approach that could teach someone how to perform a task. But we now know that observational learning is a key component of our development—humans are constantly scanning our environment, listening to conversations, monitoring others, and studying exemplars as they decide which actions are appropriate in certain contexts. Observational learning relies on *attention*, and you cannot learn if you don't have the attentive resources available to take in what is occurring. You also must have *retention* capacity (the cognitive resources available to create a memory), from which you *enact* a copy of the behavior. Finally, you must have the *motivation* to continue to perform the actions (Bandura, 2005; Grusec, 1992).

SOCIAL LEARNING THEORY: Illustrates the importance of observing, modelling, and reproducing behaviors as part of the learning process. (Bandura, 1977)

OBSERVATIONAL LEARNING: Modeled behaviors are observed by the learner, encoded by the learner, and then imitated as part of the learning process. (Bandura, 1977)

© Dmitri Disterheft/Shutterstock.com

SOCIAL COGNITIVE THEORY: Describes the role of self-efficacy in the social learning process to explore how people shape and are shaped by their environment. (Bandura, 1986)

SLT was subsumed under **Social Cognitive Theory** (SCT) (Bandura, 1986), which expanded to include more than just learning outcomes. SCT describes the process by which humans adapt their behaviors through self-control, particularly through self-efficacy and self-regulation (Bandura, 1997). SCT is used to explain how individuals harness information from the environment in order to act appropriately. Self-efficacy (covered in Chapter 3)—or one's belief in their capacity to complete a specific task—initiates goal-directed behaviors. Self-regulation provides the link between the initial enactment of a behavior and the repeated performance of that behavior. In other words, the actor first believes they can achieve the goal, and then they must summon the will to perform the behavior, even if early attempts are failures. To illustrate, think of a child learning to climb a rope ladder at a playground. The child may observe others climbing up the ladder, or a parent may demonstrate the process to them. The child then goes over to the ladder and attempts to figure out which leg goes on which rung, which arm pulls them up, etc. They may not be successful the first few times, but through the process of observing others and attempting to climb, they eventually will complete the task. We know the child has self-efficacy; without it, they would not have started toward the goal. Self-regulation is what helps them continue to try until they are successful. By observing others complete the task, the child can visualize a set of capabilities and set expectations for successful goal pursuit.

There are four approaches to learning that consistently lead to higher levels of self-efficacy in goal pursuits: mastery modeling, vicarious learning, social persuasion, and physiological/psychological/emotional arousal. *Mastery experiences* are a major component of efficacy development (Bandura, 1997). Success builds on success, particularly if there is a self-reflective component within the development process. As you build confidence and demonstrate competence in leadership opportunities, you will likely continue to seek out more challenging assignments. *Vicarious learning* assists in the acquisition of leadership knowledge, skills, and abilities (Wood & Bandura, 1989). Seeing others perform and excel at tasks similar to your own helps build self-confidence. Something as simple as seeing a similarly-sized child climb up the rope ladder will boost the belief in oneself to try the same activity. The most successful demonstrations of vicarious learning depend on the role model exhibiting a possible self for the observer (Lester et al., 2011). *Social persuasion* draws in support and encouragement from relevant others to solidify the learning process (Mellor et al., 2006). In strong organizational cultures and team settings, members are invested in each other's successes. Support from others reinforces the belief you have in yourself and may accelerate your pursuit of goals. Think of the children and parents who cheer on the child as they put one leg in front of the other on their journey to the top of the ladder. Finally, *physiological/psychological/emotional arousal*—which is found in rousing speeches or excitement over a goal—motivates action. The psychological understanding that one can perform difficult tasks boosts self-confidence. The positive emotions that arise from accomplishing a goal are powerful and help one harness a mindset of persistence toward new projects. Even the example of physiological arousal from early in the chapter regarding trying new foods—delicious food encourages one to seek out similar tastes—highlights the impact of our senses on behaviors. Physiological arousal can also highlight risks. If a project is too stressful, or if you experience physical discomfort, you may have to regroup and reassess the importance of a particular goal. All are methods that lead to positive behavioral changes (Bandura, 1997). Research finds these methods to be effective for developing leader self-efficacy in organizations (Lester et al., 2011).

SCT shows how crucial it is to transfer training from a simulated environment into real-time actions. While Bandura's work centered on role modeling in low-threat situations, which in turn allows a learner to build up behavioral skill sets to address increasingly challenging situations, *experiential* learning presents a "whole-person learning" approach to development (Hoover et al., 2010). Experiential learning opportunities merge emotional, cognitive, and behavioral impacts, thus cementing skill acquisition. These experiential opportunities—like running team meetings, holding brainstorming sessions, and giving presentations—create high involvement in the learning process and require the learner to take responsibility for learning the skills required to successfully complete the tasks (Hoover et al., 2010). Those seeking leadership development opportunities should frame their learning as whole-person learning. Doing so will help them as they explore mastery experiences, identify role models for vicarious learning, take advantage of social persuasion, and pursue psychological, physiological, and emotional arousal to adopt the knowledge, skills, and abilities necessary for successful performance. One way to tap into all four of these approaches (which may create opportunities for experiential learning) is to take part in a mentoring relationship.

Mentoring—A Specific Learning Opportunity

MENTORING:
"[m]entoring refers to a developmentally oriented interpersonal relationship that is typically between a more experienced individual (i.e., the mentor) and a less experienced individual (i.e., the protégé). (Eby, 2010, p. 505)

Mentoring is a developmental approach often used in organizations to speed learning and development. In Greek mythology, Mentor watched over and taught his friend Odysseus' son during the Trojan War and the ensuing events of The Odyssey (Homer, 1919). A mentor serves as a guide, modeling behavior that the protégé can observe and learn. Mentoring relationships are shared experiences between mentor and protégé, where the pairing meets consistently over a specified time period (Astrove & Kraimer, 2022). Those who take part in mentorship programs have the opportunity to adapt their behaviors, attitudes, and performance (Eby et al., 2008). A mentor is typically outside the protégé's direct line of report, serving as an additional support system and a safe resource to ask questions and practice skills. Mentors help protégés reflect on and learn from mastery experiences (such as simulations or role-playing exercises, which can be valuable developmental tools), serve as role models for vicarious learning, and offer social support. Guided modeling by a mentor assists in the learning process by first demonstrating the appropriate actions and then providing feedback to the protégé in a formative manner. Once a skill is mastered in a lower-threat environment, such as a simulation, the transfer of those skills to real-time opportunities completes the learning cycle. Social persuasion (i.e., encouragement from the mentor) can also assist in the transfer of training from simulations to real-world challenges and can strengthen resolve when self-regulation fails.

© Trueffelpix/Shutterstock.com

Many of the positive outcomes of mentorship programs rely on the strength of the relationship between the mentor and the protégé. To foster growth, each individual must trust the other as part of their willingness to be vulnerable in addressing their shortcomings (Kram, 1985; Wang et al., 2010). Mentorship relationships certainly benefit the protégé through role modeling and skill development, but they also benefit the mentor by expanding the knowledge of their work and developing their mentorship abilities (Astrove & Kraimer, 2022). Organizational leaders should create semi-structured mentorship programs where the mentors and protégés have the option to choose how to manage relationships. In some programs, protégés choose their mentor directly (most likely someone they have already formed a bond with)—in others, the mentor and protégé are matched based on a set of characteristics. There is evidence that input into the matching process from both the mentor and protégé can strengthen the relationship (Allen, Eby, & Lentz,

2006). The program can also set some general, overarching goals for the pairings, though beyond that should not be too prescriptive. Protégés report that the greatest career-related and developmental benefits arise from informal relationships. On the other hand, mentors accrue benefits at the same rate in both informal and formal mentorship programs (Eby & Lockwood, 2005; Ragins & Cotton, 1999).

Regardless of whether an organization offers a formal mentorship program, protégés interested in their personal development should seek out role models in their organization to act as informal mentors. This is a highly beneficial way to learn vicariously and has been shown to be quite effective as a tool for leadership development (Lester et al., 2011).

Transformative Learning

A key component of adult learning is the aspect of challenging assumptions through new experiences. During formative years, humans adopt frames of reference, habits of mind, and points of view that drive perceptions. These views are influenced by our formal education process, family cultures, social circumstances, and personal experiences (Mezirow, 1997). To continue our development beyond these structures, we must confront these frames of reference to ensure we are not hindering potential advancement. Think of frames of reference as a barrier that separates the known from the unknown. If that barrier remains untested, then a wealth of information exists beyond our current frame of reference. Habits of mind are information processing methods each individual employs—perhaps you trust someone's expertise, so your habit of mind is to listen and act based on their expertise, which drives your points of view or opinions. While opinions can change fairly easily (we are constantly taking in new information or listening to other experts), adapting habits of mind requires additional cognitive effort to disrupt the automatic evaluation of information. You must actively seek new information processing approaches. Finally, frames of reference can only be altered through a critical examination of assumptions. Transformative learning is about awareness—specifically regarding your assumptions—and revision due to your self-reflection and experiences with others (Mezirow, 1997).

Activity 1: ILT Frame of Reference

Refer to your initial leadership drawing from Activity 2 in Chapter 2. Now that you have reflected upon your meaning of leader identity, categorized the level of leader identity, evaluated your strength of leader identity, and illustrated your integration of leader identity across domains, you may be more aware of any initial assumptions you made regarding leadership. Now:

1. Write down any assumptions you see in your illustration.
2. Elaborate on your initial point of view.
3. Based on any revisions or additions to your illustration, establish your personal meaning of leadership.
4. Based on self-reflection and the discourse created with your classmates, discuss whether your meaning of leadership has transformed.
5. Characterize any transformation as a changing opinion, a new habit of mind, or a shift in your frame of reference.

> ### Activity 1: Learning Outcomes
> Your meaning of leadership drawing is a depiction of your understanding of effective leadership at a particular point in time. Over the course of this text, we have shared multiple approaches to leadership, self-assessments, and activities to challenge your initial understandings. Any changes or additions may indicate that your habits of mind have adapted and that, potentially, your frames of reference have shifted towards a new understanding of your own and others' leader identities.

Positive Organizational Outcomes

The learning process equates to building one's leader identity and generating positive organizational outcomes. Through social cognitive theory and transformative learning, we see the opportunity to build better organizations. Thus, we move beyond the systematic approach towards skill acquisition (discussed in Chapter 8) to explore what enhancing human competence at work can look like. From a rational perspective, work tasks create opportunities for individuals to acquire sets of attributes to perform effectively (Sandberg, 2000). However, these sets of elements may be too general, and the activities required for a particular job may differ based on the individual. Consider for a moment that working individuals spend most of their waking time at work. So, the extent to which people identify with and are excited by their work impacts organizational performance, team dynamics, and individual outcomes like health and well-being (Judge & Klinger, 2008). Therefore, when we think about organizational behavior and leadership, the conception of work becomes more important than completing specific tasks. The way each individual approaches work is unique to lived experiences. Instead of reducing a job to specific tasks, think of framing work challenges through past experiences that may have caused a transformation. From this perspective, leaders can infuse organizational cultures with guiding principles for the work, allow employees to innovate as they master the requirements needed for success, and help employees shift their frames of reference to take in additional information and perspectives.

Highlighting the *conception* of work shifts the focus from task completion toward positive organizational outcomes that drive performance. Common measures of such performance include job satisfaction, job engagement, organizational citizenship behaviors, and counterproductive work behaviors. Organizations that foster job satisfaction and job engagement, reward organizational citizenship behaviors, and dissuade counterproductive work behaviors set the conditions for increased identification with the work role and with the organization. These positive outcomes also reinforce that organizational leadership is invested in its human capital.

Job Satisfaction is "a pleasurable or positive emotional state resulting from the appraisal of one's job or job experiences" (Locke, 1976, p. 1304). This attitude is one of the most researched outcomes in organizational behavior and leadership research (Judge & Church, 2000). Judge & Klinger (2008) note that—because of the amount of time we engage in our work roles—job satisfaction and job dissatisfaction are prominent drivers of behavior. Pay, promotion, co-workers, supervision, work, recognition, working conditions, and management style all have an impact on a worker's overall job satisfaction. The Job Characteristics Model (JCM) presents the hypothesis that internally motivating attributes—the ability to control the work, the importance of the work, the variety of the work, the ability

JOB SATISFACTION: "a pleasurable or positive emotional state resulting from the appraisal of one's job or job experiences". (Locke, 1979, p. 1304)

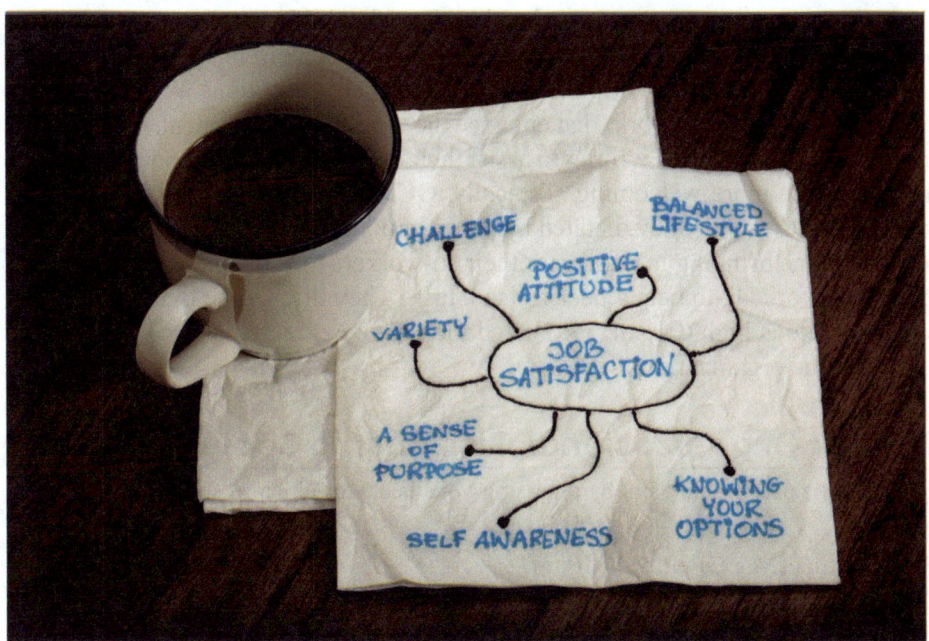

© marekuliasz/Shutterstock.com

to perform the work autonomously, and feedback regarding performance—drive job satisfaction (Hackman & Oldham, 1976). Numerous research studies support this notion, particularly the idea that the nature of the work or the extent to which one identifies with the work are the main contributors to job satisfaction (Judge & Church, 2000). This relationship is even stronger for employees who desire personal growth as part of their development (Frye, 1996). Surveys show that 60% of workers allow reciprocal spillover between their work and home lives, which highlights the importance of fostering job satisfaction (Judge & Klinger, 2008).

Work engagement refers to how effectively individuals engross themselves in their work. Personal resources are used to act on work tasks, fulfilling a sense of accomplishment. When people disengage from their work, they limit their personal resources and only perform the bare minimum (May et al., 2004). On the other hand, individuals who become engaged in their work use their emotions to enact behaviors toward their intended goals. Sometimes, engagement becomes so strong that the worker may experience "flow"—total involvement in a task (Czikszentmihalyi, 1975). Disengaged workers experience decreased commitment to their organizations, while engaged workers help decrease employee turnover (the rate of employees quitting) and increase customer satisfaction (Harter, Schmidt, & Hayes, 2002). Engagement stems from the meaningfulness of the work, how much psychological safety employees feel, and the availability of psychological resources. To a similar extent as job satisfaction, the nature and identification a person has with their work positively impact engagement. Psychological safety—the ability to show one's true nature at work without fear of reprisal—depends on the cultural norms of the organization and how supportive one's supervisors and co-workers are. Work relationships that reinforce positive interactions between co-workers are critical for building and maintaining psychological safety (May et al., 2004). Finally, engagement will depend on the cognitive resources available for an individual so they can focus on their work. Self-efficacy toward work requirements is an *internal* factor. *External* factors include physical attributes, job security, and external obligations.

> **WORK ENGAGEMENT:** 'harnessing of organizational members' selves to their work roles; in engagement, people employ and express themselves physically, cognitively, and emotionally during role performances'. (Kahn, 1990, p. 694)

ORGANIZATIONAL CITIZENSHIP BEHAVIORS: "Contributions to the maintenance and enhancement of the social and psychological context that supports task performance". (Organ, 1997, p. 91)

To maintain engagement, organizational leaders should find ways to provide support and manage externalities that might otherwise create disengagement.

Organizational citizenship behaviors (OCBs) are the actions workers take (in addition to their typical work) that enhance the working environment. OCBs come from individuals who are willing to assist their co-workers and cooperate to make the workplace more welcoming. Typically, OCBs are not rewarded by any specific schedule, nor are they dictated by organizational leaders. An OCB can range from someone bringing in donuts for their co-workers to someone staying past the end of the workday to help a peer finish a task. They often arise in organizations where morale is high (Organ, 1997), and they can be directed toward individuals or toward the organization.

Activity 2: Organizational Citizenship Scale

Rate your own organizational citizenship behaviors by assessing your behavior either at school or at work. Score each item on this scale:

1 = Never, 2 = Rarely, 3 = Sometimes, 4 = Often, 5 = Always

1. Helps others who have been absent
2. Is punctual
3. Volunteers for things that are not required
4. Takes undeserved breaks *
5. Orients new people even though it is not required
6. Attendance is above average
7. Helps others who have heavy workloads
8. Coasts towards the end of the day*
9. Gives advance notice if unable to attend
10. Great deal of time spent with personal conversations (texting, messaging, etc.)*
11. Does not take unnecessary time off
12. Assists leader with his or her work
13. Makes innovative suggestions
14. Does not take extra breaks
15. Attends activities they are not required to attend, but that help overall organization
16. Does not spend time in idle conversation

Scoring: After completing the scale, reverse score items 4, 8, and 10 (if you originally scored a 1, transpose it to 5; 2 transposes to 4, a 3 stays the same, etc.). Next, add up your total score.

Interpretation: Scores ranging from 64-80 indicate that you have high OCBs. Scores between 33-63 are average, and scores lower than 32 suggest a lack of OCBs.

Copyright © 1983 by American Psychological Association. Reproduced with permission. Smith, C. A., Organ, D. W., & Near, J. P. (1983). Organizational citizenship behavior: Its nature and antecedents. *Journal of Applied Psychology*, 68(4), 653–663. https://doi.org/10.1037/0021-9010.68.4.653. No further reproduction or distribution is permitted without written permission from the American Psychological Association.

Activity 2: Learning Outcomes

Your score on this self-assessment may highlight your tendency to enact or refrain from OCBs. While OCBs are certainly appreciated in organizations, they do not always lead to promotions or recognition. In addition, societal shifts may result in fewer enacted OCBs as individuals seek to rebalance their work-family interface during times of stress or uncertainty.

Counterproductive work behaviors (CWBs) are intentional actions by organizational members meant to cause harm (Spector et al., 2005). Negative circumstances or emotions (e.g., poor working conditions, stress, frustration with the work) usually drive this behavior, and microaggressions precede the enactment of CWBs. CWBs can be destructive; for instance, in a case where property is ruined, material theft occurs, or bullying or hostile behaviors towards others becomes common. CWBs are also related to voluntary turnover and increased rates of absenteeism (Lee & Allen, 2002). Organizational leaders need to address the conditions that lead to CWBs—if they don't, they risk facing a negative spiral in their culture, as these actions can be spread to others. Investing in training, hiring additional support staff, and providing resources can help address the conditions that might exacerbate negative emotions in the workplace (Sauter, Lim, & Murphy, 1996). Reinforcing positive leadership approaches and empowerment over how work is approached can also help avoid CWBs. If CWBs do occur, organizational leaders must address the conflict quickly to protect their workers and the culture. Clear guidance regarding the response to CWBs can ensure an organization's workforce understands the consequences of such negative behaviors (Spector et al., 2005).

While leaders are not the sole driver of these organizational outcomes, effective or ineffective leadership is often a main contributor. By developing your own leadership capabilities, you can have a positive impact on your organization and on those who work with you. Alternatively, less effective approaches to leadership (such as a laissez-faire style) clearly relate to poorer organizational outcomes. Further, actively harmful leadership approaches (such as abusive supervision) have an outsized impact both at work and in other domains. Multiple studies show increases in turnover intentions, actual turnover, decreased life and job satisfaction, increased work and family conflict, and psychological distress when individuals rate their supervisors as abusive (Tepper, 2000). The research clearly shows that positive forms of leadership generate better individual and organizational outcomes. Throughout this text, we have presented the methods by which each individual can refine their leader identity to include such positive tools. The final section of this chapter describes how a goal-setting framework offers a path toward continued leader identity development in pursuit of these positive outcomes.

Goal Setting as Identity Development

By viewing the positive organizational outcomes that come from the adoption of specific leadership capabilities, we see the importance of setting and achieving developmental goals. In Chapter 5, we reviewed the path-goal theory of leadership (House, 1971). In that relational-level theory, the leader and the follower set goals together. The leader strives to remove obstacles, thus allowing the follower to succeed. But goal-setting can often be an individual learning process. **Goal-setting theory** specifies that specific, challenging goals lead to higher task performance. The individual pursuing the goals must be committed and must have the ability to attain them while at the same time limiting distractions from other competing goals (Locke & Latham, 2006). Goal-setting is a motivational process by which the

> **COUNTERPRODUCTIVE WORK BEHAVIORS:** voluntary acts that are detrimental to an organization. (Spector, Fox, & Domagalski, 2005)

> **GOAL-SETTING THEORY:** "specific, high (hard) goals lead to a higher level of task performance than do easy goals or vague, abstract goals such as the exhortation to 'do one's best.'" (Locke & Latham, 2006, p.265)

individual's ambitions create dissatisfaction with the present state in comparison to a more pleasant future. Goals that are challenging drive higher performance due to the growth required for achievement. This growth generates satisfaction and self-efficacy. The specificity required in goal-setting ensures the individual understands exactly what steps must be taken to achieve goals. Feedback and self-monitoring help the individual track their progress toward goal attainment and can highlight when something is amiss (Locke & Latham, 1990). One final element we must consider in the goal-setting process is that of time. Goals with shorter deadlines (proximal) require immediate decisions and actions and are more likely to be achieved. Those that are further in the future are still achievable, but they require interim steps to drive persistence (Seijts & Latham, 2001). Overall, the research program on goal-setting theory recommends setting SMART (specific, measurable, achievable, relevant, and time-bound) goals (Gollwitzer, 1999; Locke & Latham, 1990).

How we frame goals significantly impacts whether goals are accomplished. Individuals are more likely to achieve challenging goals versus those they see as threatening—one supervisor may frame a new project as a stepping stone to promotion, while another may frame the same project as the only way to save your job. The former approach is more likely to be accomplished (Locke & Latham, 2006). Learning goals (those that motivate a worker to understand a process) are achieved more often than goals limited to specific performance metrics. For example, students who set out to learn specific skill sets often show higher performance than those focused solely on their GPA (Latham & Brown, 2006; Dweck, 1996). Finally, goals that are additive (i.e., we seek to add something to our skill set) are often easier than those focused on eliminating behaviors. If I tell you to avoid eating chocolate, you may immediately think of your favorite chocolate candy and then spend the next few hours trying to resist that craving. But if I tell you to add one vegetable to your eating plan each week, you may seek out new vegetables to achieve the goal and may not even think about the chocolate. Promotion-focused goals (as compared to prevention-focused) highlight potential accomplishments and maintain self-regulation towards those aims, typically resulting in more successful outcomes (Higgins, 1997).

Setting SMART, promotion-focused, learning-oriented goals is only part of the goal-setting process. Designing goal intentions—even with the criteria just presented—only explains about 20-30% of goal attainment. Humans also have problems starting and persevering on a path toward their goal (Gollwitzer, 1999). Therefore, successful goal-striving must also include planning how to minimize distractions, coping with competing goals, and sustaining effort over time until the goal has been realized. This action-planning process is anticipatory, meaning you prepare ahead of time for potential distractions or barriers so that you can immediately implement goal-directed behaviors when they inevitably arise (Gollwitzer, 1999).

Activity 3: Action Planning

Goal	• Specific goal description
Measurable Outcomes	• Knowledge, skills, abilities • Behavioral outcomes
Relevance	• Personal importance • Stakeholder impact
Achievable	• Required skill sets • Past experiences
Time Frame	• Frequency • Achieved by [date]
Specific Activities + Strategies	• Items to complete • Inviduals to approach
Feedback	• Plans for self-reflection • Reviews with trusted guides
Potential Obstacles	• Finding the time • Failing at one part of the process
Coping Plans - If/Then Approach	• IF x happens, THEN I will take y action

Step 1: Take a moment to think of a specific goal you would like to attain (e.g., improving your public speaking skills or creating a new time management system). Use the SMART goal framework and include anticipatory measures you can take to address challenges.

Step 2: Include your specific goal description, measurable outcomes, relevance to both you and other stakeholders, and evidence that the goal is achievable (e.g., prior experience). List the time frame, including the frequency with which you will enact behaviors in pursuit of your goal. Finally, include the strategies you will use to maintain focus, receive feedback, and anticipate any challenges.

Step 3: Review your action plans with others to gain feedback *before* goal striving begins. Set times and dates (preferably weekly) to receive feedback on your goal progress.

Source: Gretchen Vogelgesang Lester and Paul Lester

Activity 3: Learning Outcomes

Using a methodical goal-setting process such as the approach in this activity will help you attain your goals. Planning for potential disruptions and devising strategies to overcome barriers drastically improves your success rate. Setting time frames and reminders to review your process can also help you develop strong self-regulation skills.

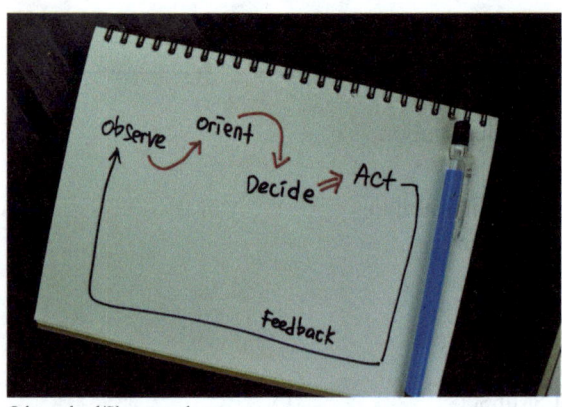
© bangoland/Shutterstock.com

By using implementation intentions during action planning, one boosts the likelihood of goal achievement (Gollwitzer, 1999). The link between expected outcomes and intentions drives goal-oriented behaviors, so the pre-planning process can help you maintain forward progress even in the face of obstacles. Regular check-ins—either through self-reflection or a reviewing process with a trusted colleague—can also increase persistence toward goal achievement. We discussed feedback briefly in Chapter 2 as a means of avoiding attributional errors. But effective feedback also reinforces whether goal-directed behaviors are working successfully or if they are distractions to forward progress. Leaders can focus their feedback on outcomes, processes, or both (Early et al., 1990).

Employing the after-action review (AAR) methodology (discussed in Chapter 4), even periodically throughout goal progression, is one approach to employing effective feedback. Even informal check-ins using a pre-scheduled structure can ensure that issues are identified before goal achievement is threatened.

In conclusion, goal-setting theory clearly highlights how one can go about their leadership development. Coupling SMART goals with pre-determined goal intentions enhances the emphasis on goal striving and goal achievement. Goal-setting theory provides evidence that proximal goals (those requiring immediate action) are more likely to result in higher performance. However, another approach suggests that when projecting identity-related goals, a future-oriented or quantum approach can be helpful for novel identity invention.

Your Personal Leader Identity Timeline

Our final activity in this text focuses on your personal leadership and organizational behavior development. This timeline activity, based on the quantum approach to identity development by Braun & Lord (2017), allows you to time travel and invent potential identities. First, you will use your current environment to make meaning of past activities (Salancik & Pfeffer, 1978; Braun & Lord, 2017). After that, you will project into the future to explore potential identities that are unconstrained by your present situation. This exploration of unimagined selves can help you break out of any current behavioral patterns. The distant future is, by definition, uncertain and undefined. The action of inventing identities can create probabilities that may eventually tie back to your current state (Braun & Lord, 2017).

While you complete this activity, we highly recommend constructing images, as they can serve as catalysts for change. You can also reflect on past identities to see if there are any you would like to reconstruct for future options.

Activity 4: Culmination of Leader Identity in Your Development Timeline

Instructions. Draw a leadership timeline (one potential approach is illustrated in Figure 1).

Step 1: Begin with your earliest memories and continue to the present. Highlight the key events (represented by the flags in Figure 1) that taught you about leadership. With these flags, note your approximate age and a brief description of the event. The other spots may be moments of transformative learning, which this reflection helps you recognize as leadership opportunities.

Describe the key milestones in your leadership journey. Here are some ideas to get you thinking:

- Examples of witnessing another's leadership (perhaps a parent, coach, or peer).
- A time when you learned about leading first-hand (perhaps a time you led a team or successfully used influence tactics).
- A character or situation in a book or film that resonated with you.
- An event you observed in the news.
- A course you took or a topic you studied.

Figure 1: Illustration of a Development Timeline (Past Reflection)

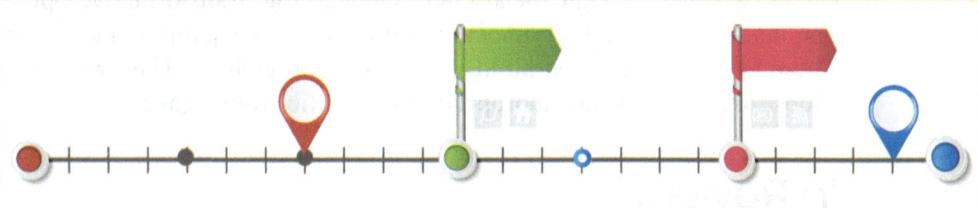

© Yganko/Shutterstock.com

Step 2: On a separate page, describe future potential invented identities. List plausible events you can envision that could influence you and your leader identity. Contemplate the distant future—20 to 40 years from now. Start with the endpoint, which will be undefined and uncertain. Then, slowly work backward to the present. The next five years may be predictable (you graduate college, launch a career, etc.), whereas 15, 20, or 30 years from now will reveal many possibilities. If you have access to it, refer back to activity 2 from Chapter 1, where you created your possible self inventory.

Some additional things to think about charting:

- An anticipated or desired promotion.
- Family milestones that might impact leadership opportunities:
  - Children moving out of the house.
  - Degree or certificate completion.
  - Retirement.
- An anticipated or desired trip.
- An anticipated or desired job change.

Figure 2: Illustration of a Development Timeline (Future Invented Identities)

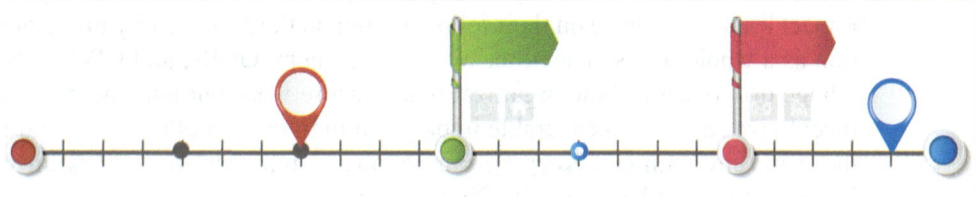

© Yganko/Shutterstock.com

Activity 4: Learning Outcomes

This activity is a form of prospecting, as you will be contemplating where your life could take you. As invented identities become plausible and possible, present opportunities become clearer and more certain, allowing you to act via the goal-setting process.

© Stokkete/Shutterstock.com

The practice of inventing leader identities helps us create opportunities that are unconstrained by present circumstances. These potential identities might solidify how our future roles relate to our past experiences. They might also help us move from the present to our envisioned state of goal achievement (Braun & Lord, 2017).

Throughout this text, we have personalized the organizational behavior and leader development process so that you can harness these tools and create the leader identity most suitable to you. Managing organizational behavior and developing your leadership skills are lifelong learning processes, whether through social cognitive learning, transformative opportunities, pragmatic goal-setting, or innovative approaches like quantum identity invention. These tools will help you build your leadership archive. They will allow you to choose skill sets that are appropriate for specific circumstances.

In Review

This chapter describes how you can learn and develop as a leader in organizations. As we note, taking a thoughtful approach to your self-development requires focus and tools to help you manage your progression as a leader. Your leader identity is shaped by your social learning and social cognition. The activities and assessments in this chapter are provided to help you identify and practice acquiring different frames of reference, skill sets and creating your own opportunities. For example, the frames of reference activity ask you to revisit your leader meaning drawing from chapter 2 to compare how your ideas may have shifted during your use of this textbook. Understanding how you challenge and adapt your habits of mind and frames of reference will help you create the conditions for additional leadership development.

Reviewing how humans learn is an important component of your identity development. Observational techniques can guide you toward the appropriate role models and even mentors to include as you embark on your goals. Using mastery modeling, vicarious learning, social persuasion, and physiological, psychological, and emotional arousal as opportunities for learning expand the opportunities you can seek out as part of your progression as a leader and followers.

We included the most studied organizational outcomes to remind you of the impact leaders can have on their followers and on the productivity of the organization as a whole. Job satisfaction, work engagement, OCBs, and CWBs can make a huge difference in how organizations measure work output. The behaviors we incentivize can have measurable impacts on individuals both at work and outside the work environment. Keeping our followers' interests in mind is an integral ingredient to a leader's overall effectiveness.

The section on goal setting presents a practical, applied process that should be of assistance in any endeavor. Learning how to use SMART goals and how to anticipate challenges and build in feedback opportunities will generate much more successful outcomes. Action planning can be geared towards individual and organizational goals.

The final culminating activity in this chapter asks you to create your own leader identity timeline from your first leadership experiences through your retirement. This activity incorporates the quantum approach to identity development, where your future possibilities are unconstrained by your current identity. As time progresses, our opportunities become more limited due to situational pressures; however, the inclusion of unfettered identities far in the future may seed some goal-directed behaviors in the moment that may allow those potentialities to one day take shape. We encourage you to include as many radical possible identities as possible in this activity; one never knows where the future will take your leader development.

Learning Objectives

Describe Social Learning Theory

Social learning theory notes that humans learn by observing others, modeling their behavior, and reproducing that behavior. We are constantly capturing information from our environment to develop new skills and abilities. To learn through observation, we need to be attentive, have the capacity to retain the knowledge, be able to enact the behavior, and be motivated to perform those actions.

Explain Social Cognitive Theory

Social cognitive theory incorporated social learning theory to describe the process by which humans adapt their behaviors. It includes the concept of self-efficacy, which is the belief in one's capacity to complete a task. It also includes self-regulation, which allows us to persist when we might at first fail at a task. We can build our self-efficacy at specific tasks by mastery modeling, vicarious learning, social persuasion, and physiological/psychological/emotional arousal. Building our self-efficacy by effectively meeting a goal strengthens the opportunity for additional skill acquisition.

Design mentoring and transformative learning opportunities

Mentoring is a specific type of social learning. In these relationships, a mentor and a protégé share experiences as they work towards the protégé's self-development. A mentor is typically outside of the protégé's line of report and serves as an additional resource for the protégé. Mentoring programs are quite effective at developmental achievements, and they also benefit mentors by increasing their own engagement and satisfaction with their work. The most effective mentoring programs are organic and protégé-directed. They also offer an opportunity for mentors to help protégés expand their frames of reference by critically examining their assumptions.

Discuss positive outcomes of effective leadership

Effective organizational leaders understand that work tasks create opportunities that go beyond the workplace and that any negative work attributes can lead to negative organizational performance. Thus, leaders who focus on creating positive work environments and meaningful work will have followers higher in job satisfaction, work engagement, organizational citizenship behaviors, and lower in counterproductive work behaviors. If the fundamentals are missing within an organization, leaders will see increased turnover, disengagement, and burnout.

Create your personal leadership timeline

The personal timeline activity requires a quantum approach to self-development, where individuals can ground their future possibilities in their past performance. Thinking decades into the future encourages creative and unconstrained thinking about possible selves; as we get closer to the present, our options become limited by our current resources and situation. The possible future selves can help motivate action towards a specific purpose.

Key Terms

Social Learning Theory (Pg. 202)

Observational Learning (Pg. 202)

Social Cognitive Theory (Pg. 202)

Mentoring (Pg. 204)

Job Satisfaction (Pg. 206)

Work Engagement (Pg. 207)

Organizational Citizenship Behaviors (OCBs) (Pg. 208)

Counterproductive Work Behaviors (CWBs) (Pg. 209)

Goal-Setting Theory (Pg. 209)

Critical Thinking Questions

1. In your own words, describe social learning and social cognitive theories. Give examples of times you have learned new skills and denote which aspects of social learning and social cognitive theory were key to that learning. How can you use these theories to help your own followers and peers develop new skills?

2. How could you design a mentoring program for your workplace? What are the most important aspects you think you should include to allow both mentors and protégés to learn from the program?

3. What would you do in a workplace where job satisfaction, work engagement, and OCBs were low? How could you address the dissatisfaction and disengagement in such a workplace? What behaviors should you enact to ensure your own workplace does not lose its positive work outcomes and organizational culture?

4. What do you think are the most important aspects of your leader timeline and action plan? What are a few of your past experiences that were seminal to your own development? What are a few possible selves you would like to someday incorporate into your leader identity? What constraints are currently limiting your forward progression toward this potential self?

References

Allen, T. D., Eby, L. T., & Lentz, E. (2006). Mentorship behaviors and mentorship quality associated with formal mentoring programs: closing the gap between research and practice. *Journal of Applied Psychology*, *91*(3), 567–578.

Astrove, S. L., & Kraimer, M. L. (2022). What and how do mentors learn? The role of relationship quality and mentoring self-efficacy in mentor learning. *Personnel Psychology*, *75*(2), 485–513.

Bandura, A. (1971). Vicarious and self-reinforcement processes. *The Nature of Reinforcement*, Academic Press: New York.

Bandura, A. (1986). The explanatory and predictive scope of self-efficacy theory. *Journal of Social and Clinical Psychology*, *4*(3), 359.

Bandura, A. (1997). *Self-efficacy: The exercise of control.* W H Freeman/Times Books/Henry Holt & Co. New York.

Bandura, A. (2005). The evolution of social cognitive theory. *Great Minds in Management*, 9–35.

Bandura, A., & Walters, R. H. (1963). *Social learning and personality development.* Holt Rinehart and Winston.

Braun, S. H., & Lord, R. G. (2017). A quantum approach to identity invention and time travel. In *Academy of Management Proceedings* (Vol. 2017, No. 1, p. 10526). Academy of Management.

Clapp-Smith, R., Hammond, M. M., Lester, G. V., & Palanski, M. (2019). Promoting identity development in leadership education: A multidomain approach to developing the whole leader. *Journal of Management Education*, *43*(1), 10–34.

Csikszentmihalyi, M. (1975). *Beyond boredom and anxiety*, Jossey-Bass.

Dweck, C. S. (1996). Implicit theories as organizers. In P.M. Gollwitzer & J.A. Barr (Eds) *The Psychology of Action: Linking cognition and motivation to behavior.* Guilford Press, pp. 69–90.

Earley, Northcraft, G. B., Lee, C., & Lituchy, T. R. (1990). Impact of process and outcome feedback on the relation of G. *Academy of Management Journal*, *33*(1), 87–105.

Eby, L. T., Allen, T. D., Evans, S. C., Ng, T., & DuBois, D. L. (2008). Does mentoring matter? A multidisciplinary meta-analysis comparing mentored and non-mentored individuals. *Journal of Vocational Behavior*, *72*(2), 254–267.

Eby, L. T., & Lockwood, A. (2005). Protégés' and mentors' reactions to participating in formal mentoring programs: A qualitative investigation. *Journal of Vocational Behavior*, *67*(3), 441–458.

Frye, C. M. (1996). *New evidence for the job characteristics model: A meta-analysis of the job characteristics–job satisfaction relationship using composite correlations* [Paper presentation]. 11th annual meeting of the Society for Industrial and Organizational Psychology, San Diego, CA.

Gollwitzer, P. M. (1999). Implementation intentions: Strong effects of simple plans. *American Psychologist*, *54*(7), 493–503.

Grusec, J. E. (1992). Social learning theory and developmental psychology: The legacies of Robert R. Sears and Albert Bandura. *Developmental Psychology,* 28(5), 776–786.

Hackman, J. R., & Oldham, G. R. (1976). Motivation through the design of work: Test of a theory. *Organizational Behavior and Human Performance,* 16, 250–279.

Harter, J. K., Schmidt, F. L., & Hayes, T. L. (2002). Business-unit-level relationship between employee satisfaction, employee engagement, and business outcomes: A meta-analysis. *Journal of Applied Psychology,* 87(2), 268.

Higgins. (1997). Beyond Pleasure and Pain. *The American Psychologist,* 52(12), 1280–1300. https://doi.org/10.1037/0003-066X.52.12.1280

Homer. (1919). *The odyssey.* W. Heinemann, G.P. Putnam's sons.

Hoover, J. D., Giambatista, R. C., Sorenson, R. L., & Bommer, W. H. (2010). Assessing the effectiveness of whole person learning pedagogy in skill acquisition. *Academy of Management Learning & Education,* 9(2), 192–203.

Judge, T. A., & Church, A. H. (2000). Job satisfaction: Research and practice. In C. L. Cooper & E. A. Locke (Eds.), *Industrial and Organizational Psychology: Linking Theory with Practice,* pp. 166–198. Blackwell.

Judge, T. A., & Klinger, R. (2008s). Job Satisfaction: Subjective well-being at work. In M. Eid & R.J. Larsen (Eds) *The Science of Subjective Well-Being.* The Guilford Press.

Judge, T. A., Zhang, S. C., & Glerum, D. R. (2020). Job satisfaction. *Essentials of job attitudes and other workplace psychological constructs,* 207–241.

Kram, K. E. (1985). *Mentoring at work: Developmental relationships in organizational life.* Scott, Foresman.

Latham, G. P., & Brown, T. C. (2006). The effect of learning, distal, and proximal goals on MBA self-efficacy and satisfaction. *Applied Psychology: An International Review,* 55(4), 6060–6123.

Lee, K., & Allen, N. J. (2002). Organizational citizenship behavior and workplace deviance: The role of affect and cognitions. *Journal of Applied Psychology,* 87(1), 131.

Lester, P. B., Hannah, S. T., Harms, P. D., Vogelgesang, G. R., & Avolio, B. J. (2011). Mentoring impact on leader efficacy development: A field experiment. *Academy of Management Learning & Education,* 10(3), 409–429.

Locke, E. A. (1976). The nature and causes of job satisfaction. In M.D. Dunnett (Ed) *Handbook of Industrial and Organizational Psychology* (pp. 1297–1343). Rand McNally.

Locke, E. A., & Latham, G. P. (1990). *A theory of goal setting & task performance.* Prentice-Hall, Inc.

Locke, E. A., & Latham, G. P. (2006). New directions in goal-setting theory. *Current Directions in Psychological Science,* 15(5), 265–268.

May, D. R., Gilson, R. L., & Harter, L. M. (2004). The psychological conditions of meaningfulness, safety and availability and the engagement of the human spirit at work. *Journal of Occupational and Organizational Psychology,* 77(1), 11–37.

Mellor, S., Barclay, L. A., Bulger, C. A., & Kath, L. M. (2006). Augmenting the effect of verbal persuasion on self-efficacy to serve as a steward: Gender similarity in a union environment. *Journal of Occupational and Organizational Psychology, 79*(1), 121–129.

Mezirow, J. (1991). *Transformative dimensions of adult learning.* Jossey-Bass.

Mezirow, J. (1997). Transformative learning: Theory to practice. *New directions for adult and continuing education, 1997*(74), 5–12.

Northcraft, G. B., Schmidt, A. M., & Ashford, S. J. (2011). Feedback and the rationing of time and effort among competing tasks. *Journal of Applied Psychology, 96*(5), 1076.

Organ, D. W. (1997). Organizational citizenship behavior: It's construct clean-up time. *Human Performance, 10*(2), 85–97.

Ragins, B. R., & Cotton, J. L. (1999). Mentor functions and outcomes: A comparison of men and women in formal and informal mentoring relationships. *Journal of Applied Psychology, 84*(4), 529.

Salancik, Gerald R., and Jeffrey Pfeffer (1978). A social information processing approach to job attitudes and task design. *Administrative Science Quarterly,* 23, 224–253.

Sandberg, J. (2000). Understanding human competence at work: An interpretative approach. *Academy of Management Journal, 43*(1), 9–25.

Sauter, S. L., Lim, S.Y., & Murphy, L.R. (1996). Organizational health: A new paradigm for occupational stress research at NIOSH. *Japanese Journal of Occupational Mental Health, 4*, 248–254.

Seijts, G. H., & Latham, G. P. (2001). The effect of distal learning, outcome, and proximal goals on a moderately complex task. *Journal of Organizational Behavior: The International Journal of Industrial, Occupational and Organizational Psychology and Behavior, 22*(3), 291–307.

Smith, C., Organ, D. W., & Near, J. P. (1983). Organizational citizenship behavior: Its nature and antecedents. *Journal of Applied Psychology, 68*(*4*), 653.

Spector, P. E., Fox, S., & Domagalski, T. (2006). Emotions, violence and counterproductive work behavior. *Handbook of Workplace Violence, 29*, 46.

Tepper, B. J. (2000). Consequences of abusive supervision. *Academy of Management Journal, 43*(2), 178–190.

Wanberg, C. R., Welsh, E. T., & Hezlett, S. A. (2003). Mentoring research: A review and dynamic process model. *Research in Personnel and Human Resources Management.* (Vol. 22, pp. 39–124). https://doi.org/10.1016/S0742-7301(03)22002-8

Wang, S., Tomlinson, E. C., & Noe, R. A. (2010). The role of mentor trust and protégé internal locus of control in formal mentoring relationships. *Journal of Applied Psychology, 95*(2), 358.

Wood, R., & Bandura, A. (1989). Social cognitive theory of organizational management. *Academy of Management Review, 14*(3), 361–384.